Attunement

AMERICAN ACADEMY OF RELIGION

REFLECTION AND THEORY IN THE STUDY OF RELIGION

SERIES EDITORS
Alda Balthrop-Lewis, Australian Catholic University
Jonathan Tran, Baylor University
A Publication Series of
The American Academy of Religion
and
Oxford University Press

WORKING EMPTINESS
Toward a Third Reading of Emptiness in Buddhism and Postmodern Thought
Newman Robert Glass

WITTGENSTEIN AND THE MYSTICAL
Philosophy as an Ascetic Practice
Frederick Sontag

AN ESSAY ON THEOLOGICAL METHOD
Third Edition
Gordon D. Kaufman

BETTER THAN WINE
Love, Poetry, and Prayer in the Thought of Franz Rosenzweig
Yudit Kornberg Greenberg

HEALING DECONSTRUCTION
Postmodern Thought in Buddhism and Christianity
Edited by David Loy

ROOTS OF RELATIONAL ETHICS
Responsibility in Origin and Maturity in H. Richard Niebuhr
R. Melvin Keiser

HEGEL'S SPECULATIVE GOOD FRIDAY
The Death of God in Philosophical Perspective
Deland S. Anderson

NEWMAN AND GADAMER
Toward a Hermeneutics of Religious Knowledge
Thomas K. Carr

GOD, PHILOSOPHY AND ACADEMIC CULTURE
A Discussion between Scholars in the AAR and APA
Edited by William J. Wainwright

LIVING WORDS
Studies in Dialogues about Religion
Terence J. Martin

LIKE AND UNLIKE GOD
Religious Imaginations in Modern and Contemporary Fiction
John Neary

BEYOND THE NECESSARY GOD
Trinitarian Faith and Philosophy in the Thought of Eberhard Jüngel
Paul DeHart

CONVERGING ON CULTURE
Theologians in Dialogue with Cultural Analysis and Criticism
Edited by Delwin Brown, Sheila Greeve Davaney and Kathryn Tanner

LESSING'S PHILOSOPHY OF RELIGION AND THE GERMAN ENLIGHTENMENT
Toshimasa Yasukata

AMERICAN PRAGMATISM
A Religious Genealogy
M. Gail Hamner

OPTING FOR THE MARGINS
Postmodernity and Liberation in Christian Theology
Edited by Joerg Rieger

MAKING MAGIC
Religion, Magic, and Science in the Modern World
Randall Styers

THE METAPHYSICS OF DANTE'S *COMEDY*
Christian Moevs

PILGRIMAGE OF LOVE
Moltmann on the Trinity and Christian Life
Joy Ann McDougall

MORAL CREATIVITY
Paul Ricoeur and the Poetics of Possibility
John Wall

MELANCHOLIC FREEDOM
Agency and the Spirit of Politics
David Kyuman Kim

FEMINIST THEOLOGY AND THE
CHALLENGE OF DIFFERENCE
Margaret D. Kamitsuka

PLATO'S GHOST
Spiritualism in the American Renaissance
Cathy Gutierrez

TOWARD A GENEROUS ORTHODOXY
Prospects for Hans Frei's Postliberal Theology
Jason A. Springs

CAVELL, COMPANIONSHIP, AND
CHRISTIAN THEOLOGY
Peter Dula

COMPARATIVE THEOLOGY AND THE
PROBLEM OF RELIGIOUS RIVALRY
Hugh Nicholson

SECULARISM AND RELIGION-MAKING
Markus Dressler and Arvind-Pal S. Mandair

FORTUNATE FALLIBILITY
Kierkegaard and the Power of Sin
Jason A. Mahn

METHOD AND METAPHYSICS IN
MAIMONIDES' *GUIDE FOR THE
PERPLEXED*
Daniel Davies

THE LANGUAGE OF DISENCHANTMENT
*Protestant Literalism and Colonial Discourse in
British India*
Robert A. Yelle

WRITING RELIGION
The Making of Turkish Alevi Islam
Markus Dressler

THE AESTHETICS AND ETHICS
OF FAITH
*A Dialogue between Liberationist and
Pragmatic Thought*
Christopher D. Tirres

VISIONS OF RELIGION
Experience, Meaning, and Power
Stephen S. Bush

WRITING RELIGION
The Making of Turkish Alevi Islam
Markus Dressler

STUDYING THE QUR'AN IN THE
MUSLIM ACADEMY
Majid Daneshgar

SYNCRETISM AND CHRISTIAN
TRADITION
*Race and Revelation in the Study of
Religious Mixture*
Ross Kane

ASIAN AMERICANS AND THE SPIRIT OF
RACIAL CAPITALISM
Jonathan Tran

THE HIGHER OBJECTIVES OF ISLAMIC
THEOLOGY
Toward a Theory of Maqasid al-Aqida
Mohammed Gamal Abdelnour

CRITIQUE OF HALAKHIC REASON
Divine Commandments and Social Normativity
Yonatan Y. Brafman

ATTUNEMENT
The Art and Politics of Feminist Theology
Natalie Carnes

ATTUNEMENT

The Art and Politics of Feminist Theology

NATALIE CARNES

OXFORD
UNIVERSITY PRESS

OXFORD
UNIVERSITY PRESS

Oxford University Press is a department of the University of Oxford. It furthers
the University's objective of excellence in research, scholarship, and education
by publishing worldwide. Oxford is a registered trade mark of Oxford University
Press in the UK and certain other countries.

Published in the United States of America by Oxford University Press
198 Madison Avenue, New York, NY 10016, United States of America.

© Oxford University Press 2024

All rights reserved. No part of this publication may be reproduced, stored in
a retrieval system, or transmitted, in any form or by any means, without the
prior permission in writing of Oxford University Press, or as expressly permitted
by law, by license, or under terms agreed with the appropriate reproduction
rights organization. Inquiries concerning reproduction outside the scope of the
above should be sent to the Rights Department, Oxford University Press, at the
address above.

You must not circulate this work in any other form
and you must impose this same condition on any acquirer.

CIP data is on file at the Library of Congress
ISBN 978–0–19–776562–3 (pbk.)
ISBN 978–0–19–776561–6 (hbk.)

DOI: 10.1093/oso/9780197765616.001.0001

To my teachers,

who opened new worlds to me, including the worlds of theology.

And to my students,

whose presence in those worlds promises the possibility of their renewal.

Contents

Preface   xi

1. Attunement   1
2. Aesthetics   31
3. Affordance   67
4. Repair   107

Acknowledgments   145
Works Cited   147
Index   163

Preface

IT IS 1988, eight years after Donna Haraway became the first tenured professor in feminist theory, when she weighs the success of feminist interventions in science studies. She and her fellow feminists have unmasked doctrines of objectivity and deconstructed science's truth claims. They have performed an "epistemological electroshock therapy" that exposed masculinist power dynamics structuring and sustaining the field all the way through its texts, which consequently no longer seemed worth engaging. They thought: "They're just texts, anyway, so let the boys have them back."[1] But showing the artifice and power dynamics of these texts did not put feminists at the center of conversations about science, nor did it give them a voice among the most powerful in science studies and philosophy of science. "Far from ushering us into the high stakes table of the game of contesting public truths," Haraway writes, the feminist critique "lays us out on the table with self-induced multiple personality disorder."[2]

This picture of Haraway rising to prominence and still diverted from the central streams of interpretation in her field is one I find both troubling and resonant. Working more than three decades after Haraway's comments in my own very different field of theology, I find that feminists are not locked out of the central conversations in the same way, nor has their critique been so thoroughly repelled. Feminists have, in fact, made major gains. Self-identified feminist theologians have taken their places at most, perhaps all, major divinity schools in the United States. Scholarly publications such as the *Journal of Feminist Studies in Religion* (1985–), *Feminist Theology* (1992–), and the *Journal of the European Society of Women in Theological Research* (1993–) dedicate themselves fully or partially to feminist theological concerns, and major academic presses such as Routledge, Bloomsbury, and Columbia University Press host series exploring gender and religion. In these ways and others, the situation Haraway evokes is not that of feminist theologians, nor is the world addressed by the feminist pioneers of the 1960s and '70s still the theological world of today.

But there are other ways of assessing the imprint of a field, some of which yield less triumphant narratives for feminist theology. In particular, tracking the content legitimized and promoted by the central institutions of systematic theology conjures a picture akin to Haraway's, in which the figures and concerns of feminist theology simply garnish the meatier conversations of systematics. Prior to July 2023, it had been nine years since *Modern Theology* reviewed a book in feminist theology, and in the last five years, only five of its roughly two hundred articles treat feminist theology in any kind of substantive way.[3] At one of the most recent events I attended in the Systematic Theology section of the American Academy of Religion (AAR), I was, by my rough estimate, one of four women in a room of about sixty men. From 2017 to 2021, the section hosted two papers centering feminist theological concerns.[4] If I point to guilty parties, I point to myself: I was on the steering committee most of those years.[5]

Yet my animating interest is not identifying guilty parties, which diminishes the matter of feminist theology's marginalization to a few bad actors in need of reform and undermines the vision of transformation that I elaborate.[6] The numbers of *Modern Theology* and the Systematic Theology section of AAR refract a much larger dynamic about feminist theology, systematic theology, and the persistence of patriarchal power. They suggest something about what is and is not considered serious and systematic, about where we scholars and students of theology learn to look for our conversation partners, and what shape we expect those conversations to take. Feminists pose and address questions we believe all theologians should take seriously, and still, with a handful of exceptions, there is an inverse relation between how marked a scholar is as a feminist theologian and the extent to which she is celebrated as a constructive or systematic theologian. Although feminist theology has made important institutional gains, many of those gains have taken hold in silos within the theological world, rather than reshaping the world's terrain such that feminist theology is seen to speak to the heart of theology. This is not to diminish the gains made. This is, rather, to voice gratitude for them and ask, what's next?

To return to Haraway, then, the problem her image identifies is not plurality—what she, writing in the 1980s, refers to as "multiple personality disorder," which today clinicians call "dissociative identity disorder" and neurodiversity advocates term "multiplicity." The problem, instead, is being laid out on the table while the real game takes place in the next room. In other words, I do not want to dispel the ambivalence, plurality, or even woundedness of being a feminist in a patriarchal world. I want to explore how feminists nevertheless flourish in this patriarchal world *as feminists*, even how they transform it. Feminist ambivalence or multiplicity registers the need for this transformation and the commitment to staying present to a patriarchal world without surrendering to the misogyny that sustains it. For what other world do we have? Even if a feminist leaves behind this particular patriarchal world—the world of Christian theology or Christianity—where can she find a world free from patriarchy? The question of how to live in *this* patriarchal world is a specified version of the question of how to live.[7] So how can a feminist carry her ambivalence and multiplicity while finding a way to go on, faithful to her deepest commitments? How can she negotiate her plurality in ways that fortify rather than flatten her?

Feminists should not have to do this work alone. It is, in a sense, deeply unfair to ask feminists to remake the theological terrain, in the way it is unfair to ask any group to assume the burden of repairing a wrong they have themselves especially suffered from. In addition to being unfair, it is impossible for feminists to change the environment by themselves. For repairs to be systemic, by definition, the mainstream has to receive them, has to be converted. And feminist theologians cannot force what Haraway calls the high-stakes game to include them. But neither can a feminist strategy succeed without feminists. This book, then, addresses two levels of audience. Most obviously, it addresses feminists by elaborating a strategy for unraveling patriarchy and transforming the theological environment to become more hospitable to women and others who are marginalized by gender in less and more extreme ways, including those who identify as transgender, nonbinary, intersex, queer, or are simply struggling within society's thick interpretation of gender. Less obviously, it addresses those who do not identify as feminist theologians, in an attempt to persuade them to take up feminist concerns as their own, to draw nearer to feminist work, to mediate it forward and outward in their own networks of interpretation.

The problem of feminist theology's marginalization is, among other things, a theological problem. That contemporary feminist theology is not widely taken as internal to systematic concerns, that it is given relatively scant institutional attention via conferences, book reviews, and symposia, suggests that we theologians are captivated by a certain picture of what counts as theology. And what might that mean for the object of our theological inquiries? Since what we take to be serious theology implies what we take to be true of God, the marginal status of feminist theology within theology more generally raises questions about the idolatries that hold us in bondage. When an anti-idolatry project like feminist theology remains siloed, what does that suggest about theology's deepest convictions about God? How can we find ourselves in the high-stakes game of publicly contesting idolatries? Perhaps it is time, remembering Haraway's words, to reclaim the texts from the boys.

* * *

The desire for feminist theology to break out of its silo is the desire for it to discover more fertile soil, to inhabit freer terrain, to move within a more hospitable environment. Soil, terrain, environment—the earthy imagery signals how and where I hope to meet this desire: down in life's literal dust and dirt, the home of the earthworm. Charles Darwin devoted his last scientific book to this humble creature, titling his 1881 monograph *The Formation of Vegetable Mould through the Action of Worms, with Observations on Their Habits*. He was interested in the social, sexual, and gustatory life of worms and, as the title suggests, their creation of vegetable mold through their secretions. In addition to creating a layer of humus through their castings, earthworms also work through the soil, aerating and sifting it, pulling leaves into it, changing its density and structure. Their work changes the physico-chemical and biological composition of soil such that it is more fertile for plant growth and better suited to their own flourishing. With a sensitive epidermis that needs warmth and water, earthworms are semiaquatic creatures initially ill suited to topsoil. But through their casting, leaf moving, and burrowing, they create an environment in which they—and much vegetative life—can thrive.[8]

While it is now well known that the environment exerts evolutionary pressures on the animal, Darwin's observations of earthworms illustrate that animals can also transform their environment in ways that are permanent and alter their own evolutionary course.[9] His nineteenth-century reflections have become important in much more recent articulations of niche construction theory. Beginning from the observation that some organisms modify their environments to benefit themselves and their offspring, niche construction theory analyzes how these organisms therefore shape the environment, sometimes permanently and significantly.[10] While "niche" is often used synonymously with "silo," niche construction theory presents the niche as importantly different from the silo: the niche is not an isolated aspect of the environment separated to maintain its distinctiveness or safety; it is that space of transformation within the environment, where changes and exchanges filter out into the broader ecological system. The phenomenon is much larger than earthworms. Snails eating lichen under rocks in the Negev Desert affect the entire ecosystem by generating tons of topsoil for plants that then feed and shelter insects and birds.[11] Bacteria can excrete substances that feed other types of bacteria, the metabolic process of which feeds still other types of bacteria, and so on, in this way bearing "immense potential for the construction of new ecological niches."[12] And no animal has been more effective in constructing niches that permanently alter the environment than humans, though many of our alterations have devastated nonhuman species.[13] All of these creatures make use of what a particular environment affords them, and in that environment, they create new affordances, altering what the environment provides both themselves and other species. The picture of evolution that emerges here is dynamic and multi-agential.

Earthworms, snails, and bacteria are not often subjects of dreams and aspirations, but they can offer inspiration for how feminist theology might move from the silo to the niche. The hope of this book is to build on the achievements of feminist theologians by offering a vision for the field's next stage of evolution that is not unlike these organisms and their environment—one of transforming the discourse of mainstream theology from within, orienting its major institutions and artifacts to the gender-marginalized. The vision turns on a mode of engaging Christianity's patriarchal inheritance that echoes, develops, and renders explicit and explicitly political a type of argumentation that, as I will show, is deep in feminist theology and the history of women and other gender-marginalized figures. Yet this mode has not been fully articulated and described, nor has its potential been fully realized. What follows is an attempt to describe and develop this mode of negotiation, to show the power it has to perform a kind of therapy for systematic theology while also insinuating the centrality of feminist theological concerns to the wider discipline of theology. The name I give to this feminist way of engaging the patriarchal texts and artifacts of the Christian tradition is *attunement*.

Attunement is an aesthetically invested and constructively oriented mode of reading and writing. Niche construction is a fitting metaphor because through attunement, feminist theologians draw on the affordances of a text or artifact to build new, positive affordances into the text. They build niches in the environments of the texts, changing what the text means for a given community and transforming the text environment to be more conducive to the flourishing of the gender-marginalized. And they build this niche through particular attention to aesthetics—the literary, artistic, and sensuous conditions and aspects of the text or artifact and the creative, artistic, and literary possibilities for engaging them.

In these ways, attunement is not primarily about the interpreter coming into tune with the text or artifact. It names the text or artifact coming into tune with feminist commitments in a way that generates a new relationship between the text or artifact, the interpreter, and the community in which that text or artifact circulates. Rather than an accommodation to the patriarchy, attunement is an act of co-creation, a niche construction, that alters the patriarchy-poisoned landscape by mediating the artifact anew.

Attunement elaborates—in both senses of articulating and further developing—the way feminist theologians, women, and other marginalized genders have always attended to the aesthetic dimensions of doctrines, arguments, and texts. Attunement is not new. Women through much of Christian history have used aesthetics as a way of making the case for their own authority, and feminist theologians have always recognized that the struggle for gender equality is fought and won in the symbolic imagination, from contesting who can represent Christ in the priesthood to examining how metaphors of fatherhood point or fail to point to God, to experimenting with images and language that might draw people closer to God and one another— as we'll see more in chapter 2. These groups have long attended to the aesthetic dimensions of doctrines and artifacts to find and make new meanings more hospitable to their own flourishing. In describing attunement, then, I am attempting to render these patterns of feminist work visible in new ways and thereby to show something about how the case for the full humanity of all genders has moved forward through investment in aesthetics, even as what feminist theorists call "malestream" modern theology has largely ignored aesthetics.[14] Like organisms receiving and changing their environment through niche construction, these individuals have made homes for themselves in doctrinal environments that would seem inimical to their presence and authority.

Attunement, then, is not new—and yet there is a way in which this aesthetically aware and constructively oriented way of reading and writing *is* new and brings newness to feminist theology. For in claiming attunement, I not only identify a pattern present in feminist theology, but I also argue for a direction that has not yet been fully realized and that bears possibilities for innovation. Drawing on the concept of affordances and the insights of actor-network theory, I develop attunement as a way of co-creating texts and images, mediating them forward differently by acknowledging the intimacy of aesthetics and politics. While feminist theology has expressed a creative and constructive impulse with regard to doctrines—and has been most successful in finding its way through to larger theological conversation when it expresses this constructive impulse—it has not fully fathomed the possibilities for attuning particular Christian artifacts to feminist concerns. The creative and substantive feminist work done on the atonement, for example, has largely come through critiquing and bracketing the most patriarchal texts, or the most patriarchal aspects of those texts, to draw on resources elsewhere for constructive work. Critical of atonement accounts that are premised on penal substitution or the glorification of divine violence, feminist theologians have plumbed the tradition and attended to the bodily lives of women. In so doing, they have developed incarnational models of the atonement that draw on happy exchange traditions (Kathryn Tanner); they have advanced accompaniment models in which God shares solidarity with suffering creation (Elizabeth Johnson); and, recognizing the raced character of surrogacy models, they have centered Black women to focus on the ministerial vision of Christ and its vindication in his resurrection and the flourishing of the Spirit in the world (Delores Williams). Their work is important, powerful, and beautiful. Meanwhile, systematic theologians continue to work on authors and theologies considered by many feminist theologians to be deeply problematic, without any engagement with feminist critiques, as if these theologians are oblivious to or casually dismissive of feminist work. This is in part a reflection of the silo-ization of theology. And this marginalization of feminist theology might, like the field of systematic theology itself, be challenged by fresh, constructive, feminist engagements with those texts and images that feminist theologians have largely neglected. The aesthetic impulse rooted deep in the soil of feminist theology can branch and blossom into this mode of engagement that sees aesthetics as enabling a range of possibilities and meanings that can allow an array of patriarchal artifacts to be reclaimed by feminists as their own. This opens up new roles and meanings for texts and images previously avoided or discarded. Over the course of this book, I hope to push the constructive impulse of feminist theologians further by suggesting that attunement offers a way beyond primarily identifying bad parts of the tradition to be avoided and good parts that might be generative—places, in other words, where feminist theologians can make a home and places where they cannot. Attunement can be a way in which feminist theologians co-create a place to flourish even in formerly inhospitable environments, though not, as I will argue in chapter 3, in every inhospitable environment. Migration is also a strategy of animal survival.

There are other, theological reasons for incorporating attunement more robustly into the clutch of feminist strategies, and this book will explore these as well, particularly in chapter 4. For attunement is a way of living in the world fitting to who we are as creatures. Critique is another strategy for responding to patriarchal texts and artifacts, one that is also fitting and can also be theologically narrated. Like attunement, it is a way of responding to sin and to the type of creatures we are: creatures that grow. Critique claims a distance that can be salutary for navigating states we are leaving behind, either because they are corrupt or because they no longer fit who we are or are becoming. But we cannot live by critique alone. Excluding strategies of attunement or claiming a methodology of *sola critica* denies something of our creatureliness, the ways we have been mothered into this world and its traditions by forces that continue to sustain us, even as such sustenance can be laced with poisons, even as our mothers wound us. If for Stanley Cavell the condition of philosophy is that of "having been a child," I similarly describe the condition of theology as that of having and becoming a mother, a condition evoked by the myriad mothers named in theological discourse, including Mother Mary and Mother Church, names resonant with the way the earth in multiple traditions is also named as a mother.[15] Both church and earth, moreover, are mothers that nourish and damage us.[16] Attunement is a way of living that does not deny but openly acknowledges this givenness, even as it can also respond to such damage and accommodate growth. As affordances can help describe the way creatures change their environment to make it more hospitable to their own flourishing, so can the affordances that attuned readings identify, augment, build, or diminish be ways of describing how women and other gender-marginalized individuals receive and renovate their church and tradition. In this way, attunement can be described as a mode of interpretation that echoes and follows the Spirit, who makes all things new.

As there are theological stakes to attunement, there remain important affinities with feminist work in non-theological disciplines. In the field of science studies, Haraway describes her feminist intervention as engendering a "self-induced multiple personality disorder."[17] Her proposal is not that feminists rediscover integration by abandoning one or the other personality. She thinks that the work of feminists in her field occurs between two temptations: on the one hand, appeal to a repristinated, feminist objectivity and, on the other hand, a collapse into total constructivism. These options were seen at the time of her writing as a dichotomy for feminists in science studies. Haraway depolarizes the alternatives as she develops her theory of situated knowledges, neither abandoning the texts to the boys nor abandoning her feminist sensibilities, which rightly perceive the texts' patriarchal commitments. The work of feminist theologians and the temptations they navigate are different from those of Haraway and her colleagues because theology is, after all, very different from science studies. But the struggle to receive well a patriarchal inheritance as a feminist is similar, as is the dilemma. How does one approach this text as one's own and as a feminist without stalling in or denying one's multiplicity? In proposing attunement, I negotiate a similar tension, suggesting a way of receiving what is there while also remaking it, creating a less idolatrous world. As a way of co-creating texts and artifacts, attunement offers a vision of going on amid ambivalence and plurality by constellating (perhaps counterintuitively) a multiplicity of texts, artifacts, and art objects around a text to let it speak anew. I elucidate attunement in the conviction that feminist theology can do a new thing, that it may continue to indulge and even expand its most creative impulses, and that it might yet be received and engaged not as second-class theological work but as a central and productive site of theology that reshapes and reimagines the current theological terrain.

We begin with Augustine.

Notes

1. Donna Haraway, "Situated Knowledges: The Science Question in Feminism and the Privilege of Partial Perspectives," *Feminist Studies* 14, no. 3 (Autumn 1988): 578.
2. Haraway, "Situated Knowledges," 578.
3. In July 2023, *Modern Theology* published Linn Tonstad's review of Susannah Cornwall's book *Constructive Theology and Gender Variance: Transformative Creatures*. I'm grateful to Katherine Ellis for this research.
4. In 2022, there were no explicitly feminist papers, but the section hosted a joint unit with the Gay Men and Religion unit and the Queer Studies in Religion unit. The Systematic Theology section also had a theme that year of "constructive proposals in queer theology" that led to three papers presented on queer theology. Again, my thanks to Katherine Ellis for this research.
5. My culpability grows: near the end of drafting this manuscript, I was asked to join the editorial board of *Modern Theology*, an invitation that I owe to the generations of feminist theologians who made representation an important part of institutional life.
6. I mention my involvement in the Systematic Theology section and *Modern Theology* because I want to avoid evoking an "us versus them" dynamic that implies that there are people, places, or institutions free of fallenness—least of all me. The belief in an unfallen people or space can, on the one hand, prevent us from coming to terms with the ubiquity of damage in our world and, on the other hand, distract us from holding out hope that any person or place yet may be redeemed. In both cases, the "us versus them" dynamic militates against the work for transformation that I am commending.

7. There is a tradition of dreaming of women-only feminist communes, for example, in Rokeya Skhawat Hossain's story "Sultana's Dream" (1905), Charlotte Perkins Gilman's *Herland* (1915), and Alexandra Kollantai's story collection *Love of Worker Bees* (1925). There is also a tradition of trying to live in separatist communities, particularly coming out of radical feminist movements in the 1960s, such as the lesbian separatist group Womyn's Land, which started in the 1970s in English-speaking countries around the world and continues in some form today. However, the enthusiasm for such movements has waned since the 1970s, with a bleaker picture of feminist separatism represented in the film *Mad Max: Fury Road*. Patriarchy lives in women as well as men, and even separatists have to practice alternative ways of life before they can achieve them. They, too, must build niches. For more on the history of separatist, communal utopias, see Kristen R. Ghodsee, *Everyday Utopia: What 2,000 Years of Wild Experiments Can Teach Us about the Good Life* (New York: Simon & Schuster, 2023).

8. These descriptions are found in Charles Darwin, *The Formation of Vegetable Mould through the Action of Worms, with Observations on Their Habits* (London: John Murray, 1881). They are recounted in Rob Withagen and Margot van Wermeskerken, "The Role of Affordances in the Evolutionary Process Reconsidered: A Niche Construction Perspective," *Theory and Psychology* 20, no. 4 (August 2010): 499–500.

9. As Withagen and van Wemeskerken write, "After all, as niche construction theory demonstrates, the evolution of animals is partly determined by the modifications that animals bring about in their environments" ("The Role of Affordances," 504). And also: "However, as we have seen, niche construction *can* alter the evolutionary trajectory. Indeed, animals have evolved specific action systems in response to the niche construction activities of their ancestors. Hence, affordances not only form the context of selection that animals *encounter*; by creating and destroying affordances, animals also *construct* this context and thereby affect the evolutionary dynamics" (503).

10. Manuel Heras-Escribano, "The Evolutionary Role of Affordances: Ecological Psychology, Niche Construction, and Natural Selection," *Biology and Philosophy* 35, no. 30 (2020): 10. The touchstone book for niche construction theory is John F. Odling-Smee, Kevin N. Laland, and Marcus W. Feldman, *Niche Construction: The Neglected Process in Evolution* (Princeton, NJ: Princeton University Press, 2003).

11. Multiple examples of niche construction, including these, can be found online at https://nicheconstruction.com/resources/. The snail example can be found in Moshe Shachak, Clive G. Jones, and Yigal Granota, "Herbivory in Rocks and the Weathering of a Desert," *Science* 236 (1987): 1098–1099. See also Clive G. Jones and Moshe Shachak, "Fertilization of the Desert Soil by Rock-Eating Snails," *Nature* 346 (1990): 839–841.

12. Magdalena San Roman and Andreas Wagner, "An Enormous Potential for Niche Construction through Bacterial Cross-Feeding in a Homogeneous Environment." *PLOS Computational Biology* 14, no. 7 (2018): e1006340.

13. This is not to insinuate that such destruction is intrinsic to human ways of living as such. There are ways of being human that do not wreak havoc on ecological systems, that can even benefit them. Along these lines, Alda Bathrop-Lewis has recently pointed me to the work of Tyson Yunporta, who calls humans a "custodial species" and identifies forms of indigenous land management that have been sustainable for more than sixty thousand years. See, for example, Tyson Yunporta, *Sand Talk: How Indigenous Thinking Can Save the World* (New York: HarperOne, 2020).

14. Mary O'Brien coined this term in *The Politics of Reproduction* (New York: Routledge, 1981). The first appearances in theological volumes seem to be in Katie Cannon and the Mud Flower Collective, *God's Fierce Whimsy* (New York: Pilgrim, 1985) and Elisabeth Schüssler Fiorenza, *Bread Not Stone* (Boston: Beacon, 1985)

15. Paola Marrati writes beautifully about the importance of this condition for Cavell in his memoir: "*Little Did I Know* is thus, among other things, one of the very few philosophical meditations on childhood whose first claim, I believe, is that 'having been a child' is a condition that none of us—no matter how different our happy or unhappy stories may be—can ever overcome, grow out of. 'Having been a child' is not a fact from the past that we may indifferently recall or forget, but rather an internal aspect of our existence that will last as long as we do. As for Heidegger, being-toward-death defines our relation to time and to ourselves as long as we exist, 'having been a child' defines for Cavell our relation to knowledge and language, hence to philosophy, as long as we live." Paola Marrati, "Childhood and Philosophy," *MLN* 126, no. 5 (December 2011): 957.

16. The damage people have suffered from church has perhaps never been more obvious than now, decades on from the initial revelations of a sexual-abuse crisis in the Catholic Church. But what it means to claim that the earth damages us may be puzzling. In making this claim, I am thinking not only about the millennia in which powers of the earth—earthquakes, floods, volcanoes, storms—occasioned fear and awe at their potential to extinguish human life. I am also thinking of how we inherit a damaged Mother Earth that consequently visits new damage upon us, in the rays of the sun, the air we breathe, and the myriad new climate-related weather emergencies we experience.

17. Haraway has a famously bleak assessment of Christian theology and particularly its views on salvation and the production of knowledge. I cannot help but wonder about the splitness she must see the feminist theologian enacting. Donna J. Haraway, Modest_Witness@Second_Millennium. FemaleMan©_Meets_OncoMouse™: *Feminism and Technoscience* (London: Routledge, 1997).

I

Attunement

TO PARAPHRASE THE nuns of Nonnberg Abbey, how do you solve a problem like Augustine? Is any theologian more offensive to feminists than Augustine? Or, except for certain documents of magisterial teaching, is any text more maddening than his *Confessions*? One collection of essays on his thought begins, "[I]t's difficult to find a figure in Western thought whose legacy is more contentious and problematic in the views of many feminists than Augustine's. . . . Augustine is the man whom feminists love to hate."[1] It's true: feminist theology cut its teeth on Augustine, exposing his gendered understanding of sin, his diminished role for women, and his captivation by the Roman ideology of the paterfamilias.[2] The misogyny of Augustine has become so canonical that it has passed into popular Christian imagination. One bestselling Christian author recently described his theology of sex and gender as "[taking] a dump on the church and encasing it in amber."[3]

What makes Augustine such a problem is not that he's the worst defender of patriarchy or that he formulates the most offensive androcentrism or even really that he's uniquely misogynist. When we compare him with, for example, Tertullian describing women as the devil's gateway, or Origen declaring that men should not listen to women, or to any number of men adumbrating the Aristotelian view of women as misbegotten males, Augustine's misogyny pales. No, it's not the depth or intensity of his misogyny that infuriates. It's how much cultural power Augustine's *Confessions* has had—and, to be very frank, how beautiful it is. For both of these reasons, it is a difficult text to stay away from as a theologian. I, at least, find myself coming back to it again and again over the years. The first time it came alive for me, I was a master's student, and I was struck by the story of separation from his unnamed partner, when his heart was left torn, wounded, and trailing blood. My imagination quickened to questions that Augustine's text could not answer but I could not ignore. Did the heart of his once-beloved also bleed? What kind of healing did she find, and how? As his star rose to become one of theology's guiding lights, she remained in shadows. I thought about her because I found his writing about women and gender problematic; I thought about her because I found his writing compelling and insightful.

What is a feminist theologian to do with Augustine's *Confessions*? Do we come to it suspiciously, ready to unmask the ways misogyny infects its story? Are we ready to pounce on evidence of its patriarchal commitments and expose its gendered expressions of power? Where and how far can such strategies take us? Might other modes of interpretation take us elsewhere? Challenging all our textual practices, Marcella Althaus-Reid presses the question of what encounters our strategies choreograph, invite, or inhibit. "If God is God, not of the dead, but of the living," she writes, ". . . our reading of the Scripture should have characteristics of life in it, such as birth, creation, recreation, movement and novelty."[4] What role do birth, creation, recreation, movement, and novelty have even in our non-scriptural texts that we take to reveal the God of the living? What role do they have in reading the *Confessions*?

In what follows, I argue for attunement as a mode of engagement bearing such characteristics of life, as a creative and generative way feminist theologians can engage texts sick with misogyny. I described attunement in the preface as an aesthetically aware and constructively oriented way of reading and writing. It engages, I noted, the patriarchal inheritance of Christianity through attention to the texts' aesthetic investments in order to augment and build positive affordances for women and other marginalized genders. Through this mode, feminists can negotiate Christianity's misogynistic inheritance without reinforcing a misogynistic framing of women and the gender-marginalized as external or peripheral to theological conversation. Unlike the interpretive modes of avoidance and critique, in other words, attunement extends the possibility of reading misogynistic texts *as feminists* while remaining internal to the streams of interpretation by which these texts continue to speak. Through attunement, feminists can claim the theological tradition as our own and so, like earthworms to topsoil, remake it. It is creative and re-creative, novel and dynamic.

In this chapter, I concretize that description of attunement, exemplifying the work it can do by engaging Augustine's *Confessions*, which I argue is a text that is itself about attunement and which, additionally, feminist theologians can through attunement claim anew, as one of *our* texts. Drawing a contrast with critique and avoidance, I also show how attunement resonates with conversations occurring in other disciplines about critique. As I adapt those insights for theology, I show how feminist theologians can build on the gains of the feminist pioneers by constructively interpreting problematic and powerful texts such as Augustine's *Confessions*.[5] I accomplish this by performing two different kinds of readings of the *Confessions* over the course of this chapter, first in the mode of critique and second, nearer the end of the chapter, in the mode of attunement. Along the way, I engage a conversation ranging across the humanities that helps describe the limits of the first kind of reading and begins to gesture toward the possibilities of the second. This is not to advocate that attunement displace critique and avoidance but to suggest the significance of attunement for feminist theology's next stage of evolution, particularly in transforming the theological discourse to be more conducive to women and others marginalized by gender.[6]

* * *

One familiar way feminists have engaged Augustine is to unmask the gender ideology funding his theological claims. Unmasking is a strategy of critique, a way of enacting a hermeneutics of suspicion that interrogates the text for its agendas. But when it comes to Augustine's *Confessions*, critique can seem derivative, defanged even, because who deploys suspicion more rigorously than Augustine against himself? Who is more committed to reading the desire behind the desire, to discerning the idol behind the sign, to maintaining the opacity of the self to herself, than Augustine? Who has more memorably captured the anxious mood than he? He's even anxious about his infant breastfeeding self.

Augustine learns about his infant self by observing other infants, and we see in his observations the suspicious mood of critique at work. "I have personally watched and studied a jealous baby," Augustine writes. "He could not speak, and pale with jealousy and bitterness, glared at his brother sharing his mother's milk."[7] Augustine watches studiously, the infant glares jealously, and the women and caretakers are blinded by sentimental attachment. As Augustine writes, mothers and nurses may smilingly tolerate this behavior, and yet "it can hardly be innocence," he insists, "when the source of milk is flowing richly and abundantly, not to endure a share going to one's blood-brother, who is in profound need, dependent for life exclusively on that one food."[8] How superior are these greedy infants, after all, to cold-blooded murderers? Not only that, but these babies are, to be honest, unrepentant manipulators, using screams and cries to obtain what they want. "At the time of my infancy," Augustine surmises, "I must have acted reprehensibly." And also: "The feebleness of the infant's limbs is innocent; not the infant's mind." Uncharmed by fantasies of infant innocence, Augustine has by this point in his observations answered a question he posed earlier: "Was it wrong that in tears I greedily opened my mouth wide to suck the breasts?"[9] For him, it was indeed wrong. It was the wrongness of original sin, an attestation of the sinfulness that would take root within him as he grew.

Augustine, really, has outcritiqued us all. He anticipates the developments of critique in modernity, when Sigmund Freud returned to the infant as a site for decoding desire and helped inaugurate a new era of suspicious hermeneutics together with Karl Marx, Friedrich Nietzsche, and later Michel Foucault—writers I have elsewhere identified as exemplars of a Baconian iconoclasm determined to dethrone idols of the mind.[10] Like them, Augustine knows that the self is not always how it appears, that idolatry can masquerade as love or fidelity, that what seems like a virtue can be a glittering vice.

What's the point in noting the sin and violence in someone who is already convinced of his own sin and violence? And the misogyny of this episode of the greedy infant is really too obvious to point out. Or is it?[11] Rachel Muers reminded us years ago that stating the obvious is an important practice of feminist theology, just as the central conviction of feminism that women are humans is both obvious and radical.[12] These insights need constantly to be reclaimed and reaffirmed in different contexts. Besides, there is (I admit) a certain pleasure in critique. Pausing in my march toward attunement, then, I offer a brief feminist critique of the *Confessions*, starting with the greedy infant of Book 1.

First is the issue of how gendered Augustine's critical observations are.[13] The posture of critique is one in which a knowing critic has epistemological priority over a naive believer or an unsophisticated interpreter—and Augustine's naive believers here are not general or anonymous. They are specifically the mothers and nurses suckling the infants, who smile obliviously and indulgently at the small sinners at their breasts. They have, quite literally, unthinking attachments to these babes. Overly sanguine about infant desire, these women with their bodily attachments cannot or will not perceive the avarice expressed in an infant's wanting. Their breasts, in these ways, both cause and exemplify their moral complacency. It takes the man observing at a distance, literally detached, to correctly see the sin of infant desire for the breast.

Beyond the question of how gendered epistemological access seems to be, what are we to make of the way Augustine chooses this episode as his first account of sinfulness in the *Confessions*? The distorted desire for nursing breasts in Book 1 foreshadows the more famous episode of the pear theft in Book 2 and his more persistent sin of lust which he worries about in the rest of the books until his conversion in Book 8. Situated between stories recounting sinful desire for a woman's body, the episode of the pear theft catches some of their resonances, so that the flesh of the fruit seems to evoke the flesh of a woman. In the section immediately prior to the pear theft, Augustine remembers how his parents relaxed their discipline and thereby allowed him to pursue sexual pleasure. His sinfulness, he writes, quoting the Psalms, "burst out from [his] fatness."[14] The next sentence introduces the pear theft, as if it erupts from his lust.

Of course, Augustine is not as interested in the pears as he is in female flesh; he describes the pears as in themselves unappealing. But the arc of Augustine's life and conversion suggests an intertwining of fruit flesh and female flesh. The pear theft episode is Augustine's retelling of the Fall narrative, his version of a paradigmatic sin. All sin, he claims, is a perverse imitation of God, and in the case of the pears, he perversely imitates the liberty of God, who is subject to no law, by *not* subjecting himself to law governing property. But when Augustine is healed from such perverse imitation, the law that he finally has to subject himself to is not about property; that battle disappears after the pear episode. The law he must subject himself to for healing is the law of sexual morality that will defeat his lust for female flesh. "Not in . . . eroticism or indecencies," he reads during his conversion in the Garden of Milan ". . . but put on the Lord Jesus Christ, and make no provision for the flesh in its lusts."[15] It is submission to this law that heals him, his encounter with these words that divinely rescues him from his storied struggle with female flesh. Shortly after his conversion, his mother, Monica, appears again to share an important religious experience and then, some paragraphs later, die. Augustine pauses in his weeping to question briefly whether his tears indicate overattachment to a woman's body. He affirms that he "could be reproached for yielding to that emotion of physical kinship and invites the reader who condemns his tears to weep in turn over Augustine's sinfulness."[16] Do his bodily connection to his mother and the tears that flow from that attachment render him uncomfortably similar to the smiling, sentimental nurses and their own liquid attachments?

Women's bodily attachments prevent them from knowing rightly, and their bodies are associated with and figure sinful desire for much of the *Confessions*. The conversion Augustine narrates in Book 8 comes by detaching himself from women and from thinking less like a woman. It's a version, perhaps more subtle, of a theme that pervades patristic theology, in which holiness entails becoming more manly, and womanhood or femininity drops away as a person embodies saintliness.[17] To diagnose sin, to renounce it, to theologize about it, is to pilgrim into more authentic humanity and saintliness by turning one's back on women and femininity.

All this is Feminist Theology 101. It takes us somewhere; but where does it leave us? Are we just replicating the suspicious gaze Augustine casts at infant babes by turning it on the writer Augustine? What do we get by looking for the sin behind the sin, the idol behind the idol? Are we left with a very Augustinian regress of sin?

In some ways, yes. And that's useful. Feminist critique renders visible to us the misogyny of the text. To identify the "incoherences in texts that both affirm the full humanity of women but imply its opposite," Muers writes, is a way of stating the obvious that sets a "process of exposure in motion."[18] That's important work that can warn us against internalizing and reproducing structures of domination. It is vital that we identify Augustine's picture of female flesh as occasioning, figuring, and preventing even the naming of sin, so that we do not let that picture colonize our imaginations about gender. But then what? For if this is the sole reading strategy of feminists, it simply confirms what we already know: women are not the intended audience of the *Confessions*, nor are they fully human subjects in the book's imaginative world; at the deepest level, women are not fully included in the world of the *Confessions*. This critique, moreover, can imply a further a claim: perhaps we shouldn't want to be. Some feminists go so far as to see a female theologian reading the *Confessions* as an attempt to authorize her voice through a problematic patriarchal inheritance. To love the *Confessions*, in this view, is to betray women or feminism. This version of critique takes us to the conclusion that we should avoid texts such as the *Confessions*, that we should seek our constructive resources for theology elsewhere.

My Feminist Theology 101 reading of the *Confessions* exemplifies a strategy of textual critique as well as the temptation of avoidance. I'll discuss the second momentarily; for now, I want to stay with the first. The reading I offered was a type of the Baconian iconoclasm I invoked earlier because it aims to expose idols of the mind and expects such exposure to effect liberation. This type of reading says of a text: You thought this was about virtue, but actually it's about power. You thought this was about atonement, but actually it's about sustaining social hierarchies. Or, in the case of my reading of the *Confessions*, the narrative presents itself as a story about a human's sinfulness and God's converting work in that life, but it's really about these understories of misogyny and patriarchal suppression. This strategy of critique focuses on the text and the dynamics within and of the world of the text, on its inhospitableness and its hostility to women.

Another strategy of critique draws on the experiences of women and LGBTQ+ individuals as sources that can be read beside and into patriarchal texts to subvert them. This has been one of the most pervasive strategies of feminist theology, which arguably began in Valerie Saiving's insight that the accounts of sin and redemption promoted by Reinhold Niebuhr and Anders Nygren were not universal human descriptions but depictions from a masculine view. The architecture of her critique went something like this: you thought this was about human sin and redemption, but actually it's about male experience of sin and redemption. This architecture became important to the development of feminist theology as a field and through its struggle with its captivation by White privilege.

There is another major form of engaging Christianity's problematic patriarchal inheritance, one complexly related to critique: avoidance. In the way that my critique of the *Confessions* might suggest feminists should seek their theological resources elsewhere, so does the mode of critique more broadly suggest as complementary the mode of avoidance. Strategies in the mode of avoidance attempt to disarm patriarchal texts by evading—and therefore not amplifying—their misogynistic claims. The strategies of avoidance are various. Feminists who broadly avoid patriarchal texts work to deprive them of their power by refusing to authorize their insights through recourse to male or patriarchal authority. They might establish their conversations in queer theory, feminist studies, ethnographic research, affect theory, or other critical theory. Some feminist theologians have a more narrow strategy of avoidance, where they might comment on patriarchal texts and writers, though without treating the more misogynistic aspects of those texts. They minimize the patriarchy of the text and attempt to enlist the author as a feminist ally. A third strategy of avoidance eschews the masculinist center of Christian theological discourse to rehabilitate women's voices at the margins. Those using this strategy might identify a countertradition more affirming to those who were themselves gender-marginalized. All of these strategies enable constructive feminist theological work by establishing new streams of conversation more generative to women and LGBTQ+ individuals, and yet, absent other modes of engagement, each risks sidelining feminist theologians from the major currents of theological discourse and cementing through their silence Christianity's problematic inheritance.

They are all ways of placing feminist theology outside the temporally extended conversations that constitute the Christian tradition. They construct silos rather than niches.

Both critique and avoidance have been important to building the field of feminist theology.[19] Critique has been a powerful and liberatory tool by which feminist theologians have exposed structures of domination. Avoidance has been a way of introducing voices into the conversation more affirming to women and the gender-marginalized. Further, sometimes, in some places, critique and avoidance are the only salutary ways to respond to a particular text or artifact. Yet, by themselves, such strategies are inadequate to the complexities of the texts and traditions we inherit. Neither critique nor avoidance proposes an ambivalent or constructive way forward with texts of patriarchy (though, as I will shortly argue, critique does express a certain type of ambivalence). They do not transform the hostile into the hospitable or expand the reach of an environment that feminist theologians might call home. So what else can a feminist theologian do? How can she find a way to engage Christian theology as *her* tradition?

Has critique, to misquote Bruno Latour's famous question, run out of steam? Has it led feminist theologians into a political and theological eddy, swirling apart from the mainstreams of theological conversation? I wonder if it is a coincidence that a recent trend of creative writing has emerged in feminist theology. No fewer than four feminist theologians have recently written novels that probe themes central to feminist theology; others have written memoirs, creative nonfiction, and dialogues.[20] Many of these writers are pillars of feminist theology, those who have helped shape the field as it currently exists.[21] And it is not only the pioneers who are thinking with and writing more like creative literature. There is a stirring on the other end of the career spectrum as well. As an early career feminist theologian, Amanda DiMiele has turned to literary studies to develop a methodology of reading White feminism as a literary figure.[22] As these few examples suggest, feminist theologians have long drawn from literary inspiration, but, as Heather Walton observed in 2007, there has been little sustained reflection on its relationship to that discipline.[23] Her comment continues to be true today, as some in the field move in more experimentally literary directions. Could this small surge in feminist theology be symptomatic of the field being ready to pursue such reflection, perhaps growing weary of academic critique? If so, such weariness is not limited to theology.[24] Various concerns about critique are currently welling up around the humanities.

Critique and the Humanities

Across the humanities over the last several years, the possibilities and limitations of critique have been reappraised. A growing number of scholars, particularly in literary theory and gender studies, find it an unsatisfying or incomplete way of relating to texts. In 2017, a volume of collected essays came out titled *Critique and Postcritique*, tracing the various dissatisfactions with critique and collating some emerging alternatives in literary studies. The year before, a special edition of *New Literary History* featured a symposium of voices across humanistic disciplines engaging Latour's *An Inquiry into Modes of Existence* and similarly looking for approaches beyond critique. Latour, after all, had written the much-cited essay in *Critical Inquiry* alluded to earlier, "Why Has Critique Run Out of Steam?," which argues that critique has lost force, spent in intellectual and political cul-de-sacs, and he exhorts academics to embrace a more additive, constructive mode of engagement.[25] Before Latour, Haraway contended that critique must be coupled with care.[26] There is a chorus of scholars who feel critique alone is not taking them where they want to go.

Much of the conversation around critique over the last decade is indebted to Eve Kosofksy Sedgwick, particularly her essay, first published in 1997, "Paranoid Reading and Reparative Reading, or, You're So Paranoid, You Probably Think This Essay Is about You." While remaining deeply appreciative of and committed to critique, Sedgwick traces the way it is saturated in paranoia even as it performs what she calls a naive hope that exposing violence necessarily mitigates it. Many recent essays reflecting on critique or considering an option of post-critique return to Sedgwick, whether to pay homage to her or to linger with the possibilities underconsidered within her essay. They ask, what exactly are the relationships, homologies, and contrasts of paranoid reading and the alternative she presents? And what does it mean that she invokes the work of psychoanalyst Melanie Klein to describe these options for reading?

Drawing on Klein's psychic position theory, Sedgwick writes of critique, "The paranoid position—understandably marked by hatred, envy, and anxiety—is a position of terrible alertness to the dangers posed by the hateful and envious part-objects that one defensively projects into, carves out of, and ingests from the world around one."[27] The full name for this position is the paranoid-schizoid position, language that recalls Haraway's reference to multiple personality disorder but is not meant pathologically. It speaks primarily to a position of infancy. The position is schizoid because in her paranoia about the object, the subject splits the object, herself, and the world into "good" and "bad." When the mother cannot meet all the infant's desires immediately, the infant splits her into the good (full) breast and the bad (empty) breast. The bad part-object frustrates; it is the object of aggression phantasies and fears about retaliatory destruction. Protected from this negativity, the good part-object can be experienced as beloved, loving, gratifying. In paranoid reading, negative affects prevail, though there is in critique, to my judgment, at least, an implied loving, too, a submerged split position, the good breast that pairs, often unseen, with the bad. The text needs to be criticized; I want to keep thinking about the text. I find the high-stakes conversation terribly flawed; I want to be in the high-stakes conversation. In this ambivalence that comes wrapped in negative affect, the critic experiences herself as split, schizoid, "laid out on the table with multiple personality disorder."[28] The problem with this multiplicity, the reasons it flattens a person, is that the good part remains unacknowledged. Critique performs without necessarily recognizing its own ambivalence.

Most of the discussion Sedgwick inaugurates treads only lightly (if at all) through Klein's psychic positions. Using a variety of vocabularies and interlocutors, Rita Felski, Toril Moi, Stephen Best, Sharon Marcus, Amada Anderson, Clare Hemmings, José Muñoz, Robyn Wiegman, Heather Love, and others have described the limits of critique through a wide set of concerns and vocabularies. Some speak specifically to the field of literary studies, but some are relevant across the disciplines. Their arguments include, for example, that critique presents a reduced version of the work it wants to interpret, that it convinces through a negativity that obscures other forms of affective attachment, that it betrays its democratic politics with an elitist epistemology, that, in fact, this epistemological elitism has been deployed by right-wing conspiracy theorists to undermine democratic politics.

James Simpson argues that there is, moreover, a kinesis to critique. Tracing the history of iconoclasm in the English tradition, he notes that iconoclasm is always an unfinished project. Smashing one image implies the need to smash others, as it is impossible to secure the world, the heart, the mind from the threat of idolatry.[29] The heir to early modern material iconoclasm, as he sees it, is conceptual iconoclasm, what I have described as a type of Baconian iconoclasm, where texts and ideas are unmasked to reveal their captivating ideologies. Such conceptual iconoclasm often targets historical accretions and traditions across time and can thereby go hand in hand with declension narratives. It identifies what we can call a negative affordance. Critique, in other words, can be helpful in dissolving destructive structures and relations, but it establishes no end to its own project, nor does it sustain constructive work.

In a world of ambivalence and ambivalent relations—communities of love and violence—we need modes of relation beyond critique. Feminist theologians especially—swimming in traditions of ambivalent texts, situated in a constructive discipline defined by its attachments—need relations beyond critique. Or, as Muers put it in 2007, we need ways of negotiating the past beyond "subservience" (not feminist), "rejection" (often critique, also avoidance), and "use and abuse (in which some of the past is designated usable, some cast aside)" (often avoidance, sometimes critique).[30] In Muers's language, we need a way of refusing disconnection, of understanding and tracing relations of past, present, and future.

Sedgwick proposes reparative reading, akin to Paul Ricoeur's restorative reading, as an alternative and complement to paranoid reading. While reparative reading also responds to a damaged and damaging world, it responds differently from critique—not just announcing the bad news and reiterating the problems but constructing a more generative and sustainable relation to the world.[31] Sedgwick describes the reparative impulse as "additive and accretive," one that "wants to assemble and confer plenitude on an object that will then have resources to offer to an inchoate self."[32] If the paranoid position splits and relates to part-objects, the reparative reassembles to relate to the whole object, though this wholeness, as Sedgwick emphasizes with italics, is "*not necessarily like any preexisting whole.*"[33] It is a "more satisfying object," "assembled to one's own specifications," "available both to be identified with and to offer one nourishment and comfort in turn."[34] This wholeness is premised not on dispelling ambivalence but on renegotiating it.

This alternative captured the critical imagination of many. Ellis Hanson describes reparation as an act of love grounded in disillusion; Wiegman as building "small worlds of sustenance that cultivate a different present and future," acknowledging a hurtful present by "respond[ing] to the future with affirmative richness."[35] Maggie Nelson draws on Sedgwick's notion of the reparative, describing particularly Muñoz's move of "misidentification" as enabling something very like how I describe attunement: a third way between "aligning with or against so-called exclusionary works of art or culture," "that allows people to transform 'these works for their own cultural purposes.'"[36] Like critique, then, reparative reading implies a kind of hope. Still, the hope of the reparative is not identical to optimism; Klein's name for this position is "depressive."

What distinguishes the reparative from the paranoid is not that they claim damage or imply hope. It is the way they perform that hope. The additive and accretive impulse of reparation moves in the opposite direction of the subtractive and unmasking impulse of Baconian iconoclasm. In the language of different types of iconoclasm, it is what I call Wittgensteinian iconoclasm. For when Ludwig Wittgenstein worries about a picture holding us captive—a picture, it turns out, of language acquisition in Augustine's *Confessions*—his strategy is not to expose or unmask in an attempt to attack and dethrone the picture. It is to proceed by example to give multiple cases of how language works otherwise; he loosens the grip that captivating picture has on our imaginations by emplacing it, in Wittgenstein's own terms in *Philosophical Investigations*, in an "album of sketches."[37]

Wittgensteinian iconoclasm does not supplant Baconian iconoclasm—supplanting is, after all, a move of Baconian iconoclasm, which says *not this but that*. Instead, Wittgensteinian iconoclasm supplements the Baconian, offering another way to respond to captivity. Similarly, Sedgwick's reparative reading does not replace critique, though it is often read that way. As George Shulman writes of Sedgwick's approach, "a truly 'reparative' view of paranoid theory or radical politics would have to value and sustain ambivalence, a tension between the hermeneutic of suspicion and quest for deep truth that characterizes 'critique,' and a generosity that seeks and welcomes possibility, in the form of unexpected changes, actions, attunements."[38] The reparative can affirm the goods of critique, can even enfold it into its own set of strategies, perhaps even enabling critique to see its own ambivalence. Besides, Sedgwick herself continued to practice critique; her concern was not about paranoid criticism per se but about the hegemony of critique and the difficulty of establishing other interpretive modes.[39]

In seeking to supplement rather than supplant, Sedgwick's reparative reading and Wittgenstein's iconoclasm are kindred. Both expand the clutch of interpretive strategies rather than tossing some out. But there is a difference between them as well. In the case of the reparative impulse, Sedgwick works not exactly by adding one sketch to another—which could suggest that the original sketch remains untouched, intact, and separate from the sketcher and beholder. It works by attuning or reattuning us to the sketch, as the sketch acquires features that can restore us.

Introducing Attunement

My use of the word "attune" is purposeful. It has also surfaced lately in literary studies, particularly in the work of Felski, as she seeks to explain how we become attached to certain texts and artifacts and how such works move us and mean for us. Attunement can speak to how our relationship to works shifts: we can become attuned to a work of art or music that previously left us unmoved, as we can become unattuned to a work that once moved us.[40] Felski takes her use of attunement from Zadie Smith's essay for the *New Yorker*, "Some Notes on Attunement," when she describes her conversion to the music of Joni Mitchell. "The first time I heard her I didn't hear her at all," Smith begins her essay. She describes her friends' and her husband's disbelief at her indifference, her resistance to their entreaties to listen again and reconsider, until one day, driving to a wedding, at a stop at Tintern Abbey, fixated on sausage rolls, she hears Mitchell on the car radio, and it undoes her. "How is it possible to hate something so completely and then suddenly love it so unreasonably?"[41] Now she cannot listen to Mitchell without weeping.[42]

Not all attunements happen so suddenly. Not all are like Smith converting to Mitchell or Augustine in the Garden of Milan. Sometimes they come suddenly, other times gradually. Sometimes by conscious practice, other times by subconscious transformation. They can come without a writer's explicit intention or because of it. Later in her essay, Smith describes more familiar, traceable processes of attunement, as when through intentional research and repeated reading, she comes to love novelists such as Fyodor Dostoevsky whom she previously didn't.

Nor does attunement happen only outside a text. It can also occur within it, can be performed by authors attempting to attune readers to the subjects they explore. Smith offers as an example of attuning readers to Søren Kierkegaard's *Fear and Trembling*—particularly the "Exordium," which is also translated as "Attunement." In preparation for contemplating the story of Abraham's binding of Isaac, *Fear and Trembling* opens with a simple man seeking to comprehend this great story. Four times the story is retold, meditated on, reimagined, and each time it ends with the vignette of a mother weaning the child from her breast. After the first telling, the mother in the vignette blackens her breast so that it will not look appealing to the infant. After the second, the mother hides her breast so that the child, in a way, loses its mother. After the third, the mother mourns with the child their new separateness. After the last, the mother has food stronger than milk ready for the child. "When I read the 'Exordium,'" Smith writes, "I feel that Kierkegaard is trying to get me into a state of readiness for a consideration of the actual Biblical story of Abraham and Isaac, which is essentially inexplicable. The 'Exordium,'" she continues, "is a rehearsal: it lays out a series of rational explanations the better to demonstrate their poverty as explanations. For nothing can prepare us for Abraham and no one can understand him—at least, not rationally. Faith involves an acceptance of absurdity. To get us to that point, Kierkegaard hopes to 'attune' us, systematically discarding all the usual defenses we put up in the face of the absurd."[43] So Smith argues that the attunement in *Fear and Trembling* prepares the reader for the philosophical-theological text that follows. It is prior to argumentation and preparatory for it, so that even if the point of any particular attunement is, as Smith understands the point of the "Attunement" in *Fear and Trembling*, to repudiate rational explanation, attunement has a complex relationship with rationality.

The types of textual or artifactual attunements Smith describes echo the larger attunements by which humans live together. Attunement names a form of deep human agreement that makes reasoning together possible, that names how it is we can know and make ourselves known to one another. That, at least, is how Stanley Cavell puts it. Our modes of thought and speech for him express "attunement in our criteria."[44] Attunement is a name for human agreement that is pre-rational in the sense that it speaks to how our arguments mean anything to one another, how they can make a claim on one another. Thinking with this Cavellian sense of the word, Felski writes, "To be born is to be thrown into a form of life, with its preferences and prohibitions, its idioms and its silences. Becoming attuned, in this sense, is a precondition of any form of being and living with others—whether we think of the young child's attuning to the gestures and facial expressions of a parent . . . or the later attuning to what counts and what matters in the world within which one must make one's way."[45] Attunement for Cavell speaks to how we reason, speak, and philosophize as separate people who can yet make ourselves known to one another.

A word like "attunement" might raise the hackles of some feminist readers who remain vigilant for ways feminist theology might become accommodated to the status quo or concerned about how, per Cavell, attunement names an "agreement" feminists should refuse. Given the history of misogyny and patriarchy in Christianity, these worries are well founded. Yet attunement's relation to agreement does not name capitulation to misogyny. When Smith describes her conversion to Mitchell, she articulates one type of attunement. The textual strategy of attunement is another type in that family. In its broadest sense, attunement identifies the possibility of intelligibility to one another. There is no line from the agreement Cavell invokes here to the particular agreements human make and share with one another. The kind of agreement Cavell identifies with attunement names, rather, the possibility of any meaningful communication, including the possibility of disagreement. The loss of attunement, then, speaks to a loss in our capacity to reason together. This is the condition that Cavell's predecessor Wittgenstein sees in philosophy: that the philosophers have lost attunement to ordinary ways of life and speaking. Wittgenstein's project, and Cavell's following his, attempt to reattune philosophy to the ordinary.[46] For philosophy to lose attunement to the ordinary is for it to lose something important about being human, which is coterminous with the capacity for attunement.

Evolutionary biologists also invoke attunement to describe our relations to one another. As they use the term, it names something related to what Felski, Smith, and Cavell mean by attunement, and it begins, for them, in our mammalian infancy. Evolutionary biologist Sarah Blaffer Hrdy invokes attunement to describe the relationships generated by more than 220 million years of maternal lactation. She tells a story in which the mammalian mother not attuned to her infant's condition would lose the baby to starvation, dehydration, or exposure, and so natural selection favored babies and mothers sensitive to each other's signals and bodies. Lactation requires a high level of attunement to the baby's appearances, smells, and sounds, and the baby co-creates this attunement, partially through lactation. The first mission of a mammal baby, Hrdy writes, is "stimulating and conditioning its mother making sure that she becomes addicted to nursing" and therefore also more attuned to the baby's signals.[47] For Hrdy, learning mutual attunement to one another begins with the attunements we learn as infants at the breast. Is it any wonder divinities such as Artemis of Ephesus appear covered with breasts or that "El Shaddai" is etymologically connected to breasts?[48] Breasts provide, in Hrdy's evolutionary story, not just physical nourishment but our entrance into human society, mutuality, and love. Even now, when new technologies mean we do not depend on breasts for survival in the same way we did for the previous millions of years, even though many of us did not nurse as infants and fewer of us have nursed infants, breasts yet reveal to us something about our creaturely mutuality and dependence on one another.

In contrast to readings that aspire to detachment or distance, attuned readings, resonant with Hrdy's descriptions of our mammalian attunements, acknowledge a type of attachment. But they also speak to an attachment that comes in the wake of new forms of separateness. The attunements of lactation are important for mammals because baby and mother have lost the attachment of pregnancy. Attunement emerges with birth, as we experience a new type of separateness, a new precariousness, that gives rise to and characterizes this new type of attachment. Because attunement speaks to our ability to be in relation to one another and the world, attunement can also speak to the negotiating of those relationships, even ambivalent ones. This capacity, too, is learned at the breast, according to Klein. As the infant transitions from splitting the mother-breast into the bad part-object it hates and the good part-object it loves, thus fearing and suspecting the breast (the paranoid-schizoid position) to discovering that the hated and loved breast are the same (the reparative-depressive position), it learns to accept the whole mother.[49] Reparation and ambivalence are bound together and to this acceptance of the whole mother, the whole inheritance. Perhaps we could also understand weaning as a loss that is also a new type of attunement, as the mother provides stronger food for the child's stronger body.

As a textual strategy, attunement arises from ambivalence. For not only do we tune out, tune in, and retune to texts and artifacts, but *we can decide to* tune out, tune in, and retune.[50] I mean that attunement is not just something that happens to us but something we can meaningfully participate in. For attunement highlights the way texts are co-created by our interpretations of them, which are themselves shaped by any number of other mediations.[51] And there can be new textual attunements when mediations are gathered and constellated. Attunement in these ways names both a mode of engaging the texts and the posture that enables such engagement, a more active and passive style of interpretation. As an argument about how to interpret, this book weighs toward the active mode of engaging texts, though the use of actor-network theory in chapter 3 will depolarize these options, to place them on a spectrum of various agencies. But conversions experienced as happening to a person are also attunements.

In addition to literary precedent, there is theological reason to turn to attunement. To return to the words of Althaus-Reid: "If God is God, not of the dead, but of the living . . . our reading of the Scripture should have characteristics of life in it, such as birth, creation, recreation, movement and novelty."[52] If God is the God of the living, then at least some of the readings of *all* our sacred texts, all those that witness to Christ, the resurrected one, the one who rebirths us into new life, should themselves bear the marks of birth, creation, recreation, movement, and novelty. What would it look like for reading to embody such vitality, such intention to renew and restore to the fullness of life?

Attunement and Interpretation

Attunement enacts Ricouer's double restoration of text and reader and Sedgwick's modification of "restoration" to "reparation." I repair the text, for Sedgwick; the text repairs me.[53] Attunement and its double, reparation, are part of Augustine's own story of conversion and growing love of scripture. Augustine turns to scripture after a mini-conversion. He reads Cicero's *Hortensius*, drawn to it by its rhetoric, and finds it inflames him with love for truth. So converted, attuned to truth in a new way, Augustine turns to scripture, eager to repeat, perhaps even intensify, his experience of reading Cicero. But he is disappointed. After the complex symmetries and dynamic tensions of Cicero, the simplicity of scripture seems crude. Later in Milan, his search for good rhetoric takes him to the preaching of Ambrose. His experience in some ways repeats his encounter with Cicero but with an important twist: Ambrose was interpreting scripture in his sermons, and so not only do the beauty of Ambrose's rhetoric and the powerful truth of his ideas strike Augustine, but hearing Ambrose, Augustine hears scripture in a new way. Ambrose's method of allegorical interpretation gives him scripture anew, and he finds it beautiful. Through Ambrose, Augustine attunes to scripture's music. Augustine is well on his way to the conversion in the garden at this point. Perhaps as a literary conversion, his story is complete. And yet the reparative moment, the moment where he can say, "The text restores me; the text repairs me," has not yet arrived.

For he is still striving with lust of the flesh, a struggle that peaks in Book 8, as Augustine is awash in a cascade of conversion stories, foremost among them Antony's, when the saint hears the words of scripture read as if directly to him: "Go, sell all you have, and give to the poor." Augustine hears a story of Antony's example inspiring an official, the official's friend, and then their fiancées, and Augustine longs to follow after them. We know how the story goes. He is weeping over his divided longings in a garden when he hears a child's voice, "Take and read," and, remembering how Antony took the words of scripture as spoken directly to him, decides to take the scripture passage he reads in the same way. When the passage enjoins him to give up lust of the flesh and put on Christ, Augustine receives the command joyfully. At this moment, when the words of scripture have been mediated to Augustine by Cicero, Ambrose, and Antony, among others, the text repairs him, restores him.

But Sedgwick and Ricouer write of two movements. The text repairs me, and I also repair the text. Augustine's relationship with scripture encompasses both. Augustine interprets scripture and, in his own interpretation, repairs it, by which I mean he bears it forward in new ways, in ways that make it more difficult for someone to encounter scripture as bald and crude as he once did and more apt to see in it the beauty that Ambrose's way of presenting scripture made obvious to him. The final book of the *Confessions* is his post-Ambrose reading of the creation narrative in Genesis, a text previously primitive and untenable to him. Augustine gives scripture to the reader anew, because attunement changes not just the reader but also the text she reads. It involves mutual restoration, mutual repair.

By claiming that an interpreter bears a text forward in "new" ways, I don't mean to stress unprecedentedness. I mean to stress the freshness, the novelty, of being re-presented from another mind, another set of mediations. All compelling readings give us texts anew, even ones that strive to be faithful to traditions of interpretation. Augustine gives us scripture anew as Kierkegaard gives us the Akedah anew in *Fear and Trembling*, as Cavell gives us Henry David Thoreau's *Walden* anew in his book *Senses of Walden*. The attunements of these readers generate for future readers new ways of attuning to the texts they interpret—a capacity I will explore further in chapter 3. The text a reader encounters is caught up in these interpretations and mediations of meaning, which are new wholes that may nourish and satisfy. Rather than a discrete object cut off from reader and world, the text is bound to both in complex ways.[54]

So perhaps it is becoming clear why I think attunement has possibilities for feminist theologians: it is a mode of engagement that participates meaningfully in traditions of textual interpretation without bracketing feminist commitment or seeing such commitment as something external to the stream of interpretation. In the case of Augustine's *Confessions*, attunement can help us approach the text not just as a narrative about attunement but as a narrative to which we, as feminist theologians, can generatively attune.[55]

Attunement and the Confessions

Let's return again to the *Confessions*, back to breasts and the denial of female flesh. How can reading that text through the mediations of literary theory, evolutionary biology, aesthetic conversions, and ancient breasted gods help us bear Augustine forward, in ways that help feminist theologians discover ourselves internal to the interpretive streams and stories of Augustine? How can we create a more habitable text?

Remembering himself as a babe at the breasts of his mother and his nurse, Augustine muses, "the good which came to me from them was a good for them; yet it was not from them but through them. Indeed, all things come from you, O God."[56] The nourishment Augustine gains from his nurse is ultimately from God, and even more: as all good gifts are, for Augustine, *of God*, so the breasts his infant self suckles are most fundamentally the breasts *of God*.

El Shaddai, the god who suckles all creation to life, stalks Augustine's text and memory.

It is not really breasts or intemperance or greed that worries Augustine in Book 1, anyway. The great anxiety of Book 1, as expressed in its summative conclusion, is peeling apart creation from Creator, loving the first as if it is separable from the second, as if it contains its own end. To fail to love gifts as if they are from a giver is for Augustine a form of idolatry. It is love stopping short of its final end. What Augustine will learn, over the course of the *Confessions*, is not to love creation less but to love it properly, as signifying the Creator, and in that process learn to love creation more. Within Augustine's narrative, it does not make sense to describe the problem of his infant self's greedy desire for breasts as excessive desire. It is, more precisely, an excess of desire in a world that has not opened to meet it. The infant Augustine cannot yet desire the breast as the breast of God.

For the infant's world is so small; the mother is the only divinity they know. The desire for the breast, in addition to being a desire for nutrition, is also proto-religious, proto-social, and proto-sexual. The desire is so large and plural, and yet it is directed toward a material object that cannot, as the infant grows, meet the largeness and increasing complexity of that desire. The infant's excess of desire, then, indicates not a sinful amount of desire but a desire that points beyond its putative object.[57] The infant's desire is correlative to a world the infant has not yet apprehended. The mothers and the nurses are right in a way Augustine the narrator does not seem to grasp: the child's coming of age does provide the opportunity for the milk greed to pass away, as the child's world grows and the child discovers objects adequate to its love. The powerful desire noted in the milk greed signals and begets the desire that will drive Augustine's quest throughout the *Confessions*. The very excess of desire is, in that way, a gift.

As the other side of a temptation is a gift, so the other side of Augustine's anxiety that all the world might become for him an idol is the great possibility that all the world can give him God. The other side of his lament about a self that departs from itself and therefore from God—a self that is, in other words, divided against himself—is a hope for a self that becomes one with God as it becomes one with itself. It is a self that comes closest to God when it gives up performing perverse imitations of God. While the drama of Augustine's struggle is at one level about two wills becoming one, about a split self finding a new whole, it is at another level about a struggle quite familiar to parents and children—and especially mothers who have gone through pregnancy. It is the struggle of one will becoming two or of one will learning its contours by learning the separateness of another. Augustine's narrative is a story not just about finding wholeness and self-unity but about relinquishing certain fantasies of wholeness—about learning that he is not God, that God's liberty is not his own, and that he can yet find his freedom through attunement to God's own.

Conversion, in this reading of the *Confessions*, is not achieved by rejecting female flesh. Giving up his beloved of ten years, I'd point out, did nothing to help Augustine draw nearer to God. All it immediately did was drive him deeper into dissipation, causing him to pursue sexual desires that were less clear, less consistent, and seemingly less fulfilling to him as he strove to drown the pain of a heart that had been left bleeding. For even if his life with his once-beloved was not a perfect choice for Augustine, he could still learn to see it, no less than his encounter with Cicero, as yet a gift from God and no less part of his healing. I wonder if Augustine, at some level, also knew that relationship as a grace, for he and his once-beloved named the fruit of their relationship, their son, a gift of God, Adeodatus.

But the *Confessions* is a story, among other things, about the difficulty of receiving gifts, even, or especially, very good ones. One way of interpreting the *Confessions* is as an exploration of how we do not know how to receive good things well, of how anxiety can be determinative of our relation to the world such that we fail to receive what we are given. Perhaps in our feminist attunements, we can see Augustine's narration differently. His narration of female flesh not as God's gift but as that which takes him away from God's gifts does not speak to the way he has to reject female flesh to be one with God. It speaks to his ongoing difficulty with receiving gifts. Perhaps female flesh is a gift feminists can help Augustine learn to receive, a way we can repair the text.

The breasts of his mother and his nurse, the flesh of his unnamed beloved, these are gifts for Augustine to help him learn his separateness from and his kinship to the world, to reattune to it. Through these gifts, Augustine experiences how deep and transforming his desire can be; he learns through them that he is not the master over himself, much less over the objects and people he desires. From his loving liaisons with women, Augustine learns the way his life and his loves most healthfully spring from a relation of dependence on the one who is life and love—which is to say, through a secure attachment. These women, their flesh, are gifts that point toward the gift of more life, more love.

The possibility of female flesh signifying the divine is raised in the *Confessions* by the presence of Augustine's mother, Monica, in Book 9. Through his rebirth in God, Augustine gains new intimacy with the one who birthed him. The rebirth does not displace Augustine's first birth but accrues to it additional meaning. Monica is received anew as gift when Augustine attunes to God as one whom Augustine is both separate from and attached to. For Augustine, the gifts of these women raise worries about a lustfulness or greed that is ultimately idolatrous, and yet their flesh is also among the sacred places where God speaks to him. For Augustine to hear the divine voice in their flesh, as for us to hear (co-create) an affirmation of women as fully human, good, and internal to Augustine's story in the *Confessions*, requires an attunement.

I repair the text. The text repairs me. I have traced the first movement—how feminist reading might repair the *Confessions*. But where is the second? How does the *Confessions* repair me? One way to answer this question is to take the "me" to refer to a feminist theologian and to point to the way Augustine's repair might be the attuned reading he models for us feminist theologians. The *Confessions* is a story about Augustine's tuning in to scripture, which he once dismissed as simple and crude but to which, through the mediation of Ambrose and Antony, he developed a powerful attachment, such that it became for him rich with wisdom and meaning. Even the creation narrative, once one of Augustine's biggest stumbling blocks to Christianity, becomes the source of his final meditation in the *Confessions*, as Augustine both receives and gives scripture anew. The repair the *Confessions* can offer feminist theologians is a provocation to creatively receive the problematic texts of our tradition so that we can bear them forward in new ways.

Another way of answering how the *Confessions* repairs me is to take the "me" more personally, to trace the claims the *Confessions* has made on *me* the feminist theologian. That is work I do in the first chapter of my book *Motherhood: A Confession*, as I work to repair Augustine's idol anxieties about breastfeeding and find that my repairs have also left me vulnerable to receiving anew his powerful insights into misplaced love. Addressing not the "you" of God, as Augustine's text does, but the "you" of my daughter, I narrate one of my own repairs in an early passage from the book:

> For a few months, everything goes well. I provide the milk you take; you take the milk you need, just as Augustine described it. I am an image of divine bounty to you, and my body signifies the unending gifts of God. It is good. Then one day . . . my body stops making enough. The babysitter brings you to me hungry, and after a minute of suckling, you begin to suckle desperately, then cry in frustration. I try different postures and techniques for generating more milk for you. Eventually you become quiet, if not content. An hour later, you're

hungry again, and we repeat the same discomfiting ritual. When I take you to the doctor two days later, she tells me your weight has dropped. We develop a plan to increase my milk supply, and she gives the plan a 50 percent chance of success. Formula is our plan for failure. I hear the word formula as if she has recommended poison. Anxiety fills me.

I become feverish in my attempts to revive my milk supply. For seven days I nurse and then pump every hour, waking up twice more at night to do the same.... I eat oatmeal and lactation cookies and give up exercise. I spin myself into worry and exhaustion, and everyone around me—your father, my students, our friends—feels it. The day I give you formula, I cry. You take the formula happily. I remain unconsoled.

Eventually, the milk supply builds back up. It is never as plentiful as before, but it is enough as you begin to eat solid foods. We continue nursing, though it's not easy, and I often feel guilty and annoyed. Why do I not release myself from my nursing anxiety to love you by other means? I have become confused about my significance—as if my milk were love itself, the abundant life you drink down in liquid form.

How many days did I deny you satiation out of my desire to reclaim my role as the abundant milk-giver? What kind of love was this that kept you hungry?...

It can be a fine line, to love the image as a way of loving the imaged, and to love the image instead of the imaged. It is easy to peel the two apart, separating image from imaged, creation from Creator, and so to seek in the first what can only be satisfied in the second.[58]

The two repairs—mine of the *Confessions* and the *Confessions* of me—are mutually implicated. Only once I can tell the *Confessions* as a story about the gift of female flesh, the way such flesh signifies the goodness of God rather than the basest impulses of human nature, can the *Confessions* help me to see the danger in my relation to my own female flesh, the way it has become implicated in a very Augustinian type of idolatry, precisely because it is such a good and powerful sign of the divine.

The stories, texts, and commitments of feminism enable a new kind of attunement of Augustine's *Confessions*, such that feminist theologians can receive it as *our* text—not just because we can repair it but because in our repairs, we receive it as a text that can repair us.[59] Haraway might describe attunement as repairing our own cars, Darwin as creating a niche. Theologically, we could describe attunement as living into the world in a way befitting our creatureliness. It is a way of acknowledging, first, that we do not create or sustain our own existence, that we are mothered into it, and second, that we are part of creating and sustaining the existence of others, that we mother others. The God who creates us invites us into the work of recreation—as Althaus-Reid puts it, birth, creation, recreation, movement, and novelty. These are the implications of creation and pneumatology.

We could also say attunement is a way of giving birth to our own mother. That language should be familiar to theologians in a tradition that turns on just this radical claim, that God who created all things from nothing created among God's children Mary, who gave birth to Jesus and became the Mother of God. Ephrem the Syrian meditates on this mystery in the voice of Mary: "The Son of the Most High came and dwelt in me, and I became his Mother; and as by a second birth I brought him forth so did he bring me forth by the second birth, because he put his Mother's garments on, she clothed her body with His glory." Mary gives birth to Christ and becomes the Mother of the God who mothered her into existence; Christ gives birth to Mary and becomes the mother of her life in and as a new creation. This image of giving birth to one who gives life to ourselves and others is one we are invited to participate in, to become mothers to the people and traditions who have given us birth, to give life to what has nourished, or at least produced, us. It is mother-becoming as a type of repair.

For another powerful image of reparative mother-becoming, I turn to a scene that pulls me like gravity in every book I write. I try to resist its lure but am a small moon, drawn again to orbit the planet of this image. At the center of the scene is Macrina, the severely loving fourth-century woman who taught her learned siblings, rebuked her brother known as "the Great," chastised another brother who memorialized her in text, and inspired her mother to turn their home into a religious community. Her breast (we are back at the breast) is sick with cancer. Her mother, Emmelia, wants to call a doctor to heal her. But Macrina can't. It seems to her too immodest, too charged with the danger of enticing a violent male desire. She knows from family lore and personal history the threat a man can pose to a woman who wants to commit to a life of celibacy. But she also does not want to pain her mother; she has seen what it is for her mother to lose a child.

Riven by these two desires, Macrina weeps and prays. I picture her on the dirt floor, prostrate in her supplications, when she receives a scriptural memory as a divine vision. Inhabited by the story of Jesus healing a man who was blind from birth, she comes to life with the memory-vision. Scooping dirt from the floor and mixing it with her tears, she goes to find her mother, Emmelia. I imagine she finds her also in prayer and that when

Emmelia turns to Macrina, she sees her daughter radiating some new energy. The daughter takes her mother's hands and says, Mother, if you will apply this tear-mud to my breast and sign the cross of our Lord, I will be healed. Emmelia trembles as she receives this grace from her daughter, the grace of being drawn into the mercy of God to repair her daughter, and she applies the balm, making that familiar sign on her daughter's tumor, following her daughter's lead in a journey of faith. The gift of healing gives Macrina new life; it gives Emmelia new life, as she, like her children, becomes Macrina's student, becomes her spiritual daughter, and so gives her daughter the grace of spiritual motherhood.

The small scar is the witness to this act of mutual healing. It is a mark, a stigma, that echoes and signifies much more famous stigmata, signs of our hope that even the most damaged parts of our world can be healed. At her sick breast, Macrina has gathered a new constellation of materials and drawn from scripture the form of a story that is given new meaning and possibilities in her life. She acknowledges the whole mother—her own mother, herself as mother, the mother lode of stories and songs that sustains her community—and in her life, from her breast, attunes the mother to sing anew.

Notes

1. Judith Chelius Stark, "Introduction," in *Feminist Interpretations of Augustine*, ed. Judith Chelius Stark (University Park: Pennsylvania State University Press, 2007), 21.
2. Augustine's misogynistic credentials were established early in feminist religious writing. See, for example, Rosemary Radford Ruether, "Virginal Feminism in the Fathers of the Church," in *Religion and Sexism: Images of Woman in the Jewish and Christian Traditions*, ed. Rosemary Radford Ruether (New York: Simon & Schuster, 1974), 150–183; Margaret A. Farley, "Sources for Inequality in the History of Christian Thought," *Journal of Religion* 56, no. 2 (April 1976): 162–176; Cornelia D. Wolfskeel, "Some Remarks with Regard to Augustine's Conception of Man as the Image of God," *Vigilae Christianae* 30 (1976): 63–71; Kari Elisabeth Børresen, *Subordination and Equivalence: The Nature and Role of Woman in Augustine and Thomas Aquinas*, trans. Charles H. Talbot (Washington, DC: University Press of America, 1981). Of course, more salutary trajectories have also been identified in Augustine's thought, and Børresen is one example of someone who has identified those along with the more problematic moments. For a summary of these—including Augustine's theology of creation, image of God, resurrection, and asceticism, see Kari Elisabeth Børresen, "Challenging Augustine in Feminist Theology and Gender Studies," in *The Oxford Guide to the Historical Reception of Augustine*,

ed. Karla Pollman and Willemien Otten (Oxford: Oxford University Press, 2013), Vol. 1, 135–141.
3. Nadia Bolz-Weber, *Shameless: A Case for Not Feeling Bad about Feeling Good (about Sex)* (New York: Convergent Books, 2019), 43.
4. Marcella Althaus-Reid, *From Feminist Theology to Indecent Theology: Readings on Poverty, Sexual Identity, and God* (London: SCM, 2004), 17.
5. I am not the only or even the first feminist theologian to approach Augustine's *Confessions* in the mode of attunement. Margaret Miles's beautiful and searching memoir also patterns her life story on and in conversation with Augustine's. Margaret Miles, *Augustine and the Fundamentalist's Daughter* (Eugene, OR: Cascade Books, 2011).
6. Through the discussion of the *Confessions*, I speak of women, a group particularly dismissed in the text, though for the purposes of articulating a strategy more broadly useful outside the gender binary to include all those marginalized by gender.
7. Augustine, *Confessions*, trans. Henry Chadwick (New York: Oxford University Press, 1992), 1.7.11.
8. Augustine, *Confessions* 1.7.11.
9. Augustine, *Confessions* 1.7.11.
10. I discuss Baconian iconoclasm in the final chapter of Natalie Carnes, *Image and Presence: A Christological Reflection on Iconoclasm and Iconophilia* (Stanford, CA: Stanford University Press, 2017). Paul Ricoeur identifies Freud along with Marx and Nietzsche as exemplars of the hermeneutics of suspicion identified as a hallmark of critique in Paul Ricoeur, *Freud and Philosophy: An Essay on Interpretation*, trans. Denis Savage (New Haven, CT: Yale University Press, 1970). Toril Moi challenges this picture of Freud as a thinker of critique and suggests instead that he conjectures based on what is right in front of our eyes in Toril Moi, "'Nothing Is Hidden': From Confusion to Clarity: or, Wittgenstein on Critique," in *Critique and Postcritique*, ed. Elizabeth S. Anker and Rita Felski (Durham, NC: Duke University Press, 2017), 31–49.
11. Some feminist commentary on this episode includes Rachel Muers's insightful "The Ethics of Breastfeeding: A Feminist Theological Exploration," *Journal of Feminist Studies* 26, no. 1 (2010): 7–24; Felecia McDuffie's sensitive "Augustine's Rhetoric of Femininity in the *Confessions*: Woman as Mother, Woman as Other," in *Feminist Interpretations of Augustine*, ed. Judith Chelius Stark (University Park: Pennsylvania State University Press, 2007), 97–118; and, more briefly and ambivalently, Sheila Kitzinger, "Commentary," in *Breastfeeding: Biocultural Perspectives*, ed. Patricia Stuart-Macadam and Katherine A. Dettwyler (New York: De Gruyter, 1995), 385–394.
12. Rachel Muers, "Feminist Theology as Practice of the Future," *Feminist Theology* 16, no. 1 (September 2007): 113.
13. I am hardly the first to point out the gendered nature of critique, which was described in the 1990s under the term "theory" rather than critique by scholars

such as Catherine Lutz and Carol Boyce Davies, who writes, "Theory, as it is reified in the academy, still turns on Western phallocentric (master) or feminist 'gynocentric' (mistress-master) philosophy." Carol Boyce Davies, *Black Women, Writing and Identity: Migrations of the Subject* (New York: Routledge, 1994), 39. Lutz points out that theory, like canon formation, is gendered, raced, and classed and that theory builds upon masculinist cults of genius. Catherine Lutz, "The Gender of Theory," in *Women Writing Culture/Culture Writing Women*, ed. Ruth Behar and Deborah Gordon (Berkeley, CA: University of Berkeley, 1995), 251, 255, 259.

14. Augustine, *Confessions* 2.3.9.
15. Augustine, *Confessions* 8.12.29.
16. Augustine, *Confessions* 9.13.43.
17. Kari Vogt makes this point, which I discuss more in chapter 2. Kari Vogt, "'Becoming Male': A Gnostic and Early Christian Metaphor," in *Image of God and Gender Models in Judaeo-Christian Tradition*, ed. Kari Elisabeth Børresen (Minneapolis: Fortress, 1995; first edition Oslo: Solum Forlag, 1991), 170–186.
18. Muers, "Feminist Theology," 113.
19. Critique and avoidance are not, of course, the only ways feminist theologians have made arguments. For a resonant treatment of how feminist theologians have and could make arguments, see Joy Ann McDougall, "Keeping Feminist Faith with Christian Traditions: A Look at Christian Feminist Theology Today," *Modern Theology* 24, no. 1 (January 2008): 103–124. McDougall draws substantially on Kathryn Tanner, "Social Theory Concerning the New Social Movements and the Practice of Feminist Theology," in *Horizons in Feminist Theology*, ed. Rebecca S. Chopp and Sheila Greeve Davaney (Minneapolis: Fortress, 1997), 179–197; Kathryn Tanner, *Theories of Culture: A New Agenda for Theology* (Minneapolis: Fortress, 1997).
20. Susan Brooks Thistlethwaite, Tina Beattie, Mary Judith Ress, and J. F. Alexander are some examples. Mary E. Hunt wrote about this trend in "Feminist Theologians Bring Wisdom to Fiction," *National Catholic Reporter*, May 29, 2019, https://www.ncronline.org/news/opinion/feminist-theologians-bring-wisdom-fiction. I discuss this further in chapter 2.
21. They are hardly the first to engage in such literary experiments. Katie Cannon's writing career, for example, has been marked by literary playfulness, the interweaving of storytelling with theorizing, and engagement with figures from literary studies such as Zora Neale Hurston. See, for example, Katie G. Cannon, *Katie's Canon: Womanism and the Soul of the Black Community, Revised and Expanded 25th Anniversary Edition* (Minneapolis: Fortress, 2021).
22. Observing the way feminist theology's strategies of reading and storytelling continually redeem White feminism by performatively divesting privilege that cannot be individually renounced meaningfully and then resolving its racism, DiMiele advocates a methodology aimed less at "solving and subverting failure than [at]

practicing creative and careful attention to it." Amanda DiMiele, "Feminist Storytelling and the Problem of White Feminism," *Literature and Theology* 35, no. 2 (June 2021): 122.

23. Heather Walton, *Imagining Theology: Women, Writing, and God* (New York: T&T Clark, 2007).
24. Philosopher Alice Crary points to the way feminists can often see damage and possibility when they are not operating from the pretended detachment of so much analytic critique. "[T]he novelist Toni Morrison and the poet and essayist Claudia Rankine," she writes, ". . . use expressive devices, the former in a fluid, literary style and the latter in a distinctive lyrical fashion, to shed light on neutrally unavailable aspects of the lives of black women in the U.S." Alice Crary, "The Methodological Is Political," *Radical Philosophy* 202 (June 2018): 47–60. The lyrical and literary are potentially generative forms for feminist writing, and these forms of writing also suggest the significance of reflecting on our forms of reading.
25. Bruno Latour, "Why Has Critique Run Out of Steam? From Matters of Fact to Matters of Concern," *Critical Inquiry* 30, no. 2 (Winter 2004): 225–248. Jennifer Fleissner points out that this essay is not the radical break Latour presents it as—that his books *Pandora's Hope* (1999) and *We Have Never Been Modern* (1993) make many of the same points. The latter even includes a section titled "The Crisis of the Critical Stance." Jennifer Fleissner, "Romancing the Real: Bruno Latour, Ian McEwan, and Postcritical Monism," in *Critique and Postcritique*, ed. Elizabeth S. Anker and Rita Felski (Durham, NC: Duke University Press, 2017), 99–126.
26. For example, Haraway, *Modest_Witness@Second_Millenium*.
27. Eve Kosofsky Sedgwick, "Paranoid Reading and Reparative Reading, or, You're So Paranoid, You Probably Think This Essay Is about You," in *Touching Feeling: Affect, Pedagogy, Performativity*, ed. Eve Kosofsky Sedgwick (Durham, NC: Duke University Press, 2003), 128. She originally published the essay in *Novel Gazing: Queer Readings in Fiction* (Durham, NC: Duke University Press, 1997).
28. Sedgwick, "Paranoid Reading," 128.
29. James Simpson, *Under the Hammer: Iconoclasm in the Anglo-American Tradition* (New York: Oxford University Press, 2010), 13.
30. Muers, "Feminist Theology," 125.
31. Ellis Hanson says something like this while elaborating Sedgwick. Ellis Hanson, "The Languorous Critic," *New Literary History* 43, no. 3 (Summer 2012): 547.
32. Sedgwick, "Paranoid Reading," 149.
33. Sedgwick, "Paranoid Reading," 128.
34. Sedgwick, "Paranoid Reading," 128.
35. Robyn Wiegman, "The Times We're In: Queer Feminist Criticism and the Reparative 'Turn,'" *Feminist Theory* 15, no. 1 (April 2014): 11.
36. Maggie Nelson, *On Freedom: Four Songs of Care and Constraint* (Minneapolis: Graywolf, 2021), 30–31.

37. Ludwig Wittgenstein, *Philosophical Investigations*, 4th ed. rev., German text with English translation by G. E. M. Anscombe, P. M. S. Hacker, and Joachim Schulte (Malden, MA: Wiley-Blackwell, 2009), 4.
38. George Shulman, "Theorizing Life against Death," *Contemporary Political Theory* 17, no. 1 (February 2018): 126. Fleissner also describes similarities and togetherness of the paranoid-schizoid and reparative critique and its alternatives in "Romancing the Real."
39. Here I repeat a point made by Wiegman, "The Times We're In," 12. Heather Love makes a similar point in "The Temptations: Donna Haraway, Feminist Objectivity, and the Problem of Critique," in *Critique and Postcritique*, ed. Rita Felski and Elizabeth Anker (Durham, NC: Duke University Press, 2017), 50–72.
40. Felski herself eloquently describes all these possibilities. Rita Felski, *Hooked: Art and Attachment* (Chicago: University of Chicago Press, 2021).
41. Zadie Smith, "Some Notes on Attunement," *New Yorker*, December 9, 2012, https://www.newyorker.com/magazine/2012/12/17/some-notes-on-attunement.
42. Smith, "Some Notes."
43. Smith, "Some Notes."
44. He uses language like this in, for example, Stanley Cavell "Excursus on Wittgenstein's Vision of Language," in Stanley Cavell, *Claim of Reason: Wittgenstein, Morality, Skepticism, and Tragedy* (New York: Oxford University Press, 1979), 168.
45. Felski, *Hooked*, 55.
46. Sanford Shieh makes this point in his reading of Cavell in "The Truth of Skepticism," in *Reading Cavell*, ed. Alice Crary and Sanford Shieh (New York: Routledge, 2006), 159–160.
47. Sarah Blaffer Hrdy, *Mothers and Others: The Evolutionary Origins of Mutual Understanding* (Cambridge, MA: Belknap, 2009), 41.
48. I describe this in Natalie Carnes, *Motherhood: A Confession* (Stanford, CA: Stanford University Press, 2020), 16. David Biale makes a convincing case for El Shaddai's meaning of "God with Breasts" based on its association with fertility blessings and a key passage in Genesis 49:25, which makes a wordplay with Shaddai and breasts (*shadayim*). David Biale, "The God with Breasts: El Shaddai in the Bible," *History of Religions* 21, no. 3 (February 1982): 248.
49. Drawing on psychoanalyst Juliet Mitchell, Jackie Stacey has an interesting description of this shift: "As Juliet Mitchell sums up: 'the baby who has hitherto been destructive of or attached to "part-objects," such as the mother's breast, is now able to take in the whole mother.' For Klein, Mitchell argues, 'How the baby manages this position—whether or not it can identify with an internalized good mother to the extent that it can repair the damage done by its destructive urges to the "bad" mother, or whether it must flee the implications of the position—constitutes the nodal experience for the infant on which its subsequent normality or psychosis depends.' ... Thus, the depressive position ... signals an acceptance of good and bad objects within the mother in her entirety." Jackie Stacey, "Wishing

Away Ambivalence," *Feminist Theory* 15, no. 1 (2014): 44. Quoting Juliet Mitchell, "Introduction," in *The Selected Melanie Klein*, ed. Juliet Mitchell (New York: Free Press, 1987), 9–32.
50. Felski describes these varied possibilities in *Hooked*.
51. Highlighting the attunements of reading resonates with Moi's observations that "reading implicates us" and calls us to "figure out how [we] stand in relation to [a text's] concepts and concerns." Toril Moi, *Revolution of the Ordinary: Literary Studies after Wittgenstein, Austin, and Cavell* (Chicago: University of Chicago, 2017), 210.
52. Althaus-Reid, *From Feminist Theology to Indecent Theology*, 17.
53. Robert Azzarello has a helpful exposition of these two moments in both Ricoeur and Sedgwick. Robert Azzarello, *Queer Environmentality: Ecology, Evolution, and Sexuality in American Literature* (New York: Routledge, 2016), 27–28.
54. In this vein, Muers writes, "We arise not from one tradition but from the crossing-over, the conflicts and unexpected interchanges of many traditions; the theological statements we inherit themselves bear the traces of their multiple origins and cannot be resolved back into singular pure foundations. Christian feminist theological engagement with patristic and medieval authors in their contexts, for example, traces such multiple origins without feeling the need either to repudiate them altogether or to identify the single 'alternative tradition' that produced feminist theology." Muers, "Feminist Theology," 126.
55. In many ways, my advocacy of attunement resonates with the work Tanner does in applying her insights of *Theories of Culture* to feminist theology. Back in 1997, Tanner drew on then-new theories of social movements and culture to argue for the way the cultural materials of feminist theology do not bear fixed meanings but can be reconfigured in more salutary and generative directions that dislodge the more common patriarchal and deleterious meanings in and of themselves; she writes that the "elements do not . . . express patriarchal interests; their service to patriarchy, or to male-dominated social structures is a function of their articulation to such interests by way of particular discursive formations. Since this is so, every element in service to a patriarchal cause has at least some potential for realignment with feminist ones." Tanner, "Social Theory," 188. She therefore calls for a "realignment of cultural items—their disarticulation from service to patriarchy and their rearticulation for feminist purposes," as "the only way to keep feminist theology from being classified as a marginal fringe movement" (188, 189). Tanner translates the possibilities for contesting "the authorizing past of patriarchal theological discourse" in three ways—one is by naming and rehabilitating a rival authorizing past (similar to what I have called a strategy of avoidance), a second is disputing the continuity of a present practice of belief with that past (a strategy of critique), and the third is "reinterpreting and rearticulating the cultural elements so designated [as an authorizing past]" (194). This last one sounds most similar to attunement but remains only as a sketch in Tanner's essay. When McDougall returns to this

essay more than a decade later, she finds this third strategy exemplified by an edited volume on Reformed theology, particularly an essay by Serene Jones attentive to the aesthetic character of Reformed doctrine and one by Mary McClintock Fulkerson engaged in an immanent critique of the *imago dei* in John Calvin's theology. Both Jones's and McClintock Fulkerson's essays are powerful and yet share more in common with critique than what I am elaborating as attunement. Tanner, "Social Theory"; McDougall, "Keeping Feminist Faith." Mary McClintock Fulkerson, "The *Imago Dei* and a Reformed Logic for Feminist/Womanist Critique," in *Feminist and Womanist Essays in Reformed Dogmatics*, ed. Serene Jones and Amy Pauw (Louisville, KY: Westminster John Knox, 2006), 95–106. Serene Jones has done work that resonates with attunement and indicates possibilities for still more attunements of Calvin in Serene Jones, "Glorious Creation, Beautiful Law," in *Feminist and Womanist Essays in Reformed Dogmatics*, ed. Serene Jones and Amy Pauw (Louisville, KY: Westminster John Knox, 2006), 19–39.

56. Augustine, *Confessions* 1.6.7.
57. I describe some of this in Carnes, *Motherhood*, 20–21.
58. Carnes, *Motherhood*, 22–23.
59. What other texts and artifacts might be reattuned? My vision of attunement is expansive, such that the question is easier to answer in the negative (as I will in chapter 3) than in the affirmative. But I wonder what feminist theologians might make with Thomas Aquinas's porous style of argumentation or what might happen to Beatrice or the circle of lust in Dante's *Divine Comedy*? I'd love to see other feminists following Elizabeth Johnson's lead by working on Anselm's *Why God Became Human* and with their own dialogues reattuning his story of the atonement.

2
Aesthetics

AT FIRST, I didn't notice how pictures preoccupied my feminist theology class. It seems obvious now that the class was filled with images. They came from students—from plays they were in, protests they were organizing, and church symbols they were pondering. They also came from the assigned readings, where printed text sometimes yielded to visual art: a uterus twisting into a crucifix and radiating light like Guadalupe, an ancient stone statue of a serpentine goddess with full hips and thick legs, a bare-breasted Madonna staring unblushingly at the viewer. For the last class, I laminated color prints and gave them to the students as mementos of our conversations together. Even then, I did not register the deep connection between feminist theology and aesthetic awareness. That insight came to me later, after I had been impelled to do my own creative feminist work, as I was reflecting on the origin of that impulse and realized I had been prepared for, and led to, such work by the texts and conversations of feminist theologians.

If attunement is a constructive, aesthetically invested engagement with the positive affordances of texts and artifacts, then perhaps the aspect of that engagement most native to feminist theology is its investments in aesthetics. Chapter 1 argued for feminist theology to do something new by expanding and developing its use of attunement as a mode of engaging its patriarchal inheritance. This chapter qualifies the invocation of novelty, emphasizing that in its aesthetic awareness, feminist theology is already primed for this mode of interpretation. For in suggesting that feminist theology turn more fully toward attunement, I am proposing that feminist theology turn toward and recognize its own founding impulses. There have always been voices in feminist theology signaling the importance, not only of images but of symbols, experiences, bodies, and songs. An awareness of the aesthetic conditions of its own existence has been a crucial part of feminist theology since it coalesced in the 1960s through the 1980s. That is not to claim that the aesthetic interests and projects I outline in this chapter amount to the fullness of the attunement I advocate in chapter 3. Even feminist theologians engaged in deeply creative and aesthetically invested work often continue to critique or avoid the most patriarchal texts and artifacts, seeking resources for constructive work elsewhere rather than reattune them. A full embrace of attunement by feminist theology would be something new and would help those in the field build new theological spaces for communion, and still, aspects of attunement—particularly, serious attention to the aesthetics of argument—are already deep in the field.

The aesthetic impulse is distinctive of feminists but not unique in the theological world. It has also played an important role in Black theology, Orthodox theology, theology and the arts, and, increasingly, environmental theology, among other fields. Even more, some level of aesthetic awareness has been present through much of the history of Christian theology. Theologians made and assessed arguments about the incarnation according to how fitting (*prepon, conveniens, behovely*) they were.[1] They invoked beauty to name God. They described the sacraments bearing "natural resemblance" to what they signify.[2]

Awareness of theology's aesthetic conditions, once so pervasive, waned in much modern thought. In her 2017 article "Imagination, Art, and Feminist Theology," Elizabeth Ursic observes that Ashgate launched its book series on Theology, Imagination, and the Arts in 2000 by asking, "What have imagination and the arts to do with theology? For much of the modern era, the answer has been 'not much.'"[3] But this is not true for feminist theology, she points out, which has from its beginning made imagination central to its questions and arguments.[4] When modern theology lost sight of itself as a thoroughly aesthetic exercise, feminist theology emerged in the recognition that theological-ecclesial battles are fought and won in the symbolic imagination.[5] For centuries, women who made themselves heard and seen as public or quasi-public figures attended to the aesthetic possibilities of their own perceptibility to the church, and feminist theology has likewise exploited, critiqued, sharpened, and expanded such possibilities, though at the level of a collective, women qua women, rather than only for individual, particular women. As gender has complexified and its complexities have been recognized, so, too, have the communities to which feminist theology is accountable, and these recognitions and expansions also come by way of aesthetic strategies. Aesthetics has been critical to the work of feminist theologians.[6]

To claim that feminist theology is invested in aesthetics is not to claim that it is purely or exclusively so invested. Such investments have, to the contrary, disclosed and affirmed the connection of the aesthetic to both the theological and the political. The terrain of feminist theology encompasses concerns about institutions, networks of power, and the material conditions of life and thought—subjects of chapter 3, where I want to argue that the field's political gains come not from backing away from aesthetic inclinations but from leaning into them as interpretive strategies embedded in particular contexts. In this chapter, I want to display how awareness of the aesthetic conditions of theological argument has been an important part of feminist theology by viewing the field through three lenses: its objects, forms, and sources. Aesthetics here encompasses both perceptibility and perceiving, the perceived and the perceiver. It involves, in other words, both what is made perceptible and a way of perceiving and experiencing such that particular objects, ideas, and modes are perceptible. As this chapter surveys feminist theology, the "aesthetics" under question also deepens, from naming perceptibility to raising questions of *whose* perception is under consideration, whose body can be a locus of divine encounter, and how taking bodily encounters with the divine seriously leads to an expansion of the theological canon to include stories, songs, and other art forms. It is not just that these creative genres are aesthetic sources for theology but that they are themselves theological works.

The deepening of aesthetics comes by attending to multiple centuries of work by the gender-marginalized to be seen and heard as fully human, even spiritually authoritative. This chapter excavates some of these stories, not only investigating the establishment of feminist theology but also scanning its prehistory. In each section, I survey a moment in the history of Christian theology and heed those gender-marginalized voices who gain some measure of presence, voice, or authority in them. I see the struggles of these individuals (all but one identify as women) as fascinating foreshadows of the struggles of feminist theologians, rhymes between the role aesthetics plays for individual women and gender-marginalized persons living before the feminist movement and for feminist theologians working in contemporary times.[7] What follows, then, proceeds by induction, gesturing to case after case of the aesthetic investments of women, the gender-marginalized, and feminists legitimating their theological voices, as I suggest the ubiquity of aesthetics in feminist theology.

Early Christian Problematics: Invisible Objects, Absent Subjects

The originating problem of feminist theology was the invisibility of women as theological objects and subjects.[8] Before feminist theology, the object of theological anthropology was "man"; relatedly, the proper theological subject—the agent of action and author of texts—was also "man." Women were thought to be included under that generic object/subject, as derivative of it, but feminist theologians argued that they were not actually identified by the *man* named in theological and ecclesial texts, nor did theologies of "man" treat women as fully human agents. The first task of feminist theology in establishing itself as a field was thus aesthetic in the sense that it aspired to render the invisibility of women perceptible and then render women actually visible, perceptible to the theological field as fully human subjects not assimilable to the category "man." What would it mean to see women as "God's agents of grace and liberation" or as narrators and witnesses of divine encounter?[9] In some ways, these questions suggest how the problem of women's invisibility in academic theology reprises the problem of their erasure in early Christian texts, where we turn next. I want to recognize that here as elsewhere in this chapter, I speak primarily in terms of women and men, which is the dominant framework for understanding gender that these individuals work with, but the strategies of these women and feminist theologians are not confined by a gender binary.

The (Not Quite) Vanished Ladies of Early Christianity

The problem of women's imperceptibility (and related mis-perceptibility) to theology is coterminous with Christian theology itself, extending back to the texts of late ancient Christianity—where appearances of women are already rare. In an essay titled after the Alfred Hitchcock thriller *The Lady Vanishes*, feminist historian Elizabeth Clark considers the difficulty of encountering women in late ancient texts. Not only do they seldom appear in the context of early Christian theology, but when they do, the lady vanishes in two senses. The first disappearance is staged by the text, the second by the historian. It is the second that concerns Clark in her article, as she grapples with the implications of the linguistic turn for feminist historians of late antiquity. Once we accept that women appear as characters in highly produced, rhetorically crafted literary texts—often in hagiography with "self-consciously literary narratives of a strongly panegyric flavor"—any simple translation from a text's character to a historical person becomes fraught.[10] If the female characters, all of whom are authored by men in early Christianity, serve literary purposes, then the attempt to discover "real women" or hear "real female voices" would seem hopelessly naive.[11] These literary women are instead "tools to think with"—devices by which male authors voice ideas unavailable in the male-centric philosophy of a time or by which they shame men with the virtues and wisdom of the weaker sex or by which they venture potentially suspect theological ideas.[12] Clark draws on Julia Kristeva, Luce Irigaray, David Halperin, and Helene Foley to suggest that these women may be "'not a true female Other' to the male philosopher but 'a masked version of the same' . . . 'a necessary female absence.'"[13] Behind the female mask, then, is another man. Twenty years after Clark wrote this article, in a world where we have become more aware of the violence of transphobia, these claims of "unmasking" an apparent woman to discover a man read differently.[14] But Clark's point is not exactly that female characters are male authors in drag but that they are tools of patriarchy used to maintain the patriarchal status quo.

What does this theory of fictional female characters as patriarchal tools mean for reading about female characters who were also historical persons? How can we find, for example, the historical Macrina in the character featured in Gregory of Nyssa's texts, which offers, according to Clark, "the most spectacular representation of a woman saint as philosopher" in late antiquity?[15] The character Macrina's long and learned discourses on Epicureanism and Stoicism do not point to educational possibilities enjoyed by late ancient women so much, Clark points out, as they allow Gregory to test a modified Origenism he expounds in later texts.[16] Clark compares Macrina to Socrates's teacher Diotima, who serves, according to Halperin, as "an alternate male identity whose constant accessibility to men lends men fullness and totality that enables them to dispense (supposedly) with otherness altogether."[17] As Diotima functions as a Trojan horse for a patriarchal ideology propagated by a male philosopher, so, too, does Macrina, regardless of her relation to a historical female person. Opening the character of Macrina like a matryoshka doll, the historian reveals her to be a false female presence, concealing the agendas and desires of and for men. Under the historian's gaze, submitted to her tools of scrutiny, the lady vanishes.

Yet Clark's claim is more nuanced than a flat assertion of female absence. In the case of Gregory's texts, she attends to the contradictions of Macrina's character and the status of late ancient women while also tracing the ways Gregory's "use" of Macrina includes affirming the spiritual equality of women, acknowledging the ways Macrina the character can embolden later generations of women, and evoking the traces and afterlives of a character like Macrina in ways that resonate with how we will discuss affordances in chapter 3.[18] The absence, then is complex: it can be a meaningful datum in itself, can continue to haunt Christianity, can conceal and create shards of presence. Clark's description of the "traces" Macrina leaves anticipates work in actor-network theory and other approaches that see texts less as true or false mirrors of worlds they represent and more as devices themselves fashioned for authorly purposes they yet exceed.[19] It also anticipates Felski's work on character years after Clark's article, when she observes that characters are hybrid entities, formed of composites like authors and characters together.[20] But if current historiographic and literary approaches attenuate the problem of the vanishing lady, they do not entirely resolve it. Macrina yet remains, in some sense, elusive to us—though so does her brother, the author-character Gregory.

The complex vanishing of the lady performed by the historian interpreting the text echoes an equally complex vanishing performed within many late ancient texts. Early Christian literature commonly identifies maleness, men, and masculinity with salvation and holiness, effacing and diminishing femaleness and femininity—as exemplified in the early Christian trope of Christians "becoming male" as they progress in sanctity, as referenced in chapter 1.[21] Vogt traces several examples of how this trope can work. Clement of Alexandria (150–215), for example, differentiates the sexes by their relation to desire. To become a man is to become blessedly free from desire, like the angels. To be like a woman, by contrast, is to be determined by desires, like a beast. Yet sex is only, as it were, skin deep, for the woman who transcends fleshly longings is "turned into a man, the woman who is no more feminine than he, the perfect, manly, woman."[22] Origen (184–253) has an even more emphatically spiritualized understanding of sex and gender, which refers to the inner man, moral categories, and spiritual realities. "Men and women are distinguished according to difference of heart," Origen writes. "How many belong to the female sex who before God are strong men, and how many men must be counted weak and indolent women?"[23] Origen names the Christian ideal through masculinity, which he associates with strength, virtue, and maturity, while also insisting that it is open to women who leave their femininity (i.e., weakness, laziness, dependence, and fleshliness) behind. As the good Christian pilgrim journeys toward maleness in these thinkers and the many who take up this inheritance, femaleness disappears.[24] Thus, when Gregory wishes to praise his sister Macrina, he writes that she seems to have transcended her sex. He wonders at one point whether it is right to call her a woman.

And still, Gregory's hagiography of his sister does not simply deny Macrina's womanhood. It also reaffirms it in some of its most dramatic episodes. As she is dying, Macrina is figured as a bride yearning after her bridegroom, echoing the text's account of her youth as a beautiful and highly sought-after potential bride. After she has died, a religious sister bares Macrina's breast to show a wound from cancer, recounting as she does Macrina's refusal to show her breast to a male doctor out of modesty. That episode itself, recounted at the end of chapter 1, turns on Macrina's relationship with her mother, a maternal connectedness expressed in her mother's joke that she carried all her other children in the usual nine months, but she carried Macrina with her "always and everywhere."[25] If Macrina has "transcended gender," it is in a very particular sense, for the disappearance of the lady into manhood or angelhood also leaves behind evidence of womanhood. It, too, is a complex absence. The case of Macrina suggests that in the field of early Christianity, it is difficult to bring women fully into focus, and yet women have not entirely disappeared from the scene. They have been erased, and at the same time, their presence is marked and sometimes celebrated in the characters some men have authored. Gregory uses the character Macrina for his own writerly purposes and yet also continually presents her as one of his two most important *didaskaloi*. She is a teacher who has marked him such that his current identity is inseparable from her own influence.

Viewing Women in Feminist Theology

Feminist historians and historical theologians have worked to name these amalgamated absences that entail disappearances and shards. As these scholars sought to bring this double absence into view, the theologians also worked to conjure a double presence: to make women visible to the subfield of theological anthropology and to make visible the patriarchal regimes of theology that diminish women and all that is associated with "the feminine." This is deeply aesthetic work, to render perceptible what has gone unseen or what has not been seen as fully human or worthy of consideration—analogous to how a poet might help a person see differently an ordinary thing such as a nest or a morning ritual or an extraordinary thing such as grief or divine encounter.[26] John Clare's "The Yellowhammer's Nest," after inspiring the reader to see bird nests she previously failed to observe, might also cause the reader's horizons to shift, such that she feels her precarious, intensely located place within the world. In the same way, many feminist theologians, seeking to make bodies appear to a field that had long excluded them, have shown the way such work involves helping the field to imagine itself differently, to feel different and differently. It brings into view new theological presences as it makes visceral those absences.

This double, amalgamated absence-presence is classically explored in Saiving's 1960 article "The Human Situation: A Feminine View." Considered the originating essay for feminist theology, it argues that when theologians such as Niebuhr and Nygren refer to "man," they do not, as they seem to believe, refer to humanity but, in fact, more specifically to men. The "feminine situation," Saiving argues, "reveals... aspects of the human situation which are present but less obvious in the experience of men."[27] Drawing on anthropological work of Ruth Benedict and Margaret Mead, Saiving points to women's experiences in the world as gestating, lactating bodies sexually differentiated from men and often involved in the lives of small children, which gives rise to a different relationship to the world, particularly in the "hypermasculine" era of anxiety and achievement that is modern life.[28] As she struggles to make women perceptible as objects of theological anthropology—as fully human subjects with stories not identical to those of men—Saiving wants to avoid essentialism while opening up the narrative arc of sin and redemption to encompass possibilities more faithful to the lives of women. To bring women into view as objects of theological inquiry means taking them seriously as theological subjects, agents in their own pilgrimages, capable of articulating complicated, sometimes conflicting desires. Saiving's struggle to make women visible as theological subjects turns into work that makes visible masculinized regimes of sin and redemption so that theology can imagine itself newly—more inclusively and faithfully.[29]

The work to make visible what is invisible to the world is difficult. How does what is invisible, what is potentially visible, come into view for the one who is theologizing? It is one thing to *know* there is an absence. It is another to see it. Delores Williams describes this struggle at the beginning of her watershed book *Sisters in the Wilderness*. Battling a double absence—as a person of color (absent even to feminist theology) and as a woman (absent even to Black theology), Williams begins, "Where would I begin in order to construct Christian theology (or god-talk) from the point of view of African-American women? I pondered this question for over a year. Then one day my professor responded to my complaint about the absence of black women's experiences from *all* Christian theology (black liberation and feminist theologies included). He suggested my anxiety might lessen if my exploration of African-American cultural sources was consciously informed by the statement 'I am a black WOMAN.' He was right. I had not realized before that I read African-American sources from a black male perspective."[30] With that insight—holding herself in view as a Black woman—her eyes opened to new possibilities.[31] Visibility begins in the concrete reality of her own life. In seeing herself and how that self has been obscured by past theological efforts, she bushwhacks a new path for theology.

The paragraph describing the difficulties and encounters that precipitated Williams's writing follows a preface in which she describes the way theological work ought to be oriented by the autobiographical. Through the autobiographical, the theologian's work becomes akin to "testifying," an experience she remembers from church as a little girl. When they testify, she explains, people witness to God's involvement in history by offering an account of the transformations faith has wrought in their lives.[32] As she testifies about her life as well as the ordinary Black women she has seen resisting oppression and rising amid adversity, she comes into her way of approaching theology. "In the midst of testifying about my own faith and marveling at the faith and courage of female progenitors, I reflect upon what it means to take seriously (as a primary theological source) the faith, thought and life-struggle of African-American women."[33] To bring Black women into view as subjects of theological inquiry, as part of discerning and constructing theological anthropology, for example, their lives must be taken seriously as sources of theology. I'll explore the significance of sources later in the chapter. At this point, I want to note two things about how Williams brings Black women into view as theological subjects. First, in one interesting strand, she aligns herself with "the ancient African theologian Augustine and the European theologian Anselm" as one of the faithful seeking understanding. But then she specifies the understanding she seeks in terms of what it means to be a Black woman in church, weaving these references as she articulates a theological strand newly named at the time Williams was writing: womanist theology.[34] Second, she then goes on to provide what is perhaps in the history of feminist theology one of the most compelling exemplifications of attunement, as she reads the story of Hagar together with the struggle of enslaved persons in the United States, enlisting the help of textual scholars such as Phyllis Trible but also surrounding the scriptural tale with the homilies of Jarena Lee and Sojourner Truth, the novels of James Baldwin and Alice Walker, and slave narratives of forced surrogacy, so that through Hagar's story, "a sense of sacredness emerges" from reflection on Black women's experience.[35] She writes that she "felt like a medium through whom representation, analysis and critique were speaking. I discovered that 'mediumship' provides what Hagar got: new vision."[36] The new vision she receives through inhabiting the person of Hagar is the vision that Williams works to impart to her viewers, as she strives to bring Black women into view as subjects of theological anthropology.

The struggle Williams articulates of identifying that which is invisible was named by Jacquelyn Grant in her book *White Women's Christ and Black Women's Jesus: Feminist Christology and Womanist Response*, written a few years before *Sisters in the Wilderness*. Grant's ultimate theological object in this book, as her title suggests, is Christ, but similar problems to those in theological anthropology arise about the exclusion and occlusions of women. Grant writes of how women's experience has been "camouflaged" and subsumed into supposedly universal male language and experience.[37] She uses this aesthetic term, "camouflage," to describe how women have vanished from sight and proposes contextualization as an important strategy for locating Christ, by finding Christ among those scripture calls "the least of these," and therefore among Black women, with their "tri-dimensional oppressive existence." In this way, she helps bring to the mind's eye what and whom patriarchal language has hidden.[38] Grant's work, then, is to help render Jesus perceptible to her readers, not as someone circumscribed by maleness but as the person who chooses to be bound to those who are poor, Black, female, and oppressed—and is found precisely by looking at poor, Black, female, oppressed people.

The work of making visible is explicitly named in some of the most influential feminist theology of the last half century. Defining patriarchy as a "graded male status system of domination and subordination" that includes racism and classism as well as sexism,[39] Elisabeth Schüssler Fiorenza points to "the silence and invisibility of women" as bound up with language, which both reflects and shapes the world.[40] The supposedly generic masculine language not only fails to make women visible to men, she writes, but it also teaches women to internalize self-alienation, marginalization, and subordination.[41] These lessons are then sacralized through masculinist language about the divine. The role of feminist theology is to liberate by rendering visible, to articulate and claim women as sites of divine presence and disclosure. In response to a church and theology that have colluded in rendering women silent, invisible, and marginal, Schüssler Fiorenza commends a "critical feminist theology of liberation" that can disrupt such patriarchal practices and help render women visible as "God's agents of grace and liberation."[42] Liberation and visibility—as well as audibility—are twined together in this early feminist work. What these feminists want is to make women appear as fully human theological subjects. As Muers writes, "Feminist theology has taken as its task, not only to bring what has been hidden (the lives, voices and experiences of women) into plain sight, but also to draw attention to the contradictions performed within theology and church life, the gaps between profession and action, the incoherences in texts that both affirm the humanity of women and imply its opposite."[43] Like Schüssler Fiorenza, Muers names an invisibility in theology repeated in church life, a connection that becomes still more important in chapter 3.

The work of rendering women visible as human, as agents of grace and liberation, is accomplished in the terrain of the imagination, and the imaginative work of feminist theology is evident again and again, particularly in works such as Kwok Pui-lan's volume *Postcolonial Imagination and Feminist Theology*, where she links decolonizing structures with decolonizing the imagination. Like Williams, Kwok begins autobiographically, about her own childhood in Hong Kong under the legacy of British colonialism. In the wake of her education into that legacy, how, she asks, can she dislodge her habitualized coloniality to claim a postcolonial intellectuality? She offers her volume as part of that process of becoming and helping others become by creating "a little more space to imagine that an alternative world and a different system of knowing are possible."[44] Her book is an imaginative tour de force, calling for the resignification of gender and gathering an array of images of Christ to help theologians imagine Christ anew. This effort to newly imagine God (and humanity) by gathering images is a strategy of many feminist theologians, who draw on various images (Wisdom-Sophia, *Christa*, various Trinitarian depictions) to bring women into view as full subjects and re-establish new forms of "resemblance" between women and the divine. Ultimately, questions of theological anthropology are never finally separable from those of Christology. But here I am venturing into the subject of theological forms, which will take us to the next section.

Before turning to that section, I want to note that the work of unmasking or exposing invisibility is the work of critique, which can also be used to make new subjects and structures visible. The type of visibility critique offers, however, is structured by displacement: not that male subject but this male-and-female subject; not that patriarchal regime of sin and redemption but this one that serves women, too. I say this to acknowledge that attunement does not have exclusive rights on aesthetics; critique also embeds and enacts aesthetic agendas and desires. But if critique is not non-aesthetic, neither does it have exclusive rights on bringing invisibilities and visibilities into view. There are many different ways of rendering perceptible, and attunement opens up paths additional to critique, paths with a wide array of aesthetic possibilities, which are oriented toward a constructive hope of rendering perceptible *as*—*as* fully human, *as* God's agents of grace and liberation, *as* authoritative, and *as* theological subjects worthy of serious attention.

Medieval Texts and Images: Queer Forms

When I first taught Julian of Norwich to my undergraduate Introduction to Theology class in the early 2010s, the eyes of even—of *especially*—my most engaged and nimble readers glazed over. Struggling to entice, cajole, or provoke them to connect with the *Showings*, I paused. "What's wrong?" I asked them. "Why aren't you responding to this?" Silence. Then one student explained, with an air of world-weariness, "I mean, I know why you assigned her. You have to put women on the syllabus. My medieval literature professor told me that's why *he* assigned her." A similar experience was repeated in my graduate class on Christology, where the conversation floundered, and then one student exclaimed, "Honestly, she's just really weird!" I learned the challenge of teaching medieval women to students whose expectations of medieval writing come only from the texts of men. Compared with the writings of their male contemporaries, there is a queerness to their writing tropes and forms not unrelated to the queerness of their gender as writing women.[45]

Because traditional, institutional means of legitimation were unavailable to them, women writing religious texts in the Middle Ages had to find new ways to claim and mediate authority. They are queer in the sense Sedgwick invokes when she writes of "the open mesh of possibilities, gaps, overlaps, dissonances and resonances, lapses and excesses of meaning when the constituent elements of anyone's gender, of anyone's sexuality aren't made (or can't be made) to signify monolithically."[46] The meshes, gaps, lapses, and excesses women used to claim and amplify their voices in a context in which women's voices were not publicly heard have interesting resonances with the way feminist theologians living centuries later have also sought to probe, explore, and play with aesthetic forms. The form of writing, in both cases, emerges under conditions in which the traditional genres and registers of writing are inadequate to the voice that is trying to speak—and the conditions under which such voices may be heard. In looking at a few medieval examples of playing with forms to authorize a voice, I believe we can illumine an aspect of feminist labor in contemporary theological writing.

Images

Even as women were shut out of the institutional ways of conferring public authority through ecclesiastical hierarchies or the developing schools and universities, and even as they were forbidden to comment on scripture, they found authorization from the highest authority of all: God. These women claimed visions, revelations, and messages directly from God. Yet though the revelation may be in one sense unmediated, the way it became authoritative was not. Most important, the (all-male) church hierarchy had to validate and frequently champion the woman visionary. Much could be said about how they claimed authority outside of the texts and artifacts they created—through the convents, confessors, and powerful men to whom they appealed. But there were other important trajectories in how their visions became authoritative, ways these revelations peddled their own legitimacy.

Many of the women writing theology in the Middle Ages—and all of the medieval and early modern women currently recognized as "doctors of the church"—stage for their readers their authority by performing their divine vision, the source of their authority. Narrating a divine encounter, they prove to the reader their legitimacy. This narration or mediation generates theologies that are themselves highly visual, centered around an image or set of images.[47] To take one of those medieval women named doctors of the church as an example: Hildegard of Bingen describes a set of images—which she had produced as visual objects—that she then interprets.[48] Exemplary of her style is *Scivias* 1.1, where she vividly describes a child before a divine figure. After she describes the scene, it comes to life, with the divine figure taking up the role of narrator. More than half of the vision is told in first or second person, the voice of the divine figure within the vision merging with the authorial voice, which mediates divine commands, sharp judgments, and bold claims—all for the purpose of authorizing Hildegard. "Pour forth therefore in a fountain of abundance," the author Hildegard reports the divine figure ordering the child, who stands in for Hildegard. "[S]tream out in your knowledge of mysteries so that those who wish to hurt you because of Eve's transgression will be struck by the force of your irrigating torrent." The divine figure anticipates objections to Hildegard's authority and then confirms that it is divinely given. "For you do not receive this profound and penetrating discernment from a human being. Rather, you receive it from the heavenly and awe-inspiring Judge on high."[49] Hildegard is not just reporting this image; she vividly describes it and then stages the divine figure authorizing her for the reader. More, she does not just report it verbally; she renders it in an image as well. In multiple ways, the reader and viewer has become a witness to Hildegard's authority by her verbal and visual image-making.

There are other examples of authority-conferring images, even from other doctors of the church. Catherine of Siena is remembered for a number of images, including God as a sea in which we the fish swim; the human soul as a tree that should be planted in the soil of humility; humanity as a vineyard in which all the vines connect to one another; and Jesus as the bridge that unites God and humanity, divided by the river of sin.[50] Teresa of Ávila, who writes in early modernity, also under conditions of patriarchal repression, explores a castle. Among the most famous non-doctor female theologians, there is Julian of Norwich, whose *Showings* receive their organizing principle from visions of the body of the suffering Christ, which occasions a series of revelations of divine love. She explores these revelations through a number of potent images for which she is remembered, especially Christ the divine mother and the hazelnut that symbolizes all of creation. The images—Catherine's various images, Teresa's castle, Julian's hazelnut and mother—gather the central theological themes of these texts, and their potency confers on the theology two types of validity. First, the insights are made aesthetically real and perceptible by these images. In this way, they have persuasive force; they show the reader the argument, so that she can see it, feel it, believe it. Second, the images repeat and thereby mediate the authority of divine revelation. In elaborating their theology through the images given by God in Godself—rather than offering a more distanced, translated interpretation of the revelation—these women make the readers witnesses to their divine encounters and thereby present their theology as bearing a divine authority.[51] In the case of Catherine, the encounter means that some of her material letters are revered as sacred objects with miraculous properties.[52]

The image that aesthetically mediated the theology and authority of many medieval women was the body—an image, I mean, of their own body, presented as an aesthetic subject and object, a subject that perceives God and an object to be perceived as the locus of sacred encounter. This is famously true of Catherine, whose body is, along with Francis of Assisi's, one of the most wondered about, discussed, and represented of the extra-biblical saints. Also like Francis, she is reported to have received the stigmata of Christ.[53] She seems, additionally, to have found ecclesiastical authority through her miraculous fasting, and the vision she reported of a mystical marriage to Christ in which his foreskin became her wedding ring is among the most popular scenes in medieval and Renaissance art. The vision of her mystical marriage to Christ turns the reader's attention to Catherine's body, as do many other descriptions of her divine encounter with Christ. She describes to her confessor Raymond of Capua being directed by Christ to drink from his side. Raymond remembers the event as if he saw it himself, inviting the reader to do the same: "[S]he fastened her lips upon that sacred wound, and still more eagerly the mouth of her soul, and there she slaked her thirst."[54] Authenticating Catherine's bodily intimacy with the divine, Raymond also thereby suggests and authorizes her spiritual intimacy.

Thematizing the body is an important and well-known trope in medieval female writing—both in texts by women and those about them. Their *Lives*, letters, and dialogues feature levitations, trances, seizures, frozenness, rigidity, uncontrolled outcrying, unwilled silence, even, as Carolyn Walker Bynum notes, ecstatic nosebleeds.[55] Female mystics describe adopting extreme ascetic measures such as hair shirts, flagellation, tight girdles, and kneeling on hard stones. Birgitta of Sweden drips hot wax into wounds on her hands each Friday, Dorothea of Montau contorts her body into positions she holds for hours.[56] Many describe bodily suffering that they did not will and imbue such suffering with religious significance.[57] Hildegard, Margaret Ebner, Margery Kempe, Julian, Gertrude of Helfta, Elisabeth of Schönau, and others all chronicle illness, aches, or physical weakness as part of their journey with God. Ebner reports mystical lactation in which she nurses a statue of the infant Christ. Birgitta describes mystical gestation in which she feels the Christ babe in her womb, which the Virgin Mary confirms in a vision as a sign of Christ's arrival in her heart.[58]

In the next section on the aesthetic sources modern women and one nonbinary individual used, I will consider the ways the body becomes a scene and locus of theology for the gender-marginalized and feminist theologians. In this section on the queer forms of medieval women, I want to note that in text after text, women claim a theological voice by rhetorically constructing and representing their bodies. In some cases, the body even structures their writing. There is a vast and fascinating literature we could review or add to—and I hope others continue to do so—but for our purposes here, I want only to emphasize that we have here yet another way aesthetics was important to women building a textual presence in the Christian literary tradition: they made their bodies newly and wondrously available to the reader and, in doing so, made the new and wondrous ways their bodies perceive also available.

Narratives and Dialogues

As women writing in the Middle Ages claim authority to speak publicly through aesthetic mediations of images and their bodies, so, too, do they make use of aesthetically invested genres, especially narrative and dialogue. Their bodies and images are legitimated through a narrative of divine encounter that makes their authority real to the reader. This is true for almost every woman whose writings circulated in the Middle Ages. Julian, Ebner, Kempe, and Angela of Foligno all used narrative. Hildegard commissioned the *Life* of her teacher and spiritual mother Jutta of Disidodenberg and wrote little narratives of her own life in letters. (Jutta's life was narrated by others shortly after her death.)[59] Catherine of Genoa did not write a narrative, but she narrated her life to a confessor, who compiled these narrations into her *Memoirs*, which became the basis for the popular "The Life of St. Catherine of Genoa" that circulated with her spiritual teachings. Catherine of Siena and Mechthild of Magdeburg also used dialogue that narrated mystical moments of their lives, with Mechthild drawing on German minnesinger poetry to create a new genre of *mystique courtoise*.[60] Marguerite of Porete's *Mirror of Simple Souls* was an allegorical dialogue. Writing in the seventeenth century, Sor Juana Inés de la Cruz made expansive use of the more self-consciously literary genres, including poetry, allegory, drama, and comedy. This use of non-didactic genres by women continues even today, as two of the most popular saints of the twentieth century, Saint Maria Faustina Kowalska and Saint Thérèse of Lisieux, lived hidden lives that became extraordinarily significant when their diaries were found and published after their deaths.[61]

Through narrative, dialogue, and other self-consciously literary genres, women worked to create their authority at a time when their authority was not given, nor were the modes of claiming authority that were open to men available to them. The authority they command through these writings is not the authority of a bishop and certainly not that of the pope. It is more akin to the authority of an artwork that arrests the beholder's gaze, a musical performance that compels attention, a divine encounter that claims the faithful's reverence. That is to say, the rhetorical and aesthetically invested writing forms did not guarantee the authority of the women writing them. Although the *Mirror of Simple Souls* was translated into multiple languages, Marguerite was burned at the stake. Mechthild retreated to a Cistercian monastery for protection from ecclesiastical authorities toward the end of her life. Kowalska's diary—which occasioned one of the most famous Christian images of the twentieth century and a dedicated day in the Roman Catholic calendar—was for decades under suspicion, on the index of forbidden books. This authority, then, is not secure, nor is it always efficacious or durable. The authority, after all, is as queer as the forms themselves, as the gender of the woman claiming it.

Authority that arises from the literary investments of the form does not have the same kind of stability that institutional authority does. These writings from medieval women work aesthetically, viscerally, affectively on the reader to stage an encounter with the divine in texts that are themselves often highly affective. The medieval texts in particular are often rhetorically extreme, featuring a subject who experiences a range of emotions from ecstasy to despondency. They foreground a way of feeling, sensing, and perceiving the world and suggest a way of reflecting on one's own feeling, sensing, and perceiving. These are texts that persuade the reader by making aesthetically real the divine encounters that authenticate them—and therefore also making the theological reflection on those divine encounters persuasive. It is an authority that can speak across centuries and at the same time one that has little recourse should the institutions of the day turn against it.

Forms in Feminist Theology

Cavell describes Ralph Waldo Emerson's "Self-Reliance" as "a theory—I wish we knew how to call it an aesthetics—of reading."[62] What "aesthetics" gives us, for Cavell, that "theory" does not always encompass is attention to what he calls the literary conditions of philosophy. Philosophy exists as language, and language can entrance, delight, surprise, rouse, dissemble, repulse, sicken. And feminist theologians, like their foresisters in the Middle Ages, are often sensitive to the aesthetics of theological claims. In the Middle Ages, each woman whose writings circulated had to make a case, implicitly or explicitly, for why her voice was legitimate. But with the birth of feminist theology, when women have some modes of institutional authority available to them to confer a level of legitimacy on their writings, they begin to make a case for why the voices of women *in general* need to be heard and taken seriously. I spent some time chronicling a few aesthetic strategies of women writers in the Middle Ages because I think versions of these strategies return with the birth of feminist theology. Specifically, feminist theology evinces its aesthetic interests through its analysis of language, its playfulness with diction, and its experimentation with genre.

One of the first feminist theologians, Mary Daly, helped shape the field beginning with her pioneering works *The Church and the Second Sex* (1968), and, after she despaired and left the church, *Beyond God the Father* (1973).

There she begins her work exposing the misogyny of church structures, symbols, and language, writing famously, "If God is male, then male is God. The divine patriarch castrates women as long as he is allowed to live on in the human imagination."[63] The battle for feminist liberation, then, must be also (though not exclusively) fought at the level of her imagination, and over her many volumes of feminist thought, Daly engages in this battle through what in *Gyn/Ecology* (1978) she calls "gynocentric" writing that seeks to cultivate a liberated and liberating imagination.[64] Early in that book, she pauses to note her wordplay, acknowledging the way she creates new words ("gynaesthesia"), uses the obsolete meanings of words ("glamour," "hag"), alters words to expose their falseness ("re-cover"), or repunctuates them to draw the reader's attention to them anew ("de-light"). She acknowledges that in her writing, she sometimes "break[s] almost into incantations, chants, alliterative lyrics."[65] The aesthetically attuned mode of writing works to enchant the reader toward a new vision of possibility, to break the spell of patriarchy by learning to "dis-spell the language of phallocracy, which keeps us under the spell of brokenness."[66] Language is so central to Daly's work that in 1987, she published *Webster's First Intergalactic Wickedary of the English Language*. It led her into further writings filled with creativity not only at the level of word but in her genres as well. In 1992, she published an autobiographical book of "spiritual adventure" that defies genre, called *Outercourse: The Be-Dazzling Voyage*. Probably no feminist theologian has used language as wondrously and creatively as Daly. In the artfulness of her word-work, she denaturalizes Christian language, inviting other feminist theologians to consider it anew.

As a field, feminist theology did begin rethinking the language it wanted to use. Two of the most influential books of feminist theology in the 1980s nodded to the importance of language in their titles. Sallie McFague published *Metaphorical Theology: Models of God in Religious Language* (1982), and the following year, Rosemary Radford Ruether wrote *Sexism and God-Talk* (1983), a locution Williams would reference a decade later in her own book *Sisters in the Wilderness: The Challenge of Womanist God-Talk* (1993).[67] Also in the 1980s, Janet Martin Soskice wrote *Metaphor and Religious Language* (1985), and she returned to language for her next book, *The Kindness of God: Metaphor, Gender, and Religious Language* (2007). Johnson subtitled her 1992 volume *She Who Is* by underscoring language as well: *The Mystery of God in Feminist Theological Discourse*. Throughout it and subsequent books, Johnson makes the interrogation and reconstruction of symbols central to her work. These feminist theologians variously analyze how language about God works, probe the registers of our language about God, evaluate various linguistic constructions, propose new language, retrieve old language, and present old language through new prisms. Feminist theology as a field consolidated around the insight that language matters, that the aesthetics of a text is not incidental to its argument. Such work continues on in texts that, like Daly's, take the imagination as an important site of creation and contestation, as in Kwok's edited volume *Postcolonial Imagination and Feminist Theology* (2005) or Namsoon Kang's *Diasporic Feminist Theology: Asia and Theopolitical Imagination* (2014). From a more historical perspective, Margaret Miles has attended to the forms of theology throughout her career, and her book on the history of Christian theology, *Word Made Flesh: A History of Christian Thought* (2004), tells the story of theology by focusing on the body of Christ—which becomes the structuring principle for her book—and incorporating both art and music so seriously that the book comes with a supplementary CD of artistic material, including images, music, and photographs of three-dimensional artifacts.[68] In the first volume of her systematics, Sarah Coakley articulated a commitment to aesthetics as part of her *théologie totale*, reproducing more than three dozen images in her book. Coakley wrote that "theological art can enable—in a way that on this supposition *only* the arts can—doctrine's creative new expression, animus, and efficacy."[69]

Given this long history of playing with the theological media of images and words, it should perhaps be unsurprising that feminist theologians have also turned toward experimentation with genre. In addition to Daly with *Outercourse*, a number of feminists have turned toward autobiography. Ivone Gebara has been writing memoir,[70] and Miles wrote one titled *Augustine and the Fundamentalist's Daughter*, which she put in conversation with Augustine's *Confessions*. Walton has promoted a genre she calls autoethnography, in which an author analyzes her own self and experience of the world as a way of gaining insight into culture. It pays attention, in other words, to the self as a mediator of the world and experiences of the divine.[71] Soskice turned to creative nonfiction to write *Sisters of Sinai*, a story of two learned and adventurous sisters who in the nineteenth century discovered a manuscript in the monastery at Mount Sinai. Johnson mimicked an Anselmian dialogue in her ecofeminist book *Creation and the Cross*, which replaces Anselm and Boso with Elizabeth and Clara even as she replaces Anselmian focus on atonement for human sin with a more creation-centered account of salvation. Then there are feminist theologians who have taken to writing novels. After her last work of traditionally genred theological writing focused on the violent contestations of women's bodies, Susan Brooks Thistlethwaite wrote a series of detective novels featuring a female religion professor who investigates cases of violence against women. After years of both more traditional and experimental writing, including an account of the Last Supper through the eyes of Martha and Mary,[72] Tina Beattie has taken her feminist religious writing into fictional forms as well, her recent trajectory beginning with a thriller titled *The Good Priest*.

One thing these more explicitly literary genres do is provide the opportunity for writers to appeal more directly to the imagination. When writing about violence against women's bodies, for example, that violence can become an abstraction; the very act of writing about it as a category or problem can deflect from the concreteness of the violence itself. But a story about violence against women's bodies that describes that violence and traces its sources can communicate the violence viscerally, so that the reader feels it as a concrete reality.[73] Novels and more self-consciously creative genres can mediate powerful images in a manner not dissimilar to how medieval women writers use images, narratives, and forms. These more aesthetically invested forms of writing can be more affectively engaging and thus can retune our affective engagements with aspects of the world and God. For example, Beattie's *The Good Priest* raises the questions of demonic work, narrates female prostitutes, and proclaims the ultimate nothingness of evil—features it shares with much Christian hagiography (and particularly *The Life of Antony*). And yet the female prostitutes are not demons (as in old hagiography) but fully orbed humans who receive mercy, give mercy, are misused, drive the action forward, and invite the reader to attach to them. And these creative genres write women into the tradition differently, finding ways to make it their tradition, to claim Anselm's mantle while modifying his theology and discarding some of his less desirable claims, for example.

There is another way of describing the significance of this genre experimentation, which Linn Tonstad has been exploring in her work on disciplinarity, truth, and genre in systematic theology.[74] She points out that theologians often reduce differences to issues of representational diversity regarding gender, race, and sexuality—which obscures the way difference runs all the way through the epistemological and methodological. To require a class in medieval theology to include *a woman* on the syllabus is to reduce difference to representational diversity—and virtually ensure that her theology will be seen as inferior, as a misbegotten version of the theology done by the men of her day. To face the true challenge of difference is (at least) to ask why Julian's or Ebner's writing does not appear to some as proper theology and consider what that reveals about the disciplinarity of theology. It is to make visible the regimes by which theology becomes and is received as theology—and thereby to open up possibilities for receiving the work of Ebner, Kempe, Angela, Marguerite, Mechthild, and Sor Juana as theology. The different genres of writing in theology point to and emerge from different ways of knowing and being in the world—and these are differences that feminist theology continues to pursue and make visible, if often in more muted ways than their medieval foresisters. We are, after all, in the guild in a way they could not be.

Modern (American) Claims: Aesthetic Sources

The different genres and forms pursued by medieval women theologians are not fully separable from the different sources of their theology. Of course, some sources are shared with malestream theology. In their arguments, images, and forms, medieval women drew on scripture, liturgy, and some canonical theologians. But they also took their own lives and bodies seriously as sites of divine revelation, ones that could help them to interpret other theological sources. With the medieval women, I explored the rhetorical construction of the body as an important authority-conferring image. Here I am interested in the subtly different point that bodily life for early modern women and nonbinary preachers reveals something about God's plans for a person, community, and world and about where and how God is moving within it. For many of these individuals, taking their bodily life seriously leads them also to consider art and song as sources for theology. The importance of lives, bodies, and art as sources of theological reflection continues in the modern world, as women began to compose in theological genres historically reserved for men (particularly homilies) and make arguments for their conducting theological work as women, through appeals both to divine revelation and to human reasonableness. In other words, though these preachers continue to make cases for their theological authority by referencing their own particular divine callings, we also begin to see something more. In demonstrating to the reader or auditor that discrimination against them is not *reasonable*, these preachers gesture toward broader arguments against discriminating by gender.[75]

The Body as Source for Early American Preachers

Some of the first women Christian preachers—ones who spoke in the services of institutional churches—are found in the young United States. The ministry of the Public Universal Friend (1752–1819), formerly Jemima Wilkinson, commenced, in fact, in 1776, just a few months after the country declared its independence. Wilkinson became gravely ill, and as her family prepared for her death, she one day rose up and declared Jemima Wilkinson had died and been reborn as the Public Universal Friend. The Public Universal Friend's androgynous presentation proved their new identity as one who had transcended gender and therefore whatever gender constraints prevented them from preaching.[76] Their body and dress—male clerical roles, female shoes, long hair—became proof of their authority and a source for their theological reflection on the work of God in the world, the central conviction of which was this: Christ is coming soon. The androgyny of the Public Universal Friend witnessed to the imminence of Christ's return, the way the Friend had transcended gender and thereby testified to a resurrected state in which there is neither male nor female and no one is married or given in marriage. Their body was in this way a source of theological reflection, an illustration of their theology, and its confirmation.

While the Public Universal Friend left behind few writings, we have many more from Jarena Lee (1783–1864). In justifying her call to preach in the African Methodist Episcopal Church, Lee wrote the *Religious Experience and Journal of Mrs. Jarena Lee, Giving an Account of Her Call to Preach the Gospel*, which opens with an epigraph from Joel 2:28, "And it shall come to pass . . . that I will pour out my Spirit upon all flesh; and your sons and your *daughters* shall prophesy." Marking the Spirit's work as inspiring daughters as well as sons, she goes on to narrate her body, her tremors, her emotions, as proof of the Spirit's work in her and as making her the kind of person who can well perceive the Spirit's work in the world—both importantly related to her calling as preacher. When she faces church authorities, she frequently trembles in anticipation—proof that she is not proud or initiating her own calling— and is then stilled by the Lord, in one case filled with "sweet serenity, a holy joy of a peculiar kind, untasted in [her] bosom until then," evidence that God has indeed called and prepared her for her work of preaching.[77] Visions often reaffirmed and underscored her divine calling. And again and again, this Black woman, who preached to both Black and White congregations over the course of her life, describes the fruit of sermons by tracing bodily evidence of divine work: tears of contrition, shouts of joy, groans and sighs, happy amens. Once, a "whole set of females, by the power of God, as the rushing of a wind, were all bowed to the floor, at once, and screamed out."[78] Her own body and the bodies of those to whom she preached offered these evidences of the Spirit's work and also illumined how the Spirit worked, suggesting God's overcoming of the limitations of gender and race. A motif Lee repeatedly sounds throughout her *Religious Experience* is the Lord's almightiness, which contrasts with humanity and thereby subtly implies human equality in the face of such unfathomable power. Her narration of the Lord overcoming the prejudices of gender and race in order for Lee to preach further displays and promises social transformations, as human convention falters and shifts before the all-powerful Lord.

In her appeals to the body, the emotions, and the direct work of the Spirit in convicting a heart, Lee works within the shifting religious landscape of early America, which was seeing a rise in enthusiasm and populist impulses within Christianity—and those very transformations also helped women to find a voice and authority. That authority is wielded with particular power by the formerly enslaved woman and abolitionist Sojourner Truth (1797–1883), perhaps the most well-known female preacher of the nineteenth century. In her famous speech "Ain't I a Woman?" she appeals directly to her body to break open images and perceived limitations of womanhood. "Look at me! Look at my arm!" she commands the audience, before describing the work her arm had done, the amount she had eaten to support such labor, the lashes she had suffered—and the thirteen children she had borne.[79] Childbearing then sets up her Christological riposte, in which she addresses an argument that women should not have equal rights to men's because Christ was a man. She asks: "Where did your Christ come from? From God and a woman! Man had nothing to do with Him." And Jesus authorizes Truth's theology. Grant narrates her responding to a preacher that she could not read, but "When I preaches, I has jes one text to preach from, an' I always preaches from this one. My text is, 'When I found Jesus!'"[80] It is a text that locates Jesus in her own story of conversion and that births in her a love so powerful that she "can love, *even de white folks!*"[81] Truth's authority and theology both derived from, pointed back to, and were confirmed in her storied body and the way it proved and displayed divine freedom and love.

Many early American female preachers embroidered their claims by drawing on hymns and songs as homiletic sources, which were not mined for theological content so much as for their capacity to bring the bodies of the congregants into the activity of preaching. They sang to inspire others to sing and exhorted congregants to stamp, clap, join hands, and shout in what Catherine Brekus calls an "alternative form of prayer." They wept for sin and ranted at sinners, planned hand gestures and vocal inflections, and were often highly emotional. Drawing on bodily choreographies of contrition, praise, and joy, they made their own sermons affective, aesthetic events. In this way, the female preachers used aesthetically rich sources to create aesthetically attuned forms.[82]

The Body, Art, and Other Sources of Feminist Theology

The turn to bodies in the early American female theologians is just one way women have claimed a voice through aesthetic sources. We could go back to the medieval theologians to look at the way a statue of the crucifix figured prominently in the story of Ebner or the significance of wearing a white dress in the book of Kempe. As feminist theologians have sought sources that might contain possibilities beyond those available in the mainstream patriarchal conversations of Christian theology, they have also looked to aesthetic objects, turning to sources as diverse as ancient statues (Carole Christ), visual representations of the Trinity (Coakley), hymns and spirituals (Grant), or contemporary art of the cross (Kim Power). All of these art objects, often seen as "merely" aesthetic or insufficiently theological or intellectual, when used as sources for theology expose and help theology come to terms with the aesthetic conditions of its own existence. The sources in this way are deeply related to writing form, as they help expand the canon of what counts as theology. But of all the aesthetic sources feminist theologians considered, they have drawn on none so frequently and so forcefully as bodies—and perhaps no stream of feminist theology has done so more compellingly than womanist thought.

Grant eloquently thematizes the relation of sources to the disciplinary exclusion and inclusions of Black women in *White Women's Christ, Black Woman's Jesus*, where she writes, "Feminist theology is inadequate for two reasons: it is *White* and *racist*. Feminist theologians are white in terms of their race and in terms of the *nature of the sources* they use for development of their theological perspectives." Feminists do not speak to *women's experience* but to *White women's experience*, and White women's participation in the reality of slavery and its afterlives created "a gulf between these women."[83] What feminist sisterhood can White women claim when they have physically, psychologically, and financially abused Black women? Theology must be written out of encounters with Christ, who always, Grant affirms, leads us into facing the challenges of our particular contexts.[84] That means taking seriously the witness of Black women—their prayers, their hymns, their sermons, their narratives, their biographies.[85] This difference in sources is not purely formal. It shifts the theological lens from a more remote and ethereal Christ of feminist theology to the Jesus who shares in the suffering of the afflicted. These prayers, hymns, sermons, and narratives, moreover, are not pre-theological sources to be made theological; they are engaged as already theological sources.

Shawn Copeland traces similar themes in *Knowing Christ Crucified*, glossing Francis of Assisi's claim that the cross is a book. But this book is no hermetic object. As she writes, she draws beautiful images into beautiful images. Opened with "love and intelligence," the book of the cross gives us "traces of the crucified Jewish Jesus" in those suffering from injustice, in those who sing and dance in the face of oppression or fear, and in those who speak the truth of their own painful journeys.[86] If the cross is a book, it is one that is always expanding its own canon to include the lives of truth-telling, defiant joy, and suffering on the margins of life. The book opens to the world. To claim these human realities as a book is to press theological scholars to take them as seriously as the libraries of their more usual texts. It is no coincidence that Copeland's litany of traces of the cross includes song, worship, prayer, and dance, for she points to song as a healing practice in the Black church and prayer as sustaining and cultivating the "inscape" of Black people's desire for God under the absurd and death-dealing conditions of slavery.[87] Uniquely formed by the cross, Black people in the United States have uniquely witnessed to Jesus. The relationship between Jesus and the suffering of Black life for Copeland is not symbolic but material and is intrinsic to the work of theology. The body of Jesus, she writes, "impels us to place the bodies of the victims of history at the center of our theology."[88] Christ's love calls us to break from sinful human bondage and imagine ourselves—imagine the marginalized—as God's own flesh. Christ calls the enslaved to freedom, calls the marginalized to know herself as Christ's very body.

Black bodies are central to Christian theology for Copeland and Grant because Jesus's body is central to Christianity. And returning us to Black bodies also becomes an activity in exorcising our imaginations. Williams, insisting that the experience of Black women is an important point of departure for Christian theology, points out the way our imaginations are deformed by their associations of positivity with white and negativity with black and performs the way an imagination re-formed by what Copeland calls the book of the cross can receive that other book—the book of scripture—anew in her reading of the story of Hagar and Sarah.[89] Recognizing that Paul read Hagar as the paradigmatic outsider, Williams reads her through the lives of the marginalized, vulnerable women and therefore as a daughter of God who participated in her own liberation.[90]

The way feminist theology has learned to make the bodies of the marginalized central has become one of its hallmarks. The litany is long and distinguished, but a sampling of works from the last decade or so include

Serene Jones's *Trauma and Grace* (2009), Copeland's *Enfleshing Freedom* (2010), Eboni Marshall Turman's *Toward a Womanist Ethic of Incarnation* (2013), Thistlethwaite's *Women's Bodies as Battlefield* (2015), Kelly Brown Douglas's *Black Bodies and the Black Church* (2012) and *Stand Your Ground* (2015), Mayra Rivera's *Poetics of the Flesh* (2015), Beattie's four-part essay "A Mother Is Born" (2015), Hannah Bacon's *Feminist Theology and Contemporary Dieting Culture* (2019), Karen O'Donnell and Katie Cross's edited volume *Feminist Trauma Theologies* (2020), and O'Donnell's recent monograph *The Dark Womb* (2022). Then there are Latin American feminist theologians such as Althaus-Reid and Gebara who for decades expanded the work of liberation theology to center their theologies on the invisible bodies of poor and sexually marginalized women. Sometimes feminist theology is generalized under the heading of contextual theology and described as appealing to the authority of "experience," but that generic term obscures the way it is bodily being in the world, enfleshed perception and perceptibility, that centers much feminist theological reflection.[91]

To take the body as a source of theological reflection is aesthetic in three senses: it is itself an aesthetic object that can be aesthetically judged or marginalized, visibilized or invisibilized, as Williams notes; it is an aesthetic subject that can be made to envision and perceive what was previously invisible; and it invites reflection on those objects and activities produced by and sustaining our bodily lives together, including art and song. This turn to women's bodies, particularly in the womanist and liberationist traditions, is also a turn to the social, political, and economic conditions registered in and partially created by those bodies. When womanist theologians demand that theology be adequate and accountable to Black women's lives, feminist theology is summoned to reflect more deeply on its own political conditions—and the claims such conditions make on the feminist theologian. Drawing on Walker, who coined the term "womanism," Grant identifies womanism with "the active struggle of Black women that makes them who they are.... [W]omanist just means *being* and *acting* out who you are."[92] Even here in this definition of womanism, the aesthetic investments of feminist theology point to and are consummated in other investments beyond aesthetics or theology.

Conclusion

I have been displaying here the way feminist theology has invested in aesthetics in ways that have prepared the field to articulate what Cavell calls an "aesthetics of reading" and which I am suggesting is consummated in the mode of attunement. For a guiding, if often implicit, insight of feminist theology has been that theology is made and made persuasive through its aesthetic investments, through its work in symbols, images, diction, structure, syntax, metaphor, narrative, rhythm, and bodies. It is through aesthetics that women throughout Christian theology claimed presence, authority, and voice, and it is through aesthetics that feminist theologians pioneered the existence of their field. It is through aesthetics, moreover, that sensibilities and subjectivities can be remade and reattuned so that a person desires, becomes, lives out the flourishing of all. So while aesthetics can name a bourgeois flight from political conditions, aesthetics can also in this way and others be yoked with politics. For Cavell, they are yoked because the literary conditions of philosophy invite a response of acknowledgment that recognizes the social conditions of philosophy and life, of taking responsibility for oneself and another in a community of interlocutors.[93] For feminist theologians, too, awareness of aesthetic investments means that feminist theology is not sheltered from the questions, demands, and entanglements of the political but is more radically exposed to them. It is to this relationship with the political that I turn in chapter 3.

Notes

1. As I discuss in my book *Beauty*, the category of fittingness (*to prepon*) was central to early Greek debates about the incarnation—prominent in Irenaeus, Athanasius, and Gregory of Nyssa. In the Latin tradition, *convenientia* was famously a term of art for Bonaventure, Anselm, and Thomas Aquinas. Julian of Norwich is among those who brought it into the English theological tradition through her use of *behovely*, which has gained theological attention since Denys Turner's article (and subsequent book on Julian), "'Sin Is Behovely' in Julian of Norwich's *Revelations of Divine Love*," *Modern Theology* 20, no. 3 (2004): 407–422. Natalie Carnes, *Beauty: A Theological Engagement with Gregory of Nyssa* (Eugene, OR: Cascade, 2014), 55–58.
2. Citing Thomas Aquinas's commentary on Peter Lombard's *Sentences*, *Inter Insigniores*, the Roman Catholic declaration authored by the Congregation for the Doctrine of the Faith reaffirms the medieval argument that the "natural resemblance" between the sacrament and the signified means that only men can be priests. Congregation for the Doctrine of the Faith, *Inter Insigniores*, 1976, 5.12, https://www.vatican.va/roman_curia/congregations/cfaith/documents/rc_con_cfaith_doc_19761015_inter-insigniores_en.html.
3. Elizabeth Ursic, "Imagination, Art, and Feminist Theology," *Feminist Theology* 25, no. 3 (2017): 310. The copy she quotes from the publisher is, as of this time of writing, still on the series website, though Ashgate has since been bought, and so

the series is now Routledge Studies in Theology, Imagination and the Arts. https://www.routledge.com/Ashgate-Studies-in-Theology-Imagination-and-the-Arts/book-series/ATHEOART.
4. Ursic, "Imagination, Art, and Feminist Theology," 310.
5. Elizabeth A. Johnson exemplifies this powerful insight in her interrogation and reconstruction of the symbols of theology. See, for example, *She Who Is: The Mystery of God in a Feminist Theological Discourse* (New York: Crossroad, 1992).
6. In an essay advocating theology as poetics, Rebecca Chopp writes toward this vision: "Theology now explores domains of imaginative discourse, understanding its ordering discourse as reworking language, symbols, codes, images. In this work, theology is not simply adding or subtracting metaphors but reshaping the moral imaginary." Rebecca Chopp, "Poetics of Testimony," in *Converging on Culture: Theologians in Dialogue with Cultural Analysis and Criticism*, ed. Delwin Brown, Sheila Greeve Davaney, and Kathryn Tanner (New York: Oxford University Press, 2001), 66.
7. In this structure, I am influenced by my own introduction to feminist theology as a sophomore in Professor Sarah Coakley's Feminist Theology class at Harvard. She divided the syllabus into two parts: the first looked at the issues of sex, gender, and sexuality that arose in particular historical periods; the second mirrored the first but took up questions and issues doctrinally rather than historically.
8. Invisibility is an originating problem for many discourses of the marginalized and oppressed; for example, it is invoked in much Black theology, Dalit studies, and disability studies—particularly in the moment these fields are materializing and gaining initial momentum. For examples, see Judith Weisenfeld, "Invisible Women: On Women and Gender in the Study of African American Religious History," *Journal of Africana Religions* 1, no. 1 (2013): 133–149; Shubham Pandey and Priyanshi Nagarkoti, "An Anthropological Analysis of the Invisibility of Dalits of India in the Environmental Discourse: A Tale of Subjugation, Alienation and Resistance," *Contemporary Voice of Dalit* [online early view], April 19, 2021; Mary Carlson, "Making the Invisible Visible: Inviting Persons with Disability into Life with the Church," *Horizons* 45 (2018): 46–73.
9. The phrase "God's agents of grace and liberation" comes, as we will see, from Elisabeth Schüssler Fiorenza, "Breaking the Silence: Becoming Visible," in *The Power of Naming: A Concilium Reader in Critical Feminist Theology*, ed. Elisabeth Schüssler Fiorenza (Maryknoll, NY: Orbis, 1998), 172.
10. Elizabeth Clark, "The Lady Vanishes: Dilemmas of a Feminist Historian after the 'Linguistic Turn,'" *Church History* 67, no. 1 (March 1998): 18.
11. Clark, "The Lady Vanishes," 15.
12. Clark, "The Lady Vanishes," 27. Quoting Peter Brown, *The Body and Society: Men, Women, and Sexual Renunciation in Early Christianity* (New York: Columbia University Press, 1988), 153. Clark notes that Brown himself here borrows this phrasing from Claude Lévi-Strauss.

13. Clark, "The Lady Vanishes," 26. She explicitly quotes David Halperin's analysis of the role of Diotima in Plato's *Symposium* in his book *One Hundred Years of Homosexuality and Other Essays on Greek Love* (New York: Routledge, 1990), and she quotes him quoting Kristeva.
14. There is an interestingly related though different anxiety about the identity of novelist Elena Ferrante, in particular a desire many women have that the author be a woman. Elisa Sotgiu writes insightfully about this desire in "Have Italian Scholars Figured Out the Identity of Elena Ferrante?" *Literary Hub*, March 31, 2021, https://lithub.com/have-italian-scholars-figured-out-the-identity-of-elena-ferrante/.
15. Clark, "The Lady Vanishes," 23.
16. Clark, "The Lady Vanishes," 27.
17. Clark, "The Lady Vanishes," 26; quoting Halperin, *One Hundred Years of Homosexuality*, 151.
18. Clark, "The Lady Vanishes," 30–32.
19. Clark's sophisticated understanding of traces and their role in constructing new identities resonates with her own work using social network analysis to illumine the Origenist controversy in a book that came out a few years before "The Lady Vanishes." Elizabeth Clark, *The Origenist Controversy: The Cultural Construction of an Early Christian Debate* (Princeton, NJ: Princeton University Press, 1992).
20. See especially the third chapter of Felski, *Hooked*, and also Amanda Anderson, Rita Felski, and Toril Moi, *Character: Three Inquiries in Literary Studies* (Chicago: University of Chicago Press, 2019).
21. As Vogt writes, "the 'becoming male' metaphor indicates in all contexts a development from a lower to a higher state of moral and spiritual perfection." (171) The elevation of masculinity and maleness is not unique to Christian writing; it is everywhere in antiquity: Aristotle, Plato, the Stoics, the Gnostics, and so on, naturalized by centuries of texts, practices, and institutions repeating and reaffirming the normativity of maleness. Vogt, "'Becoming Male,'" 171.
22. Vogt, "'Becoming Male,'" 175; quoting Clement of Alexandria, *Stromateis* VI.100.3.
23. Vogt, "'Becoming Male,'" 176; quoting Origen, *Homilies on Joshua* 9:9.
24. Rosemary Radford Ruether describes Augustine tracking a similar line when he says that woman bears the image of God "as nongendered intellect but does not 'represent it' as woman." Rosemary Radford Ruether, *Women and Redemption: A Theological History* (Minneapolis: Fortress, 1998), 73. Ruether references *On the Trinity* 7.7, 10, in which Augustine denies that a woman has the image of God in herself when considered part of the couple, and *The Work of Monks* 40, when he claims that women do not symbolize the image of God in their bodies but instead image the concupiscent part of the soul. During a recent trip to Puebla, Mexico, I was visually reminded of this tradition while staying at a former convent, where I came across a Baroque painting of a figure robed in red and blue, wearing a crown, holding a lily, and carrying a child also crowned. It was Mary's traditional

iconography, except that a beard covered her face—a male attribute meant to evidence her unique holiness among women.
25. Gregory reports this joke in his *Life of Macrina,* trans. Kevin Corrigan (Toronto: Peregrina, 1998), 25.
26. This is not to claim that visibility itself solves the problem. The work of rendering visible is both aesthetic and political, such that rendering visible raises the question of rendering visible *as what?* In the case of feminist theology, the issue is now to render women visible as fully human subjects and as authoritative (over their own experience, in their own body, with interpreting scripture, for the church). But visibility can also go wildly awry, as I explore in Carnes, *Image and Presence,* 124, 132–137.
27. Valerie Saiving, "The Human Situation: A Feminine View," in *Womanspirit Rising: A Feminist Reader in Religion,* ed. Judith Plaskow and Carol P. Christ (San Francisco: Harper & Row, 1979), 27. It was originally published in the *Journal of Religion* in April 1960 and is generally considered the inaugural essay of feminist theology.
28. Saiving, "The Human Situation," 36.
29. Engaging political theorist Linda Zerilli, Nicholas Norman-Krause writes about how perception is an achievement made in words that reflect and enable collective judgment. "Objects can only appear to us, can only come into view, as they do so in language, which involves these faculties of perception.... This coming to see an object in common is the work of building a 'common sense,' or *sensus communus.*" Nicholas Norman Krause, *Political Theology and the Conflicts of Democracy,* PhD diss., Baylor University, 2021, 236.
30. Delores S. Williams, *Sisters in the Wilderness: The Challenge of Womanist God-Talk* (Maryknoll, NY: Orbis, 1993), 1.
31. Williams in this way performs Stanley Cavell's insight, as Toril Moi articulates in her essay exploring his influence on her own work as a feminist theorist: "I knew that Cavell was right: one simply cannot write if one cannot find one's inheritance and if one cannot find the courage to say what one sees. Only by speaking can we discover if there is a community for us. Muteness is separation, and oppression. And he was right to insist that autobiography and philosophy are 'internal' to each other." Toril Moi, "Philosophy and Autobiography: How Stanley Cavell Welcomed Me into Philosophy," *ABC Religion and Ethics,* January 7, 2019, https://www.abc.net.au/religion/stanley-cavell-philosophy-and-autobiography/10696038.
32. Williams, *Sisters in the Wilderness,* ix.
33. Williams, *Sisters in the Wilderness,* xi.
34. Williams, *Sisters in the Wilderness,* xi–xii, xiii.
35. Williams, *Sisters in the Wilderness,* 235.
36. Williams, *Sisters in the Wilderness,* 236.
37. Jacquelyn Grant, *White Women's Christ, Black Women's Jesus: Feminist Christology and Womanist Response* (Atlanta: Scholars, 1989), 10.

38. Grant, *White Women's Christ*, 217.
39. Schüssler Fiorenza, "Breaking the Silence," 163.
40. Schüssler Fiorenza, "Breaking the Silence," 169.
41. Schüssler Fiorenza, "Breaking the Silence," 169.
42. Schüssler Fiorenza, "Breaking the Silence," 172.
43. Muers, "Feminist Theology," 113.
44. Kwok Pui-lan, *Postcolonial Imagination and Feminist Theory* (Louisville, KY: Westminster John Knox, 2005), 3.
45. This is true of many new forms of art, which seem initially queer. Felski references Smith making a similar point, for Smith admits she would have been "nonplussed, maybe even a little scandalized," if she saw Pablo Picasso's *Demoiselles d'Avignon* in 1907. Yet in her life today, it is "obviously beautiful" to her. This is certainly true of early Picasso and many artists in the history of visual art, but we could find similar examples in other art forms as well—the first performance of Igor Stravinsky's *The Rite of Spring* with Vaslav Nijinsky's choreography or middle-aged adults relating to the music of the next generation. Felski, Hooked, 52–53; quoting Smith, "Some Notes, 113.
46. Eve Kosofsky Sedgwick, *Tendencies* (Durham, NC: Duke University Press, 1993), 8.
47. Carolyn Walker Bynum points out that mystical men such as Bernard of Clairvaux also have visions that are frequently physical, but she notes that "men's writing often lacks the immediacy of women's; the male voice is impersonal." Carolyn Walker Bynum, *Fragmentation and Redemption: Essays on Gender and the Human Body in Medieval Religion* (New York: Zone Books, 1992), 190. Women, on the other hand, narrate an event that happens to them alone. I am suggesting that is because men like Bernard of Clairvaux, already institutionally legitimized and powerful, do not have the same kind of need to authenticate their visions in their writing by vividly reproducing the experience in the way women do.
48. Revelations can also be received aurally, even when they are visual, as Rosalynn Voaden points out for Hildegard of Bingen. Rosalynn Voaden, "Mysticism and the Body," in *Oxford Handbook of Medieval Christianity*, ed. John Arnold (Oxford: Oxford University Press, 2014), https://doi.org/10.1093/oxfordhb/9780199582136.013.024; quoting here Hildegard of Bingen, *Scivias*, trans. Columba Hart and Jane Bishop (New York: Paulist, 1990), 60.
49. Hildegard of Bingen, *Scivias* 1.1, in *Hildegard: Selected Writings*, trans. Mark Atherton (New York: Penguin, 2001), 132–135.
50. Emily Ann Moerer writes, "Saint Catherine achieved some of her most profound visionary experiences while contemplating visual images, such as her miraculous receipt of the Stigmata of Christ, and therefore images were vital to her sanctity. However, Saint Catherine was not officially canonized until more than eighty years after her death, and during this time visual images again played a key role in creating her sanctity." Emily Ann Moerer, "Catherine of Siena and the Use of Images in the Creation of a Saint, 1347–1461," PhD diss., University of Virginia,

2003, https://doi.org/10.18130/V36P83. Lisa Tagliaferri quotes a passage from Sarah Ahmed describing queering as disturbing the order of things, and she continues, "Catherine, as someone marked as woman, inhabiting various edges of society—located in spaces that are not typically authorized for someone of her sex, class, education level—disturbs the order of things." Lisa Tagliafelli, "Lyrical Mysticism: The Writing and Reception of Catherine of Siena," PhD diss., City University of New York, 2017, 51.

51. For more on the way witness and authority yield the importance of both asceticism and art in the Christian tradition, see the chapter in the forthcoming book from Natalie Carnes and Matthew Whelan, "Bearing Witness," in *Why This Waste? Art and Poverty in the Christian Tradition*.

52. Martyn Lyons, "Celestial Letters: Morals and Magic in Nineteenth-Century France," *French History* 27, no. 4 (December 2013): 496–514, https://doi.org/10.1093/fh/crt047.

53. Bynum notes that while Francis of Assisi and Raymond of Capua are the only male saints to have claimed all five visible ones, "dozens of such claims are made by medieval women," and only for the women did the wounds periodically bleed. Bynum, *Fragmentation and Redemption*, 187.

54. This narration comes from Catherine of Siena's confessor's narration of her life. Raymond of Capua, *The Life of Catherine of Siena*, trans. Conleth Kearns (Wilmington, DE: Glazier, 1980), 156. A similar passage is found in the first person in Angela of Foligno's writings: "I saw and drank the blood which was freshly flowing from his side. His intention was to make me understand that by this blood he would cleanse me." Angela of Foligno, *Complete Works*, trans. Paul Lachance (New York: Paulist, 1993), 128.

55. Bynum, *Fragmentation and Redemption*, 186. Bynum also notes that these various bodily events rarely, if ever, appear in the *vitae* of male saints.

56. Voaden, "Mysticism and the Body," 407.

57. Bynum also reports that men were less inclined to attribute religious significance to their own illness or suffering. Bynum, *Fragmentation and Redemption*, 188.

58. Birgitta, *Revelaciones Lib. VI*, ed. Birger Bergh (Stockholm: Almqvist & Wiksell, 1991), 247. Translated by Claire Sahlin in "A Marvelous and Great Exultation of the Heart: Mystical Pregnancy and Marian Devotion in Bridget of Sweden's Revelations," in *Studies in Saint Birgitta and the Brigittine Order*, ed. James Hogg, (New York: Edwin Mellen, 1993), Vol. 1, 108–109.

59. Godfrey of Disibodenberg had also started a hagiographical work that remained unfinished but was incorporated into a *Life* by Theoderic of Echternach. Anna Silvas, *Jutta and Hildegard: The Biographical Sources* (University Park: Pennsylvania State University Press, 1998), 122. John Coakley, "A Shared Endeavor? Guibert of Gembloux on Hildegard of Bingen," in John Coakley, *Women, Men, and Spiritual Power: Female Saints and Their Male Collaborators* (New York: Columbia University Press, 2012), 45–67.

60. Ruether makes this point in *Women and Redemption*, 100, drawing on the work of Barbara Newman, *From Virile Woman to Woman Christ: Studies in Medieval Religion and Literature* (Philadelphia: University of Pennsylvania Press, 1995), 137–167.
61. For Saint Teresa of Calcutta, the relationship was reversed: her intense fame pressured the publication of a diary she had wished to remain private. Mother Teresa, *Come Be My Light: The Private Writings of the Saint of Calcutta* (New York: Doubleday, 2007).
62. Stanley Cavell, "Being Odd, Getting Even: Threats to Individuality," *Salmagundi* 67 (Summer 1985): 110.
63. Mary Daly, *Beyond God the Father: Toward a Philosophy of Women's Liberation* (Boston: Beacon, 1973), 19.
64. Mary Daly, *Gyn/Ecology: The Metaethics of Radical Feminism* (Boston: Beacon, 1978), 24. The importance of language to her work comes at least partially from Luce Irigaray.
65. Daly, *Gyn/Ecology*, 24.
66. Daly, *Gyn/Ecology*, 4.
67. More recently, Wilda Gafney in Old Testament/Hebrew Bible studies has taken a similar tack, drawing from Black preaching traditions to highlight and reinterpret female characters in scripture. Wilda Gafney, *Womanist Midrash: A Reintroduction to the Woman of the Torah and the Throne* (Louisville, KY: Westminster John Knox, 2017).
68. Other examples in her highly prolific career of attending to images, bodies, and emotionality as a lens into history and theology include Margaret Miles, *Image as Insight: Visual Understanding in Western Christianity and Secular Culture* (Boston: Beacon, 1985); Margaret Miles, *A Complex Delight: The Secularization of the Breast, 1350–1750* (Berkeley: University of California Press, 2008); and Margaret Miles, *On Memory, Marriage, Tears, and Meditation* (New York: Bloomsbury Academic, 2021). In this way, Miles keeps good company with a number of feminist historians of Christianity, including Patricia Cox Miller, particularly *The Corporeal Imagination: Signifying the Holy in Late Antiquity* (Philadelphia: University of Pennsylvania Press, 2009); and also Susan Ashbrook Harvey, particularly *Scenting Salvation: Ancient Christianity and the Olfactory Imagination* (Berkeley: University of California Press, 2006) and Susan Ashbrook Harvey and Margaret Mullett, eds., *Knowing Bodies, Passionate Souls: Sense Perceptions in Byzantium* (Washington, DC: Dumbarton Oaks, 2017).
69. Sarah Coakley, *God, Sexuality, and the Self: An Essay 'On the Trinity'* (Cambridge: Cambridge University Press, 2013), 191.
70. Gebara has said that she does not see her memoir as part of her theological work but as a way of "honoring my ancestors and their history" and as a "gift I give myself of the memory of my ancestors." I defer to her judgments and yet cannot help but see her memoir as theological in a broad sense, inasmuch as it is one of the most

significant living theologians reflecting on her own origins—similar to how, for example, Stanley Hauerwas's memoir *Hannah's Child* is taken as theological, though it contains little explicit theological reflection. Personal interview with Gebara over Skype, March 4, 2021.

71. Heather Walton, "What Is Autoethnography and Why Does It Matter for Theological Reflection? *Anvil: Journal of Theology and Mission* 36, no. 1 (n.d.): 6–10. https://churchmissionsociety.org/resources/what-is-autoethnography-theological-reflection-heather-walton-anvil-vol-36-issue-1/. This is part of her broader reflection on theological genre in Heather Walton, *Writing Methods in Theological Reflection* (London: SCM, 2014).

72. Tina Beattie, *The Last Supper According to Martha and Mary* (New York: Crossroad, 2001).

73. This is not to say that creative genres necessarily elicit a fitting response to the depiction of violence; a reader may find the violence arousing rather than disturbing, for example. This is a risk of fiction writing, and it more broadly points to the risk of any writing, or being, in the world.

74. This summary of insights is culled from Linn Marie Tonstad, "The Place, and Problems, of Truth," *Literature and Theology* 35, no. 1 (March 2021): 4–21; Linn Marie Tonstad, "(Un)wise Theologians: Systematic Theology in the University," *International Journal of Systematic Theology* 22, no. 4 (October 2020): 494–511; Linn Marie Tonstad, "Writing Theology," paper presented at Christian Theology Senior Seminar Programme, University of Cambridge, February 10, 2021, https://www.facebook.com/2215193512141417/videos/743542639919348..

75. Catherine Brekus chronicles the way many women not only preached but did so while arguing for the right of women to do so. Catherine Brekus, *Strangers and Pilgrims: Female Preaching in America, 1740–1845* (Chapel Hill, NC: University of North Carolina Press, 1998).

76. The Public Universal Friend generally eschewed gender, though some of their followers used "he," and the detractors almost invariably used "she." Due to the difficulty of avoiding pronouns altogether, I will use "they," which seems closest to communicating the transcendence of gender central to the Public Universal Friend's theology. For more on the gender transcendence of the Public Universal Friend and their life, see Scott Larson, "'Indescribable Being': Theological Performances of Genderlessness in the Society of the Publick Universal Friend, 1776–1819," *Early American Studies* 12, no. 3 (2014): 576–600; Paul B. Moyer, *The Public Universal Friend: Jemima Wilkinson and Religious Enthusiasm in Revolutionary America* (Ithaca, NY: Cornell University Press, 2015); Susan Juster, "'Neither Male nor Female': Jemima Wilkinson and the Politics of Gender in Post-Revolutionary America," in *Possible Pasts: Becoming Colonial in Early America*, ed. Robert Blair St. George (Ithaca, NY: Cornell University Press, 2000), 357–379.

77. When Lee describes her first encounter with a church authority about her vocation, she also offers a remarkable theological justification of her calling as a woman.

She begins by affirming that nothing is impossible with God and then linking her theology of salvation with one of calling: "If the man may preach, because the Saviour died for him, why not the woman? . . . Is he not a whole Saviour, instead of a half one?" She goes on to cite the example of Mary as the first preacher of the resurrection, to defend that her proclamation was indeed preaching, and to bring her justification back to her original point that God can accomplish anything: "If then, to preach the gospel, by the gift of heaven, comes by inspiration solely, is God straitened: must he take the man exclusively? May he not, did he not, and can he not inspire a female to preach the simple story of the birth, life, death, and resurrection of our Lord, and accompany it too with power to the sinner's heart?" To leave no doubt that her preaching is the gift of God, she points to its fruit: penitent sinners, contrite tears, converted hearts. When she herself doubted that her gift would continue, a vision of an angel confirmed her in her faith that "nothing could have separated [her] from the love of God, which is in Christ Jesus." Jarena Lee, *Religious Experience and Journal of Mrs. Jarena Lee, Giving an Account of Her Call to Preach the Gospel* (Philadelphia: Jarena Lee, 1849), http://www.umilta.net/jarena.html.

78. Lee, *Religious Experience*.
79. It is a tragic irony that Truth can point to these "manly" features of strong arms, hard labor, hearty appetite, and capacity for physical suffering because slavery has made them visible, that she was treated as a "lady" because she was not treated as a human. It is remarkable that in this speech, Truth leverages the injustices of one form of oppression against another.
80. Grant, *White Women's Christ*, 214; quoting Olive Gilbert, *Sojourner Truth: Narrative and Book of Life* (1850 and 1875; reprint ed. Chicago: Johnson, 1970), 119.
81. Grant, *White Women's Christ*, 214; quoting Gilbert, *Sojourner Truth*, 122.
82. Brekus, *Strangers and Pilgrims*, 199–201.
83. Grant, *White Women's Christ*, 195.
84. Grant, *White Women's Christ*, 121, 120
85. Grant, *White Women's Christ*, 196, 213.
86. M. Shawn Copeland, *Knowing Christ Crucified: The Witness of African American Religious Experience* (Maryknoll, NY: Orbis, 2018), xxiii.
87. Copeland, *Knowing Christ Crucified*, 6. Copeland, *Knowing Christ Crucified*, 26.
88. Copeland, *Knowing Christ Crucified*, 80.
89. Williams, *Sisters in the Wilderness*, 84.
90. Williams, *Sisters in the Wilderness*, 7, 5. In this approach, Williams describes the influence of Elsa Támez and Latin American feminists.
91. The new womanists are even more ecumenical in their sources and sometimes interreligious in their conversation. As Monica Coleman notes in the introduction to her edited volume *Ain't I a Womanist, Too?* many of the third wave womanists take as their point of departure not the work of pioneering womanist theologians Grant, Williams, and Cannon but that of novelists such as Alice Walker and Toni

Morrison as they speak from and to multiple kinds of religious commitments. Monica Coleman, "Introduction," in *Ain't I a Womanist, Too? Third-Wave Womanist Religious Thought* (Minnesota: Fortress, 2013), 17–27.
92. Grant, *White Women's Christ*, 205.
93. In her essay on Cavell, Moi quotes Cavell writing along these lines, saying, "The autobiographical dimension of philosophy is internal to the claim that philosophy speaks for the human, for all; that is its necessary arrogance. The philosophical dimension of autobiography is that the human is representative, say, imitative, that each life is exemplary of all, a parable of each; that is humanity's commonness, which is internal to its endless denials of commonness." Moi, "Philosophy and Autobiography"; quoting Stanley Cavell, "Philosophy and the Arrogation of Philosophy," in Stanley Cavell, *A Pitch of Philosophy: Autobiographical Exercises* (Cambridge, MA: Harvard University Press, 1996), 10–11.

3
Affordance

SEVEN YEARS BEFORE describing her sudden attunement to Joni Mitchell, Zadie Smith explored another unforeseen aesthetic conversion in her novel *On Beauty*.[1] The protagonist is Howard Belsey, an art history professor whose Marxist commitments lead him to skepticism about Rembrandt and the cult of genius that shadows him. He says things like "Prettiness is the mask that power wears." And "Art is the Western myth by which we both *console* ourselves and *make* ourselves."[2] Howard's nemesis is Sir Montague "Monty" Kipps, a professor and conservative public intellectual who has written a book extolling the genius of Rembrandt. Monty claims, "Art [is] a gift from God, blessing only a handful of masters," and derides programs such as affirmative action as an affront to the blessed meritocratic order.[3] If Howard represents a historicist perspective in which artworks are understood through powerful social forces such as class, inequality, and power, Monty exemplifies a formalist one in which art has an intrinsic value that holds across epochs and empires. As an academic, Monty is much more successful than Howard, though he, no less than Howard, uses Rembrandt as a means to an end: to attain scholarly and critical acclaim and to prove his ideological commitments. Neither man's philosophy, or his life course, is particularly appealing.

It is at the end of *On Beauty* that Howard finds himself in a moment of conversion. His marriage and career are collapsing. At a last opportunity to salvage the latter, Howard readies his lecture slides and prepares to give his well-worn arguments deconstructing Rembrandt's genius and, with it, the concept of the human that Rembrandt is said to have helped birth. As the PowerPoint begins, Howard looks out to the audience. His eyes fall on his wife, Kiki. He sees her hair braided with a scarlet ribbon, her "bare and gleaming" shoulders.[4] What kind of gaze is this? I think of Sappho's poem with the looping purple ribbon and James Wright's poem "Sappho" which returns three times to the beloved's "pure, bare shoulder."[5] Something has shifted. Howard looks back at the slides, dumbly, as they roll on, noticing, almost surprised, as figures appear in the images, and then he arrives at the last slide, when he finds his voice only to name the image, croaking, "*Hendrickje Bathing*, 1654."[6]

The audience awaits explanation, but Howard only gazes at the woman in the painting, who looks away into the water, "considering whether to wade deeper" and "not . . . certain of what lurked beneath."[7] He and Kiki look at each other. "The woman's fleshiness filled the wall."[8] "The woman" is the bather, but she has taken on the "fleshiness" so often associated with Kiki. Howard smiles at his wife. Echoing the bathing woman, Kiki looks away, smiling, as Howard looks back at Hendrickje, Rembrandt's beloved, and there is some understanding, or some promise, that seems to be developing between Howard and Kiki, as his lecture slips away from him. The book ends, "Though her hands were imprecise blurs, paint heaped on paint and roiled with the brush, the rest of her skin had been expertly rendered in all its variety—chalky whites and lively pinks, the underlying blue of her veins and the ever present human hint of yellow, intimation of what is to come."[9] So concludes not only the book but the section titled "On Beauty and Being Wrong."

In the final moment of the book, the beauty of Rembrandt and the beauty of Kiki speak to Howard—sing to him—in a new and powerful way. This is clearly a moment of conversion, but conversion to what or to whom? One way to describe the transformation under way would be to claim Howard is repudiating his Marxist, historicist position in favor of Monty's conservative, formalist approach that can appreciate Rembrandt. We could in this spirit describe Howard as won over to Rembrandt's genius despite himself, as the formal qualities of the painting overcome his attempt to reduce the image to dynamics of power.

But that doesn't seem quite right. After all, Monty and his view are presented as problematic throughout the book, refracting into a life with his family even more selfish and damaged than Howard's.[10] Further, the ending is not a moment apart from the narrative of Howard's life, as if a renunciation of it tout court, but its culmination, the moment his life has led him to. His investments and de-vestments in the academy and its rewards, his betrayal of his love for Kiki, his abiding love for her despite those betrayals, his ongoing conflict with Monty, his family's entanglements with Monty's family—they are all caught up in and help to make sense of this moment of conversion. He maintained his pre-conversion self through denying and suppressing aspects of himself and his loves; the conversion opens a different way of being that is not a rejection of historicism so much as an opening up of his own history. In the final scene, the self-narratives that he had committed so deeply to—the ones that required him to forget his love for *The Great Gatsby* and *Taxi Driver*—are smeared and then rinsed from his eyes, as he sees, stupefied, the beauty before him.

In "Some Notes on Attunement," Smith begins the story of her conversion to Mitchell: "The first time I heard her I didn't hear her at all."[11] And it is as if Howard has not seen these paintings, has not fully seen his wife, before this moment.[12] His gaze shifts between the two sites. *Hendrickje Bathing* invites Howard to see his wife anew. Or is Kiki inviting Howard to see the painting differently? There is some relation between Hendrickje and Kiki, as the form of the painting reframes his wife, and the sight of his wife confers for him new vitality on the painting.[13] He is disarmed. But his vulnerability to the beauty of Rembrandt is not a retreat into formalism, nor is it evidence of a timeless canon innocent of power dynamics. It is a presentation of art's power as activated by various persons, organisms, and objects in the world, of art as coming alive through the mediators that carry it forward. It is not a timeless relation to art because it is marked by its particular place in time, its relation to a past and possible futures. This vision of art as complexly entangled in the world—its politics, theology, academics, and aesthetics—shapes the work of this chapter, in which I continue to explore the possibilities of attunement, with one slight difference from Smith's described episodes. Though it can be the happy accident that Howard and Smith experienced it as, attunement can also be an intentional practice of reading and writing that gives rise to new meanings and politics. This is, in fact, one of the gifts of actor-network theory (ANT)—that its sense of agency as distributed across multiple actors and actants blurs the distinction between more passive and active understandings of attunement, making sense both of how it can operate like Smith's sudden conversion to Mitchell and Howard's to Rembrandt but also how it can be like Smith's slower, more intentionally cultivated love for Dostoevsky and Kierkegaard's attempts to attune the reader in the "Exordium" of *Fear and Trembling*.

What is new in this chapter relative to the earlier ones is not a claim for the intentionality of attunement but my explicit exploration of its political possibilities. In chapter 1, I argued that attunement provides a way for feminist theologians to build on the achievements of critique and avoidance while also helping to move the field forward in new ways; it is a mode in which feminists can engage the patriarchal inheritance that constitutes the bulk of the Christian tradition as our own *and* as feminists. In chapter 2, I argued that for feminist theology to turn toward attunement is for it to turn toward its own impulses—specifically toward an aesthetically aware and invested mode of reading and writing that feminist theologians have long expressed, echoing centuries of women and other marginalized genders doing the same. In this chapter, I want to use the category of affordances to elaborate why attunement's aesthetic investments yield new political possibilities. Having learned from the insights of those working in ANT (and literary scholars such as Felski who take an "ANT-ish" approach to literature), I trace some of the connections among texts, transformations, aesthetics, and politics, first in the process of attuned reading and then in the process of attuned writing (or making)—acknowledging that the difference between the two is not a firm or stable one.

If ANT helps to describe the plurality of agencies that co-create a text or artifact, giving it possible ways of being in the world, the concept of affordance helps to describe how these possibilities arise in the reader's relation to the text. I find "affordance" immensely helpful as a way of taking texts seriously as texts—as not, for example, reducible to politics—while insisting that the way texts mean is inevitably caught up in myriad actants and forces. Affordances can help make sense of at least one layer of Howard's conversion, as he gazes at *Hendrickje Bathing* and perceives in the painting a form that *affords* him new recognition of his wife's beauty, and the way Kiki's presence, which holds for him all the gorgeousness, unforeseeability, and humanness of their love, *affords* for him a way of seeing these qualities in *Hendrickje Bathing*. These are offerings of the text and of his wife's presence that emerge in Howard's dual relation to them. Before I begin to trace what an attuned reading and writing can do and give, I will begin by exploring the history and meaning of this term "affordance" and outline the ANT-ish approach to art and theology that I intend when I invoke it.

Affordances in Context

I borrow the concept of affordances from the field of psychology, where it was first proposed by James J. Gibson in a 1966 essay and expanded in his 1979 book *An Ecological Approach to Visual Perception*. Gibson wanted to describe what the environment offers or provides (affords) the animal as well as the immediacy by which an animal perceives that offering. A surface that is sufficiently horizontal, flat, extended, and rigid, he points out, affords terrestrial animals support for walking, standing, and running. Whether it is sufficiently rigid (to take one aspect) is judged with reference to a particular animal. A rhinoceros, for example, requires a different level of rigidity for support than a squirrel does. Or, more different still, water affords support and stridability for certain water bugs, while for humans, water affords drinking, pouring, bathing—but not respiration. Air affords respiration for us but not for a fish. As these examples suggest, an affordance speaks to physical properties but only emerges relative to a particular animal, for it requires an animal that can make use of a feature of the environment to become what it is.[14] Affordance, then, references the complementarity of an animal and its environment in a way that sidesteps the divisions of subjective and objective. It names a relationship.

The relationship affordance names between the animal and its environment is stable but not static. The stability is necessary for the evolution and survival of a species. The dynamism in some ways results from the complementarity that affordance names, as an animal learns to make a suitable environment still more suitable to its particular needs, thereby altering the environment to create new affordances, as in niche construction. Gibson points out the ways the shapes, substances, and media of the environment have been altered by humans to change what it affords us, to make it easier to feed, clothe, shelter, and warm ourselves (while in the process making life more difficult for almost all other animals).[15] This idea that we can use current affordances to create new ones will be important to the last part of the chapter as I develop the work of attunement in writing and making.

The dynamic generativity of affordances is one reason I find the concept of affordances helpful in articulating what it means to attune to a work of theology. Appropriating Gibson's work more explicitly to describe niche construction, scholars of psychology Rob Withagen and Margot van Wermeskerken describe the construction of a niche as the perception and use of affordances that create and destroy "other action possibilities." "Indeed," they continue, "animals bring about changes in the affordance layout and this modified layout is passed on to the offspring. Thus . . . the 'ecological inheritance' encompasses an inheritance of affordances."[16] Affordances specify how the transformations of the environment yield an "ecological inheritance" passed down to offspring in turn shaped by that inheritance and so, in this way, illustrate a dynamism that has real evolutionary significance.[17] And the way this inheritance is both received and co-created (altered for future generations) illumines the dynamism of Christianity's patriarchal inheritance.

A second reason I find the concept of affordances helpful is the way "affordance" already embeds within itself an investment in aesthetics that honors and extends the history traced in chapter 2—the way attention to perceptibility, alternative forms, artistic sources, and embodied knowing have been an important part of feminist theology. Inasmuch as affordance theory arose out of a theory of "ecological perception," an affordance is already theorized aesthetically. Gibson developed affordance theory as an alternative to the understanding of perception as the apprehension of abstract images to which we subsequently assign meaning. Rejecting that approach, Gibson described perception as the direct apprehension of what bears functional significance to us.[18] An affordance names what is perceived by the animal, and if the animal transforms the environment by augmenting, creating, or destroying an affordance in response to that perception, it also alters the perceptual capacities of its offspring. In the case of humans, we could say that altering affordances also alters the material of and capacities for aesthetic judgment. The dynamism of affordances—of perception, creation, transformation, and new perception—is, among other things, an aesthetic dynamism.

A third reason I find affordances helpful pertains to negative as well as positive possibilities that the environment offers the animal. For humans, a cliff, as Gibson points out, affords falling off—and there is no shortage of cliffs in the texts of Christian theology. Sometimes a particular part of the environment becomes so toxic that the best chance of the animal flourishing is migration.

In plundering this concept of affordances from ecological psychology for feminist theology, I am far from the first humanist to find Gibson's concept fecund. It is a concept that has only gained followers over the ensuing decades. From 1966 to 1979, 280 articles or books mention affordance or affordances according to Google Scholar. In the 1980s, there are 1,340; in the 1990s, 7,970; in the 2000s, 34,600; and in the 2010s, 79,100. The next decade looks sure to surpass those numbers, for from 2020 to August 2023, there were 77,100 references to affordance or affordances in scholarly research, which puts it on track to top 200,000 references in the 2020s.[19] No small share of responsibility for this uptick lay with Donald Norman, who saw the concept's implications for design theory in the 1980s and elaborated it in his bestselling book *The Design of Everyday Things* (1988), priming affordance theory for its enormous popularity in technology studies. But affordance also shows up in an array of other disciplines, including philosophy, dance studies, literary theory, disability studies, and even a bit in theology.[20] Latour himself mentions affordances, and many of those influenced by his work have picked it up at least lightly.[21]

The field of literature has taken up affordances in a way that has been especially influential for my understanding of attunement and the interpretation of texts. For as literature has taken up affordances and translated it into its own discipline, the concept has shifted and expanded in important ways. Texts are not exactly like water, air, and cliffs. As Eleanor J. Gibson, James Gibson's wife, noted herself, "The structure of a text is nested, like events in the world."[22] She writes, "A text may afford finding out how to bake a Genevoise cake, or the telephone number to call a broker in San Francisco, or words and music for singing a hymn."[23] And they may do so, moreover, even when these affordances are not an author's intention or within the genre conventions of what the text might be expected to offer. As literary scholars such as Namwali Serpell, Peter Khost, and Caroline Levine have drawn on affordances, they have worked on the term to render it adequate to their subject. Their work on affordances has helped me imagine and translate it into feminist theology. It is, in this way, an example of the dynamism affordances can describe.

Work on affordances is just beginning to take off in theology. Douglas Knight invokes affordances to describe the porousness of the creature to creation in his work on eschatology.[24] In an article on the affordances of doctrine, Hanna Reichel draws on Norman's application of affordances to design theory to probe the role of the systematic theologian as a type of designer who can be held accountable for how doctrines of sin might damage a person or community.[25] Recently, they have expanded their insights into a book that aims to help theology move past its wars of method and toward a better theology, one more faithful to an unruly reality and ineffable God.[26] Andrew Davison has published a popular article for the *Church Times* reflecting on home as a set of affordances that can be intentionally furnished and arranged to afford ways of living and moving more conducive to the life one hopes to live.[27] David Brown and Gavin Hopps work more in the Gibsonian tradition of affordances that found its way into musicology as a way to resist dichotomies of immanent and constructed meaning. For them, Gibson provides language to describe how music can *afford* authentically epiphanic experiences.[28] Victoria Lebzyak uses affordances to talk about the perceptibility of the sacraments in the theology of Alexander Schmemann.[29] And in his 2023 book *The End of Theological Education*, Ted Smith invokes affordances to think about the end—and potential new beginnings—of theological education.[30] These diverse and recent uses of affordances suggest that perhaps in theology, the concept of affordances has a robust future.

Actor-Network Theory

ANT provides a way of seeing the multi-agential character of affordances. Affordance does not name a single relationship—one, say, between animal and the environment—for "environment" itself contains multitudes: landforms, air, water, plants, bacteria, other animals. ANT notes the plurality of relationships that are part of niche construction, the way the animals are not the only agents acting on, against, and with the environment. The earthworm does not transform the environment just for itself but for microbes, water, air, earth, plants, animals, and so on—all of which take on roles sustaining (or altering) the new ecological system. The dynamism is fugue-like, as change can ripple through an entire ecological system. The plurality of agents implicit in niche construction theory and underscored by ANT turns out to be immensely important to acknowledge when learning how a text means in the world—and, in fact, the role feminist theology plays in the world.

Alive to the complex entanglements of the world, ANT can disabuse us of our investments in false purities, directing us to the mediations and processes by which art, academic discourses, and feminist theology are made—and how they might be made different.[31] While researching this book, I interviewed Margaret Miles. She mentioned taking a position at Harvard in the late 1970s, as women's and gender studies programs were beginning to spread across the nation, energized by the women's liberation movement. When she proposed starting a new doctoral program that focused on feminism and religion, some at Harvard Divinity School worried that the term "feminist" was not sufficiently scholarly. In their minds, feminism was activism, politics rather than academics. So instead, they titled the program "Religion, Gender, and Culture."

On the one hand, the anxiety of these faculty members does get at something real. Feminist studies *did* emerge out of the women's liberation movement, and many women's studies programs remain deeply invested in political issues that pertain not only to current events but to the situation of women on campus.[32] But that anxiety assumes that political investments render a discourse less academic or less intellectual. ANT helps us to come to terms with all academic work as hybrid, as invested in processes, institutions, and sociopolitical commitments that sustain it and make it plausible. Women's studies, like feminist theology, is different from many fields in that it foregrounds its politics. It is a field invested in exposing the politics that would suppress it, that delineates the ideas, institutions, and forces that enforce gendered regimes and discipline women as a class of people. In that way, it has a particularly explicit relationship to politics. But all discourse, all art, is co-mediated, and politics is inevitably part of such co-mediation.

To see feminist academic discourse and women's liberation as related is not to claim their relationship is a straightforward one. It is and has been in many ways fraught. In her book *Disciplining Feminism*, Ellen Messer-Davidow posits that as it became established as an academic discipline, women's studies was also drained of its radicalism. She tells a story in which women's studies is "formatted by the academy's intellectual and educational venues," shaped by the incentives, rewards, and promotional guides of the academy so that, in her blunt estimation, "the project that had set out to feed social change became a discipline that fabricated esoteric knowledge."[33] In Messer-Davidow's narrative, as the women's liberation movement sought the resources and intellectual power of the academy, it was also changed by the academy. The relationship between women's studies and the women's liberation movement fractured and separated over time, as the movement that sought to transform academia was instead, as Messer-Davidow avers, transformed by it.[34] Yet as early as 1975, one of the founding mothers of feminist theology, Elisabeth Schüssler Fiorenza, was reporting and refusing the view that the goal of women's liberation should eclipse concerns about publication in mainstream journals.[35] For her, the goal of liberation is entwined with feminist theology's mainstream success, inasmuch as the effectiveness of feminist theologians at liberating women within the church depends partially on their ability to move the church and those who take the church seriously.[36] Such dependence reflects how ideas filter out of the academy; that academic theologians often train pastors, priests, and ministers; and how ideas move through the world, are given life and power, through networks and institutions that connect, sometimes more tenuously, sometimes more stably, academic and political realities. Political and academic relationships may not go the way we foresee or hope they will go. But discourses and art nevertheless exist by and through these relationships and mediations. One powerful way to see how these mediations occur and the possibilities they open and close is through attention to affordances, which I turn to next, first as a strategy of reading and then as a strategy of writing and making. In these two movements, the concept of affordance can illumine a future for feminist theology.

The Affordances of Form

The model of attunement I am proposing is an aesthetically invested mode of reading and writing that develops textual affordances in ways generative to women and other marginalized genders. But what exactly does it mean to look for affordances in texts? In the following sections, I turn directly to this question, naming three ways to think about the affordances of theological artifacts: through form, attention, and doctrine. Each provides opportunities for historical and concrete engagement that allows for moving beyond the grip of patriarchy.

In chapter 2, I reflected on "forms" as a way of identifying how women and feminist theologians have claimed authority in their texts and artifacts. Here I want to explore "forms" as potential affordances for attuned reading. Why can "forms" do so much work? Levine's book *Forms: Whole, Rhythm, Networks* addresses that question, using the concept of affordances to highlight the aesthetic and political significance of form. Pointing out the way forms pertain not only to texts but also to prison cells, national boundaries, patterns of time, and routines of a factory, among other examples, Levine notices that social forms name arrangements intentionally crafted and that impose order, "just like art objects."[37] By considering form as an affordance, Levine narrows the gap between formalist and historicist approaches to literature, as attending to the aesthetics of a text becomes a way to study a text's life in the world.[38] She sets up her approach to form as affordance by looking at what forms in texts do, asking, "What is a walled enclosure or a rhyming couplet *capable* of doing? Each shape or pattern, social or literary, lays claim to a limited range of potentialities. Enclosures afford containment and security, inclusion as well as exclusion. Rhyme affords repetition, anticipation, and memorization. Networks afford connection and circulation, and narratives afford the connection of events over time."[39] Organizing her discussion around four types of forms, Levine acknowledges the significance of interstices, disruptions, and other non-form elements of a text but argues for her approach by claiming form is an underdiscussed aspect of how texts work in the world.

The structural similarities between forms in texts and forms in the world are striking, but Levine insists that the formal and historical, artistic and political, are not merely connected as analogies. Because the affordance that all forms share is *portability*, the political, formal, artistic, and historical all influence one another via forms, as they migrate and are translated across different domains, opening possibilities previously unforeseen or unavailable. In their migrations and transpositions, forms change; differing contexts matter for the work that forms do. Even as forms expand or shift over time, new, unexpected affordances can arise in response to a person's desire or need: the shoe jammed under my door that serves as a lock, the pencil that also holds my hair back in a bun. The same is true for the affordances of texts. In a book published three years after Levine's, Khost writes of these unexpected affordances as guerrilla uses of texts, as when Kristie S. Fleckenstein uses Lewis Carroll's literary invention of the bread-and-butterfly as a conceptual metaphor for her proposal of "cyberethos." The image, Khost points out, renders her complex argument intelligible, convincing, memorable, and even moving, but the capacity of the image to perform such work emerges only in relation to Fleckenstein's concept of cyberethos.[40]

The translations of forms into new contexts and the new affordances that emerge in their context-crossing mean that texts and artworks can have exciting lives in the world. In the Christian tradition, the movement of forms can precipitate a conversion (as it does, in a secular key, for Smith's Howard Belsey), which then disseminates that form to do more work in the world. One example of this is Augustine's *Confessions*, which, in the book leading up to his own conversion, chronicles story after story of conversion that haunts Augustine, particularly the conversion of Antony, which causes him to see his life anew until he finally adopts Antony's narrative shape as his own. As Antony was converted to the life of poverty by hearing scripture as if given directly to him, so Augustine decides to interpret the next scripture he reads as if given directly to him. Imitating the form of Antony's conversion, Augustine records what becomes one of the most memorable and influential accounts of conversion in Christian history, one that shapes conversion stories for centuries. Years later, the form that precipitates the conversion of Saint Francis is not narratival but visual. Specifically, it is the San Damiano crucifix, an image of the suffering Christ, by which Christ calls the saint into a life of repair among the least of these. In the wake of this conversion, images of the suffering Christ eclipse images of the triumphant Christ as the dominant crucifix style of the Middle Ages, affording new forms of piety, new relations, and new art forms. Approximately three centuries after Francis, Bartolomé de las Casas famously described his conversion away from the Spanish encomienda system as seeing Christ crucified not once but ten thousand times in the indigenous. The form of the suffering Christ affords in this case recognition of the brutal atrocities he was participating in and solicits Las Casas's own conversion.

The form of the cross, in which the glory of God is revealed in the form of abjection, is one example of how pre- and early modern women in their marginalized, humble statuses were able to claim a voice for themselves by emphasizing their humility. This is the case, for example, with Margery Kempe, who meditates on the cross and reflects on the crucifix as a devotional object as she adopts its inversion of power and humility, glory and abasement, to authorize her own voice. The crucifix is not just an abstractly known form, either, but a tangible, visible form, realized in the devotional objects of Kempe's life. In a powerful article, Laura Varnam traces the way Kempe's relationship to devotional objects, particularly the pietà and the crucifix, enables her to inhabit the roles of Christ and Mary in a way that confers spiritual legitimacy on her voice. It is, in other words, the fact that these roles she adopts have particular forms, recognizable shapes, that her authority can be recognized, even when the traditional modes of authority are closed to her because of her gender and marital status.[41] The form is portable, migratable from the statue to Kempe's performance of it, so that the authority recognized as belonging to the figures in the statue can also migrate to Kempe. The form of the crucifix, then, affords both recognition and the portability that enables Kempe to live and move through the world differently: to wear white, to go on pilgrimage, to write a book. This pattern repeats in the stories of multiple female mystics and authorities, including Julian of Norwich, Margaret Ebner, Birgitta of Sweden, and Catherine of Siena. They inhabit recognizable Christian forms and devotional objects and in their performance of them acquire a version of the authority ascribed to the object.[42]

The migrations and translations of forms can be both conservative and radical. They are conservative in that they are conserving something—a form—and radical in that what they conserve does something utterly new. Even more, it is often the very conservation that enables the radicality, for it is the recognizability of the form that gives it such potency for conferring authority. Finding a form of writing adequate to her gender, authority, and theology, for example, Hildegard adopts vision descriptions and elaborations, a form both embedded in Christian scripture and transformed by Hildegard's heavily theological interpretations. Concerned about Anselm's theology of the atonement, Johnson adopts its form of a dialogue between teacher and pupil to proffer her new account, relying on the legible authority of Anselm's account to claim a seriousness for her own.

This is not to say, of course, that forms necessarily do radical work. Forms can bestow authority while also denying female bodies, as, for example, in the case of the ancient Christian Perpetua, who in her text of martyrdom displays her holiness through dreaming herself into a male body. In this way, the association with maleness is reinforced rather than opened up, demonstrating the way forms can occlude as well as reveal, the way the form (the male body) can also problematically suggest what is deformed (the female body). But the meaning and work of a form can also shift, grow, and move in unforeseen ways, particularly as feminists decide to put them to new types of work, and in this way, forms are potentially, not necessarily, generative affordances of texts, images, and artifacts.

The Affordance of Attention

Forms are one important type of affordance in theology and religious studies. But there is perhaps an even more familiar one, even if not commonly associated with the language of affordance. It is the concentration and absorption that certain texts or ideas solicit. How many teachers in theology or religious studies early in their syllabuses invite their students to read Simone Weil's essay "Reflections on the Right Use of School Studies with a View to the Love of God"? Weil argues that geometry or Greek may have nothing to do with divinity in subject matter, but studying those subjects, which are so rigorous, so outside of one's own ego, so demanding, cultivates in the student a capacity for attention akin to prayer. We are venturing into a more abstract understanding of affordances here—one in which affordances beget affordances— but we could say that learning Greek affords a quality of attention that itself affords prayerfulness.

Any type of scholarship or literature—even those less rigorous than complex mathematics or ancient languages—affords some level of attention. Or, to put the matter more precisely, in the words of Yves Citton, "a specific type of attention . . . constitutes a text as literary."[43] The type of attention cultivated through literature (and theology texts engaged as literarily interesting) cultivates a receptivity so that unforeseen categories can emerge. And there are latent political possibilities simply in this act of looking. As Citton, like Levine, draws on affordances to think about interpretation of texts, his meditations, like Levine's, take him at one point to Jacques Rancière. Rancière emphasizes *looking* and claims that the type of looking important to an aesthetic experience is a form of action. The spectator "observes . . . selects . . . compares . . . interprets . . . links . . . composes his own poem with the elements of a poem provided him" and thereby "confirms or transforms the pre-existing distribution of positions."[44] To read a poem, Rancière insists, is to compose a poem from the elements given.[45] Drawing on the French similarities of *lire* (to read) and *lier* (to tie), Rancière describes this composition as an act of binding different things together. Aesthetic looking, in other words, is a complex act of meaning making, like Howard Belsey looking at his wife, Kiki, at the end of *On Beauty*, noticing her purple ribbon and her bare, gleaming shoulders in a way that evokes the poetry by and about Sappho. He looks at her as if she were a poem or a subject for a poem he is composing. Is his encounter with *Hendrickje Bathing* affording for him this gaze at his wife?

There is an interesting harmony here between Rancière's description of aesthetic looking as active and political with Pope Francis's hope articulated in his encyclical *Laudato si'* that looking might midwife a new politics. Early in the encyclical, the pope points to his namesake Saint Francis, who insists that part of the friary garden remain uncultivated, to be set apart from use and consumption, so that in looking at this beauty apart from functionality and appetite, the mind might be raised to God. It is a different type of looking from ordinary seeing and not unlike Rancière's aesthetic looking. We are thick in the dynamism of affordances here. If affordance theory insists that we perceive based on what we need or desire, then what kind of need or desire drives perception of a plant when food is taken off the table? In the case of Saint Francis's rule about the uncultivated portion of the garden, we might ask, what new affordance might arise from that rule?

Wanting to encourage a different way of looking, Pope Francis turns to the saint's *Canticle of the Creatures*, from which the pope's encyclical gets its title. The pope is worried about the depth of the environmental crisis, the way even our attempts to "solve" that problem will reinforce our desire for mastery of the world. So Francis's song of praise that turns to the various created things in wonder is not aesthetic ornamentation but aesthetic transformation, an attempt to shift humanity's relationship to creation in a way that enables new forms of action, paths for moving through the ecological crisis by undergoing our own conversions.

Aesthetic looking is an affordance that literature presumes, one akin to attention, an affordance that geometry and the ongoing memory of ancient texts presume. These affordances can in turn beget new affordances, new bonds, new political arrangements. Learning the attention that a text requires of us can help us look with more care at people and arrangements in the world.[46] Of course, aesthetic looking can, like forms, also give rise to more sinister possibilities. It can harden toward objectification and elicit an illusion of mastery. Yet it is not incidental, it seems to me, that so many of the medieval women who claimed a voice did so by performing and thereby inviting the reader into aesthetic looking. Julian, for example, attends to an image of the suffering Christ, describing and rehearsing her gaze at the image, and the reader who follows her text attends to the image as well, which helps to bring the suffering Julian herself into view. This type of looking is often not entirely separable from forms. For example, Hildegard, in the opening image of

Scivias, describes an image (later created) that depicts her with flames over her head, receiving divine visions. The reader and the beholder look at this aesthetic object, the vividness, intricacy, and commandingness of which solicit attention, and in such attention, the form comes more clearly into view. By the form, the beholder or reader is invited to confer authority on Hildegard, to read her into a history of Pentecost and other stories of divine inspiration. In another image, a picture of the universe pointing to God is strikingly vaginal, affording the reader a way of looking at femaleness and femininity that elevates them and shifts the reader's relationship to them and the divine. There is a dialectical relationship between attention or aesthetic looking and forms: attention can enable one to see forms, and the forms can elicit our attention. Through both these sites of affordance and the relationship between them, I want to emphasize that reading and beholding are latent with political possibilities—which can be plumbed or ignored.

Doctrinal Affordances

Unlike form and attention, doctrine is not an obviously nor intrinsically aesthetic category. However, to consider the affordances of doctrine in the context of attunement is to consider the act of perceiving the possibilities of doctrine—possibilities for how it means and what it does—and acknowledge such possibilities as co-created. It is, in this way, to acknowledge the taking up of doctrine as aesthetic and to encourage creativity in the dramatization and co-creation of the affordances of doctrine. Through the lens of attunement, in other words, we see engagement with doctrine's affordances as at least minimally aesthetically invested, and we see the possibilities for new affordances with heavier investments in aesthetics.

Many of the women and feminist theologians described in chapter 2 could be pictured as acknowledging the claims of texts and artifacts of Christianity to discover, note, and expand their affordances. Catherine of Siena and other mystics who claimed direct divine revelation, without mediation, echoed and were credible because of the claims that God creates ex nihilo, which identifies creation without mediation. Jarena Lee drew on Joel 2:28's picture of a Spirit poured out on all flesh to justify her preaching career. Sojourner Truth worked with the virgin birth to justify and make sense of her call to preach Christ. These women found some indentation in a cliff of the tradition, and it became for them a handhold they used to climb up and then build a platform for themselves. They perceived in these doctrines new affordances, new ways they could use them, and thereby made the doctrines usable in new ways, often using images and bodily testimony, as traced in chapter 2, to make the affordance vivid and compelling.

Feminist theologians have also participated in the emergence of an affordance by discovering in older doctrinal commitments new uses and possibilities. Responding to Catholic arguments that women cannot be ordained because only men can stand *in persona Christi*, Johnson drew on Gregory Nazianzen's Christology—adopting his famous argument against the Apollinarian heresy that what Christ did not assume that Christ did not heal—to point to the way Nazianzen affords an argument for women's ordination: if women are saved by Christ, then women's flesh has been assumed by Christ as well as men's. If Christ has assumed the flesh of women so that women might be one with Christ, what, then, is the problem with women standing *in persona Christi*? It is not accidental that it takes sixteen hundred years for this affordance to emerge from Nazianzen's text. It required certain political and theological conditions—dropping Aristotle/Thomas Aquinas's argument that women are inferior to men from magisterial texts, the availability of formal education to women, the consolidation of feminist theology as a field—to become an affordance of this text. This argument is just one example in a deep history of women and feminist theologians making use of affordances in a way that opens up history to future possibilities.

The work of opening up, reusing, and transforming is important and coexists with another tendency in feminist theology to unmask problems, which are cast in a story of negative accretions, which is to say, a declension narrative. So many feminist theologians and historians, from pioneer Ruether to recent champion Beth Allison Barr, hold together their feminist commitments, their commitment to Christianity, and their realism about the patriarchy of the church by narrating patriarchy as a fall from an egalitarian moment that misogynistic forces quickly crushed. As appealing as this approach can be—it provides a way both to condemn and to salvage Christianity—the declension narrative introduces its own problems. It requires some scholarly gymnastics to defend anything like a pre-Fall moment, relatively unsoiled by patriarchy, and attempting to do so strains feminist theology's relationship to history, where the sources and engines of declension lie. A temptation arises to leave history and concrete communities behind, as if they can be shed, in favor of a flight into symbol, as the theological is construed as a counterpoint to history, or as if floating above its own historical conditions. But thinking broadly about affordances means considering potentialities that emerge with certain readers in particular contexts. That deflates the temptation to search for a moment free of negative affordances and returns the reader to history, to the contexts and communities in which readers actualize the potentialities of the text, inspiring her, one hopes, to engage in the work of activating more positive potentialities. To put this charge theologically, it is to seek the Spirit's work in history and to be en-Spirited for such work in the present, catching glimpses of the kingdom that we pray will come.

Affordances in Their Environment, or Attunement as Time-ful, Concrete, Worldly

Nikolas Kompridis argues for the importantly historical or time-sensitive character of what he calls disclosure, which in its orientation toward aesthetics and possibility is akin to attunement. His work illumines how attunement need not be a repudiation of critique but can in some ways be its complement, for in his book *Critique and Disclosure*, Kompridis proposes disclosure as an alternative *and companion* to critique that is also vital for critical theory.[47] Working from the Frankfurt School and building on Martin Heidegger's discussion of art as world-disclosing, Kompridis contrasts the normative clarifications of critique with disclosure's capacity to suggest new perspectives, alternative possibilities, and enlarged meanings. Disclosure is appealing to him because it is time-sensitive, meaning it speaks to our condition as creatures in time, preserving an unclosed past by moving toward an unclosed future, which protects against both "reactionary nostalgia and vanguardist euphoria."[48] Disclosure extends possibilities of renewal and transformation at a time when the utopian energies that fund critique have been exhausted and "[s]kepticism and despair . . . have outstripped hope."[49] The renewal disclosure promises comes about, moreover, through what Kompridis describes as the "de-centering of the self," which does not mean a facile transcendence of the self and its parochialism or a rejection of one's partial perspective to arrive an impartial view.[50] Instead, he writes, "it is about an enlargement of self, opening it up to what was previously closed."[51] Kompridis is here intervening in a conversation about Jürgen Habermas, but his description of the work of disclosure as staying with a past while allowing it to remain open to future possibilities is resonant of what I have been suggesting of attunement and the relationship to history and the work of the Spirit. We could say that through attunement, we as time-sensitive creatures move through an unclosed past and an unclosed future, finding sources of renewal not in self-transcendence but by opening the self where it had been closed.

One of the helpful things about a time-sensitive posture such as disclosure or attunement is the way it encourages attention to the concrete, returning us to life with political and institutional realities that co-mediate textual affordances. It is not just that textual affordances can give rise to new political and institutional realities but that these textual affordances emerge in tandem with political and institutional realities. We see that again and again in the history of feminist theology. When I interviewed feminist theological pioneer Mary Hunt about the early years of feminist theology, she pointed to six-week living-and-learning programs in Grailville, Ohio, in the 1970s as instrumental to gathering the will, momentum, and support for feminist work. Women in seminaries and graduate programs met to exchange ideas and develop networks of support that continued to sustain them for decades.[52] Grailville shows up again in Messer-Davidow's book *Disciplining Feminism*, where she describes an Industrial Areas Foundation–led training at a "retreat managed by radical nuns."[53] This togetherness of political organizing and feminist theologizing echoed the wider togetherness of the women's liberation movement and the emergence of women's studies programs in the 1970s. But it also speaks to a long tradition in which institutional/political spaces and theological authority go together in a way, as we saw, that Schüssler Fiorenza recognized. The same divine visitations that authorized Hildegard's theological work also authorized her to claim some independence for her convent over and eventually against the bishop.[54] And this independent space also enabled Hildegard to keep producing her theology and art with minimal interference from ecclesiastical authorities. Her visions afford both theological authority and some measure of institutional autonomy, which in turn afford more opportunities for theological and artistic work.

I have myself experienced the surprising ways in which political/institutional realities and theological texts can co-create affordances. In one recent experience teaching feminist theology, I asked the students why they were taking the course. I ask some version of this question at the beginning of every class I teach, as a way of gauging the background and interests of my students. But this time, I did not get the usual sorts of answers. The first student replied that she had been a victim of sexual assault in her conservative, patriarchal church, which had handled her trauma poorly. After she shared, student after student in that class disclosed their own experiences of sexual violence and the refuge, meaning, and healing they were seeking in feminist theology. Every woman in that class had a story. I listened—present, receptive, and stunned. This had not been my intention for the activity or for the class in general. My goals were that they learn the history, texts, and methods of feminist theological discourse, and I asked the question to assess how much background they had in the field and discern how to pitch our conversations. Yet the class was not a simple expression of my intention. I had put together a list of texts and a course description, which gave rise to a particular shape and composition of the class, which then became a space of spiritual struggle and comradeship, which in turn energized the papers the students wrote and the themes they took up. Throughout this class, I saw firsthand the way social, institutional, and textual affordances mutually constitute each other. Amid the togetherness of the class, the syllabus, the private room, and me, the students perceived and enlarged a new affordance.

Composition and Creating Affordance

We arrive now at the hinge, from reading attunement to writing it. As reading can be an act of attunement that responds to the aesthetic affordances of a text and tradition, so can writing and making be acts of attunement that intentionally create and augment generative affordances. But we have already been discussing composition, particularly in the section on doctrinal affordances. The distinction between perceiving and creating, reading and writing, is not a firm one, for attuned writing builds on the way attuned reading is compositional, the way it, as interpretation, also makes meaning. Citton exemplifies this compositionality of reading that so easily tips over into writing and making when he writes, "The point is . . . to reorient the interpretive performance of the texts toward a more explicitly constructive use of its affordance. Instead of asking what our interpretation can *undo* (totalitarianism, capitalism, colonialism, sexism, mastery, fundamentalism, etc.), we are invited to ask what it can *make* (a platform of negotiation? a mapping of controversies? a handbook of strategies? a lexicon of sanity?)"[55] Attuned writing responds to those questions of what a text can make by *making*—making, I mean, something not just for oneself but for others, for a public that can find in the work new affordances.

The attunement model of writing and making that is compositional, constructive, and positive is a more fleshed-out version of (or a larger genre inclusive of) what I, in a previous project, referred to as Wittgensteinian iconoclasm, in contrast to Baconian iconoclasm. I visited this briefly in chapter 1. Where Baconian iconoclasm is motivated to dethrone the idols of the mind to expose the reality underneath (like critique), Wittgensteinian iconoclasm responds to a picture that has held us captive by surrounding it with an album of sketches. The power of the captivating picture is deflated as it is reinterpreted through situating it among other pictures. Baconian iconoclasm can become an eddy of shame that one had been duped, had perhaps taken pleasure in something without recognizing that it was not worthy of pleasure. But Wittgensteinian iconoclasm, like attunement, operates in a more constructive mode. In Wittgensteinian iconoclasm, it is the artist, not the demolitionist, who performs the iconoclastic work, as making becomes a form of breaking and energies are released forward into new visions and possibilities. Similarly, in attunement, we see a mode of critical yet constructive engagement modeled on art, which funds political action and imagination. In the next three sections, I trace some examples of how that can work.

Finding a Place and Composing a Play: Ivone Gebara and Feminist Theology in Brazil

Brazilian nun Ivone Gebara is a luminary of feminist theology. Early in her career, she connected the degradation of women, the earth, and the poor. Her life and work express both conviction and brilliance. As the 2009 Pat Reif lecturer at Claremont College, however, Gebara looked back on her career and struck notes of lament rather than celebration. She spoke of a "great distance" opening up between academic feminism and women's social movements, between feminist theology and the lives of most women in the church. In that lecture, she describes feminist theology as a difficult, "romantic struggle believing that sufferings and arguments can move hearts for a significant change in the traditional institutions of the Church."[56] Yet the arguments of feminist theologians did not move hearts, she acknowledges, at least not very much. Surveying the Catholic church in Brazil, Gebara sees that the church hierarchy remains patriarchal, that it continues to use scripture to solidify the standing of the most powerful rather than respond to the world with mercy, mutuality, and tenderheartedness.

Part of the problem is not just that patriarchy is something out there, outside of us, but that it has taken root within us. We are, Gebara insists, "colonized by it." Even if we have broken free from oppression in some ways—perhaps, she acknowledges, we have made some progress away from Augustine's essentialized gender roles—freedom is difficult because we are bound to the past in complex ways, in ways that call for what Kompridis calls time sensitivity. She says, "Our body is built on a connected past history, a past heritage, past ways of speech and expression of our values, on past words that have defined ourselves. The 'I' becomes an 'I' only among a 'We.' It is this complex web of past, present and future as well as the confluence of different traditions that we can define some aspects of our identities. Inside my 'I,' I can find lots of different 'I's' in harmony or conflicting among them."[57] Oppression does not live in abstractions or only in systems or in other people; it is in our bodies, our communities, our individual and collective identities. In this acknowledgment, Gebara resists the temptation to find a pure, untainted time or space. Her unblinkered perspective of the ways we are bound to patriarchy also makes clear that finding a way through and beyond oppression will be charged with difficulty and complications. There is no facile way of breaking free.

Measuring the work of feminist theologians against her hopes for it, Gebara voices disappointment. Looking back on her decades working with other feminist theologians, Gebara says, "We did new theology, biblical studies, wrote lots of books and articles, and did new liturgies.... But most of our work was frequently in the margin of our original churches. As feminists we were not integrated as part of the ministry and magisterium of our churches. For a long time in spite of our suffering we did not care. Now, after many years we have begun to think about the flourishing of our labor.... [W]e have to think more about our methods of working and our new concepts in order to leave a nourishing heritage to the new generations.... I feel that with our feminist theological past history we still need to work in new simple language and new forms of expression."[58] From her perspective in Brazil, Gebara outlines two problems with the way feminist theology has fallen short of its hopes. First, it has failed to move the patriarchal church, leaving male hierarchies and strategies of domination firmly entrenched. Second, in failing to move the church, it also failed to move many women in the church, particularly the poorest women, whom Gebara believes should be at the center of feminist theological reflection. Feminist theology, in fact, widened the gap between the educated, financially stable women writing feminist theology and the poorest women among us—a betrayal of her deepest commitments.

Coming to terms with what she called the painful reality of feminist theology's shortcomings, Gebara pressed in the quotation above for reflection on new methodologies and concepts. But what are these new ways of working? The question would not let me go, and so I wrote to Gebara asking if I could interview her. We spoke over Skype, where she continued her note of lament, though I also found an energy in her that expressed hopefulness, or at least the possibility that things might be otherwise. In our conversation, she turned repeatedly, emphatically, to the placelessness of feminist theologians in the church in Brazil and the ways they have been marginalized ecclesially and academically. "We have no place," she repeated five times in succession. But she also spoke of ways she had found a place, had constructed a niche, we might say—first by forging connections across denominations and religious traditions and second through the arts.

In describing how the arts could help feminist theologians find a place, Gebara spoke of work with musicians and theater people, including a play on the life of her close friend Dom Hélder Câmara. She first saw a play about him in which all his close collaborators were portrayed as male. Afterward, when the director began to speak to the public, she raised her hand. "I can't agree with this," Gebara remembers saying. "If I take a close look at the life of Hélder Câmara, I see first he lived with nuns in convent, [where] his room and food were prepared by nuns; second, he had two women secretaries writing all day with him; and third, when he was in the [Second Vatican] Council while bishop of Rio de Janeiro, a group of women were his closest confidants. There are letters now published that show this, and there are small schools of Hélder Câmara, with only women working there. If you take the library of the diocese, it was organized by women; and [there was] me, too!"[59] The director was struck by her remarks and invited Gebara to meet with the theater people once a week to teach them more about that history and about feminist theology, their work culminating in a play that was shown over the internet.

Amid the placelessness of feminist theology, one way Gebara created a place was through participation in theater. In the community formed by the process of making a play and in the audience who received their art, Gebara found one way she as a feminist theologian could inhabit new spaces. Another way was in the nature of what they produced. Rather than allowing the narrative of women as outsiders to be entrenched through yet another story of all men doing important work in the church, Gebara provoked the theater to tell a new story, which could itself do new work in the world. Through plays, a person can register, correct, and cast a way of seeing and feeling the world generative of a better community; they can be part of an aesthetic and therefore political transformation. We could say that Câmara's high valuation of women and their talents, the inclusive way he ordered his life against an entrenched patriarchal order, is an affordance the play amplifies and helps to spread, though it could just as easily have been suppressed, hidden as in the original play that occluded women's roles.

While the Brazilian churches and academies in which feminist theologians lived and worked relegated them to the margins of those institutions, Gebara found in the arts a community that accepted her centrality and helped her retell the story of women's work for theology that rendered visible and perceptible the ways women already were central to the church and the academy. The hope was that the play could both energize her and feminist theologians to sustain them in their work and also pry open the imaginations of church and university officials as well as laypeople to help them conceive of women, church work, and theology differently. The arts here represent a hope for new "methods of working," "new forms of expression" that can "move hearts for significant change," offering a way for feminist theologians in Brazil to create a place for themselves as they work to claim their place in church and university life. The substantiveness of this hope is underscored by a recent study of Orthodox Jewish women authored by two politics and policy graduate students and which found that art was a way for Orthodox Jewish women to express feminist commitment, broadcast feminist revisions, and carve out, both personally and collectively, a different space for women in their religious communities.[60] Art enabled them to find and make a better place for themselves, and this weighty hope for the political work of art extends, I think, to aesthetically invested forms of writing as well.[61]

Aesthetic Encounters and Political Work: The Virgin of Guadalupe as Image, Play, and Symbol

As the affordances of theater and play production help Gebara create a place for feminist theology in Brazil, so do the affordances of theater amplify and extend the affordances of the Virgin of Guadalupe. Nichole Flores's recent book *The Aesthetics of Solidarity: Our Lady of Guadalupe and American Democracy* testifies to the political significances of the Guadalupe, whose story turns on multiple aesthetic encounters. An Indigenous peasant, Juan Diego (Cuauhtlatoatzin in his native language, Nahuatl), receives at the Hill of Tepeyac an apparition of the Virgin as a brown-skinned girl, who tells him in Nahuatl that she wants a church built at that location. When the bishop does not believe Juan Diego, the Virgin appears to him again, giving him unseasonal flowers as a sign that she has charged him with this summons. When Juan Diego unfurls the *tilma* carrying his sign from Mary before the bishop, the flowers roll away to reveal a miraculous image. That image is the Virgin of Guadalupe, patroness of the Americas.

Flores acknowledges throughout *The Aesthetics of Solidarity* the multiple ways the Guadalupe image has been used. It has a complex legacy. But she spends much of her book tracing the generative work it is doing, and to that end, she opens by discussing a play, *The Miracle of Tepeyac*. Written by playwright and activist Tony Garcia, *Miracle* laments the loss of a Chicanx neighborhood in Auraria in Denver and the hierarchy's decision to close St. Cajetan's, a Chicanx church there. Garcia's play interweaves Guadalupe's symbol into the stories of fictional parish members of St. Cajetan's and so, as Flores describes it, connects the struggles for recognition and justice of Juan Diego with that of the Chicanx community. Drawing on the way Guadalupe embodies Mary's prayer that God lift up the lowly, Garcia makes use of this affordance of Guadalupe—an image with the capacity to render perceptible the work of lifting up as divine. Through Guadalupe, the play can dramatize and question the way the Chicanx community is sacrificed for economic "progress" and probe the "emotional, spiritual, and political" aspects of their removal from Auraria.[62] The image itself already has deep emotional, spiritual, and political resonances with many Chicanx and Latinx people, and the play enlarges the resonances that have been found in Guadalupe and builds on them to make a political claim.

The aesthetic is not just one dimension alongside the political in this story but is imbricated with it. Juan Diego's encounter with Guadalupe, which, as Flores continually points out, is aesthetic, is both a personal conversion and a political shift, where Juan Diego is empowered and elevated relative to the ecclesiastical-colonial hierarchy. As we saw with so many female mystics, an aesthetic encounter with the divine that is mediated in such a way as to repeat the aesthetics of the encounter authorizes the lowly one who first receives the encounter. Every time someone sees the Guadalupe image, she is afforded a glimpse at the one who lifted up Juan Diego, who gave herself as an image to authorize Juan Diego over and against the church hierarchy. The play builds on that work because of how it weaves Juan Diego's story with the fight for St. Cajetan's in a way that also, Flores notes, invites the audience to plait "their own experiences of oppression into the braid."[63] The way the colonial structures of power that Juan Diego faces are drawn into the story of the neocolonial structures the Chicanx characters face invites a further reflection on the varieties of oppression the audience members face in their own lives. The aesthetics of the play afford new forms of solidarity and suggest new possibilities for political action.

The Miracle at Tepeyac is just one example of Guadalupe aesthetically affording a politics of solidarity for Flores. In her book, Flores points to others, such as the United Farm Workers in California and Los Comités Guadalupanos in New York City, each of which uses what Flores calls "Guadalupan grammar" to criticize unjust political and economic arrangements. Even as they draw on the affordances that emerge from acknowledging the Virgin of Guadalupe, they also draw on her affordances of form. Flores continues, "Simultaneously these justice movements marshal the aesthetic dimensions of Guadalupan images, narratives, and liturgies to invite society at large to join them in their campaign."[64] This does not mean that Guadalupe cannot be deployed to nefarious ends or that deployment of the image toward liberation guarantees success. It means that Guadalupe is an important source of generative affordances, as she offers the capacity to fashion new forms of solidarity that are, in words of Flores that echo the hopes of Gebara, "necessary for changing minds and changing hearts."[65] As the ability to cultivate solidarity such that hearts might be changed is an affordance of Guadalupe, so the ability to change hearts and minds about gentrification, immigration, or labor exploitation are affordances created by particular deployments of Guadalupe in arts of protest. The affordances give rise to the possibility of further affordances.

Answering a Crisis in Representation: SPEAP

Where Gebara speaks to co-creating a home in relation to Mother Church and Flores explores co-creating with the Mother Mary, Latour occupies himself with a different mother—Mother Earth—or, as he prefers, Gaia. Gaia has been a major preoccupation that galvanized a new program founded in 2010 at the Sciences Po Paris. Created by Latour and Valérie Pihet, the Experimental Program in Political Arts (SPEAP) seeks to address what Latour calls a "triple crisis" in representation that spans not only art and politics but also science as this last field seeks to renew its methodologies, practices, and questions. In an essay articulating the motivation of SPEAP, Latour points out that when something like the environmental catastrophe calls for collective decision-making, our failures to represent who we are, what we might become, and the challenges we face in a way that is "precise, sensitive, sensible, and shared" is particularly acute.[66] SPEAP's ambition is thus to reforge the lost links between political, artistic, and scientific representation, "*to compose* a common world, and to rekindle what has always been the great ambition of politics—to create a livable and shared public space" through collaboration, mutual learning, and collective action. The program is necessarily interdisciplinary as it canvasses artistic practices for methodologies that might aid in interpreting a social issue for political action. SPEAP invites professionals, artists, and researchers to join in this experimental endeavor to "create new forms of representation of public affairs and reinvent the relationship between the different social actors."[67] Representation and social action, in Latour's articulation of

SPEAP's ambition, are bound up with relationships. How might work born from these motivations, ambitions, and commitments approach a particular crisis of representation?

In 2014, shortly after the launch of SPEAP, Latour gave a lecture at MIT for the Center for Art, Science, and Technology, in which he explored projects that embody the interdisciplinary, creative spirit of SPEAP and answer the theme of his lecture, "How do we make ourselves sensitive to Gaia?" This question, Latour reflects, is aesthetic "in the original sense" in that it asks about capacity for sensing phenomena. In asking how we render ourselves sensitive to Gaia, Latour also asks what forms might render Gaia sensible to us. Only in our sensitivity to a phenomenon can we receive it, but becoming sensitive (rendering sensible) for Latour means overcoming Western philosophy's centuries-long captivity to Dutch still life as a representation of objects and relations in the world. (We have not traveled far from Rembrandt after all.) In looking at a Dutch still life, we are subjects who stand at a distance from objects untouched by time, flattened into two dimensions, stilled to a halt. The relation of an observer to the objects in a still life is in many senses extracted from the ordinary conditions of space, time, and movement in which we live with those objects. Within this relation, we observers have all the agency. We are the living ones; the objects are still, dead. They are abstracted in a way that can create a beautiful representation that may suggest myriad insights about life; but to take still life as a paradigmatic representation of our life with objects is a mistake that engenders a false and problematic relation to Gaia, who appears to us inert, distanced, outside of us. So what forms of representation might help us to receive Gaia anew, more fully and truly?

Latour's lecture offers a series of examples of artists and scientists creating better representations that might help us receive Gaia. One example is Tomás Saraceno's project *On Space Time Foam* (2012), which renders those who engage it newly sensitive to the earth, shifting the subject-object relation. Inviting people onto its large, air-filled, translucent membranes, *On Space Time Foam* renders those who answer its invitation unable to walk. They can only crawl across the membranes, like babies, subjects who experience the ways they are subject to the object and to the conditions of space and time that it establishes.[68] The illusion of human life as apart from Gaia, as outside nature in the way the subject is distanced from the Dutch still life object, fades. As people crawl and move across it, the membrane vibrates like a drum, rendering space audible. The conditions of existence, movement, life—usually invisible to us—are literally perceptible in a new way.

Latour gives example after example of projects sensitizing us to receive Gaia or depicting the difficulty of such sensitizing. A puppeteer named Olivier Vallet dramatizes submission to the puppet, the puppeteer being moved by that which he or she moves, to question subject/object dichotomies. Writer Pierre Daubigny and directors Frédérique Aït-Touati and Chloé Latour, advised by a team of scientists, invent a play, *Gaïa Global Circus: Une Tragi-Comédie Climatique* (2014), staged beneath a billowing, moving canopy to shift the sense of space-time and provoke reflections on the "abysmal distance between our little selfish human worries and the great questions of ecology."[69] Physicist Alain Podaire presents in his work a model that registers the problem of making a model of the oceans, reflecting how color can represent the oceans, their history, and their salinity and demonstrating the similarity between the questions of artistic and scientific representation—a similarity only highlighted when juxtaposed with artist Adam Lowe's project *Terra Firma* (2014), which, in attempting to create a new projection of the earth, distorts the areas of the oceans to depict the exact proportion of the surfaces and depths in a way that presses the question of the future of cities such as London and New York. Philippe Squarzoni composes a graphic novel, *Climate Changed: A Personal Journey through the Science* (2014), which explores in word and image the immense difficulty of discussing climate change in that medium, and scientist Oliver Morton writes a scientific book on photosynthesis called *Eating the Sun*, in which the words are energized by an attempt to present a "Gaia-esque" view of the earth. All of these projects are different ways of attempting to render us sensitive to Gaia as more than an object, to renew a relationship with Gaia, and thereby to help us to receive the earth anew in a way that is necessary if we are to address the climate crisis. (And in Latour's conviction that our looking at the earth, our configuring of relationships, must change in order to address the climate crisis, he sounds very much like Ranciére or Pope Francis in *Laudato si'* or someone who has recognized the affordances of attention.)

SPEAP continues Latour's long legacy of collaborating with artists, of seeing the methodologies, questions, and even the crises of art affordances that emerge in relation to crises faced by scientists and politicians. He continually returns to art in his work. Over the course of his career, Latour cocurated three exhibitions and received the Nam June Paik Art Center Prize. Even when he is not explicitly engaging art, his investment in aesthetics as intimate with both scientific work and political change shows up in the form of his writing. His style is animated and lively—so lively that it occasionally breaks into dialogue, as in a small chapter composed of a student-teacher dialogue for *Reassembling the Social* or briefer interludes in essays such as "Why Has Critique Run Out of Steam?" Frequently, he'll meditate on words or the inadequacy of certain expressions he nevertheless uses (he's famously frustrated with "actor-network theory"). Describing the way Latour frames a moment of technological history in the genre of a murder mystery, Francis Halsall writes that his creative writing is not some stylistic trick but is part of advancing aesthetics as a way of exploring the world not inferior to science, law, or ethics.[70] His practice of thinking and writing, Halsall notes, conceptually rhymes with the practices of contemporary artists. In these and other ways, the form of Latour's writing consistently reiterates the validity and necessity of aesthetics. As Latour explicitly says in an interview with Halsall, "If politics is the art of the possible ... then we need political art to open this up, this 'possible' or to multiply this possibility."[71] Thus, when Graham Harman considered what a re-envisioned, Latourian humanities would look like, he ends his essay, "Among other things, a Latourian humanities would entail the writing of vivid and persuasive prose, not the endless hedging of fifty-page exercises in pretending to subvert everything while actually moving nothing a single inch."[72]

Literary Turns in Feminist Theology

Latour's conviction that art can open up "the possible" for politics underscores the significance of the pioneers of feminist theology currently embracing the literary conditions of theological work. In chapter 2, I spoke about how these novels, memoirs, and experimental genres appeal to the reader's imagination, write women differently into the tradition, and help visibilize women's bodies. But I want to stress not just how these literary feminists are reading the tradition and using its affordances to construct a more habitable place within it but also how, in doing so, they are writing new affordances into the tradition as well. As discussed in chapter 2, writers such as Thistlethwaite and Beattie use an affordance of art—presence—so that we encounter violence against women's bodies but in a form that *sees* the violence, that registers it as horrific, and thereby affirms the value of women's bodies. Johnson's Anselmian dialogue has given us a female version of "A" in Anselm's dialogue, and so the tradition now has a new character with which to imagine a future. The aesthetic investments of their writing help them to extend through it new affordances that could not emerge from more traditionally expository theological writing. In this way, we can see the value of early Christian texts about women that have questionable relations to the historical persons they supposedly depict.

Thecla, the companion to Paul in the apocryphal *Acts of Paul and Thecla*, gave Gregory of Nyssa a way to understand the powerful intelligence, witness, and independent-mindedness of his sister Macrina, whose literary representation as a teacher and miracle-performing Socratic figure in turn gave rise to new ways to imagine and understand women in the Christian tradition where her story was told. Late ancient acts, martyrologies, and hagiographies of women could, like the recent literary turns in feminist theology, add to the landscape of theology, offering the possibility of shelter or handholds for climbing further on, offering the possibility of creating niches and, over time, changing the landscape, making it more hospitable to the flourishing of women.

Negative Affordances

Landscapes, of course, are not all shelters and handholds. When Gibson introduces the concept of affordances, he is clear that there are both beneficial and injurious affordances. An ingested substance, he explains, can afford nutrition, but it can also afford poisoning. A knife can afford cutting or being cut; a cliff can afford walking along or falling off; the flesh of another can afford comforting or cruel touch.[73] So far, I have discussed a mode of engaging a tradition primarily through positive affordances, both making use of them and writing and making with an eye toward them. But what of negative ones, especially brutally negative ones? What do we do with those texts that afford poisoning, laceration, and violence?

In a patriarchal tradition, negative affordances for women and other marginalized genders are rife. There are texts that conceal, diminish, and deride women and the gender-marginalized, affording silencing, oppressive hierarchies, and domination. They are sometimes produced, moreover, by men who even outside their writing *did* silence, oppress, and dominate women, sometimes cruelly. So what can we do with their work? With attunement, I have been advocating a strategy of composition, of responding to and building affordances generative to women and other marginalized genders. Now I want to think both about what attunement can do with negative affordances and about the limits of attunement. The genre and circumstances of the negative affordances I consider are all too familiar in the wake of #MeToo and #ChurchToo. In the words of Claire Dederer's 2017 piece for the *Paris Review*, "What Do We Do with the Art of Monstrous Men?"[74] Dederer posed this question as her title, and Sarah Stewart-Kroeker followed suit, quoting it as her own title in a 2019 article in *De Ethica*.[75] Given what we have learned about Woody Allen, Roman Polanski, Kevin Spacey, and myriad others, they ask, what kind of relationship to their work do we, should we, have? Is their work contaminated? Are we when we enjoy it?

Dederer articulates the complexity and subtlety of the dilemma—probing the possible relationships between artist biography and work, the harms or benefits of consumption and abstention, the multiple types of monstrosity—and Stewart-Kroeker offers some terms for thinking through it. Her framing concept is *aesthetic involvement*, and she puts the term to work identifying the multiple ways a work forms (or deforms) those who love it, other artists and works, the common artistic record, and social judgments about gender, sexuality, and morality. It bears similarities to acknowledgment in that both presume the intersubjective dimension to engaging art and texts. What becomes clear throughout Stewart-Kroeker's careful attentions and distinctions is how unavoidably particular and personal the judgments about the work of a monstrous man are. Eschewing temptations to offer what she calls a "single normative principle," she instead poses questions relevant to seeking a path forward, asking about the nature of the artist's actions, the effects on the viewers of the art, and the way engaging the art affects those directly damaged by the artist, as well as questions to consider if one decides to engage the art.[76] The outcome of facing such questions might be to abandon the artworks, to refrain from watching, consuming, or writing about them again. Or it might be to watch them again. Stewart-Kroeker notes film critic A. O. Scott's lament that he cannot "unwatch" the Allen films he's seen; they have become part of his critical cinematic imagination, and so he chose to watch them again, with different eyes, to see and interpret them differently, and to write about them differently, that they might live differently in the world from how they currently do.[77]

Perhaps Scott's situation and response open up a possibility of a Wittgensteinian iconoclasm with regard to the monsters. As Dederer and Stewart-Kroeker note, Allen often uncritically pictures an older man with a young woman, where the older woman is "brittle" and the young woman vital and open, the difference between the women justifying or absolving Allen/the character of abandoning the former for the latter. In a passage that Stewart-Kroeker quotes, Scott observes as he returns to Allen's oeuvre, "The Woody Allen figure in a Woody Allen movie is almost always in transit from one woman to another, impelled by a dialectic of enchantment, disappointment and reawakened desire. The rejected women appear shrewish, needy, shallow or boring. Their replacements, at least temporarily, are earnest, sensuous, generous and, more often than not, younger and less worldly than their predecessors. For a very long time, this was taken not as a self-serving fantasy but as a token of honesty, or freedom from sentimental conceptions of domestic love."[78] Instead of allowing the film to stand as a freestanding picture of "freedom from sentimental conception of domestic love" or what fully adult women are like and why men might be pardoned for sleeping with teenagers, a Wittgensteinian iconoclasm could resituate this picture in an album in which it is newly received as a picture of the human propensity to justify our misuse of others by casting the misused in roles convenient for our wishes. The film might register for us the temptation of a man to claim that a woman is worthy of rejection by painting her as difficult and shrill. It might also show us how that portrait also follows from an attempt to justify his desire for an underage teenager (as in Allen's *Manhattan*) by painting *her* as wanting, deeply wanting, to be educated by and sexually involved with him. In this way, we could receive these movies as raising powerful questions about self-deception and justification. Maybe one day, this reassessment might lead to retelling these or similar stories through the women's points of view in ways that might bring into focus what the narrator occludes.

But on the whole, I don't think now is the time for such renewed attention to Allen's corpus, even as it may be important for particular individuals such as Scott.[79] Partly, I wonder if we are still too caught up in the deception that Allen's movies exemplify, so that returning to the films may once again bewitch us. Mostly, though, I think the movies of Allen needs to be given a rest because of the issues raised by Stewart-Kroeker's questions, not least of which is the ongoing damage suffered by Dylan Farrow. Farrow has described the nausea and retraumatization that public attention to Allen gives her, and it is past time to take her suffering seriously.

The focus on the survivor as a way of assessing the ongoing consumption of art is an approach adopted by the organization Into Account. Offering support and advocacy for victims of sexual trauma and their allies in Christian settings, Into Account has developed a set of questions for working through one's relationship to the art and work of perpetrators of sexual violence not unlike the ones Stewart-Kroeker articulates. The organization was active in the prosecution of David Haas, a music minister and composer whose popular songs have been sung in myriad churches across the United States and also a sexual predator who raped, assaulted, and molested dozens of women and children from 1979 to 2020. For some victims, the songs are retraumatizing; and in some songs, Haas embedded messages for his victims. What is to be done with these songs, many of which have become important to people's worship lives? Into Account recommends a survivor-centered approach to sexual assault, so that if a victim in one's community is injured by the music, the community should cease singing them.[80] Will there be a day when they can be sung again?[81] Maybe. Maybe not. That is for communities to discern as they continue to prioritize survivors and seek the health and flourishing of the most vulnerable among them.

Many of the women on the team for Into Account come from communities deeply affected by the sexual assault and exploitation perpetrated by John Howard Yoder, whose predatory behavior caused a crisis and ongoing reckoning in Christian theology and especially the Mennonite community. While there is not complete consensus about what do with Yoder in theology, most theologians recommend either not engaging him or engaging his thought with a "hermeneutics of suspicion."[82] I raise this now to outline the limits of attunement. It is a powerful way of negotiating a patriarchal inheritance, but it is not meant to replace avoidance (such as not singing a Haas song or not engaging Yoder) or critique (such as exposing the exploitative elements present in Allen's movies or Paul Tillich's theology).[83] Adopting the attunement approach to a patriarchal tradition does not commit a person to repairing any particular text, artifact, or artwork, and it certainly does not commit a person to repairing all of them. Sometimes niche construction is not a viable option, and animals turn toward migration for survival. There are times and places when a song simply cannot be reattuned.

Conclusion

To approach the texts and artifacts of Christianity through their affordances is to appreciate the historicist and formalist aspects of meaning making—the way, that is, formal aspects of the text can move and act powerfully on both reader and world but only in and through mediations (actors and networks) that are inevitably historical. In this way, attunement's attention to affordances can help to resist sharp divisions between aesthetics and politics, insisting instead on their multiple connections. By outlining the affordances of form, attention, and doctrine, this chapter articulated a vision for affordances in attuned reading and writing that it went on to flesh out in particular examples, such as Gebara's play, the Virgin of Guadalupe's multiple iterations, Latour's Experimental Program in Political Arts, and recent literary turns in feminist theology, all of which connected politics and aesthetics. It concluded with a reflection on the limitations of attunement, which cannot itself become the only mode of engaging Christianity's patriarchal inheritance. Sometimes the most salutary way forward is on to new terrain.

Transformations are complex, sometimes mysterious, both in how they begin and in what they open up. I wonder what might have happened in the next chapter of Howard Belsey's life. What might his life have become if he were to keep faith with his moment of epiphany? How might he interpret his conversion, and what way might he find to go on from it? Perhaps he would not deny the encounter he had with *Hendrickje Bathing* and Kiki the way he had denied the grip *The Great Gatsby* and *Taxi Driver* had on him or the significance of his boyhood encounter with Rembrandt's *The Staalmeesters*. Or perhaps he could hold that encounter, the *presence* of that artwork, together with the knowledge he had accumulated over his lifetime about the economic, political, and intellectual systems that co-produced it. Perhaps the way his epiphany about Rembrandt and his epiphany about Kiki came together would draw him to a closer attention to his own life and the myriad actants and winding paths that led him to that moment. The beauty, he might see, is fabricated by threads and weavers almost too intricate to trace. But fabrication is not deception or falseness. The beauty is true enough for him to change his life and real enough for him to give up his last effort at academic stability and respectability. It speaks, in both these ways, to our humanness and the ways in which our humanness is always embedded in and co-constructed by what is nonhuman.

I have been elaborating in this chapter attunement as an aesthetically invested reading strategy that attends to the affordances of a text to build more generative affordances into the tradition. In doing so, I have attempted to trace ways art and aesthetics can have political and theological significance, how art and aesthetics can bear affordances for political and theological transformation. I want in chapter 4 to specify what that might look like in a particular case. I want to consider attunement and its political implications and imbrications by considering a subject important for feminist religious thought: Mary, a figure that seems to promise so much hope for feminist theology but has brought the field so much disappointment.

Notes

1. Zadie Smith, *On Beauty* (New York: Penguin, 2005).
2. Smith, *On Beauty*, 154.
3. Smith, *On Beauty*, 44.
4. Smith, *On Beauty*, 442.
5. The Sappho poem is "Don't Ask Me What to Wear," and a good translation can be found in Mary Barnard, *Sappho: A New Translation* (Oakland: University of

California Press, 2019). Wright's poem "Sappho" can be found in James Wright, *Above the River: The Complete Poems* (New York: Farrar, Straus and Giroux, 1990), 33.

6. The verb "croak" is Smith's own, as Howard's journey to rediscover his own full humanity apparently requires a froglike turn. Smith, *On Beauty*, 442.
7. Smith, *On Beauty*, 442.
8. Smith, *On Beauty*, 443.
9. Smith, *On Beauty*, 443.
10. One important virtue Howard has that Monty lacks is openness to the possibility of conversion. When Monty faced his own crisis—his wife's death—he, too, was invited into a different way of perceiving the world, through news of his late wife's personal bequest of a precious painting to Kiki. But Monty refused this invitation, choosing instead to harden himself with deception. He attempts to keep the painting from Kiki.
11. Smith, "Some Notes."
12. It is as if he sees Rembrandt for the first time, at least, since boyhood, when he has a compelling encounter with *The Staalmeesters*. "How many times has Howard looked at these men? The first time he was fourteen, being shown a print of the painting in an art class. He had been alarmed and amazed by the way the Staalmeesters seemed to look directly at him" (Smith, *On Beauty*, 384). The energized encounter contrasts sharply with his current interaction with the painting, a lecture with old, often-repeated ideas that "makes him very tired. He slumps in his chair" (Smith, *On Beauty*, 384).
13. Even their names associate them. The ending of "Hendrickje" evokes Kiki, while the H nods to Howard.
14. James J. Gibson, "A Theory of Affordances," in James J. Gibson, *An Ecological Approach to Visual Perception* (Boston: Houghton Mifflin, 1979), 129–130. In Gibson's words, an affordance "points both ways, to the environment and to the observer" (129). Anthony Chemero extends Gibson's thought that an affordance is "neither of the person, nor of the environment, but rather of their combination" (187). Anthony Chemero, "An Outline of a Theory of Affordances," *Ecological Psychology* 15, no. 2 (2003): 181–195.
15. Gibson, "A Theory," 129–130.
16. Withagen and van Wermeskerken, "The Role of Affordances," 505.
17. Heras-Escribano, "The Evolutionary Role of Affordances."
18. Harry Heft, "Affordances and the Perception of Landscape: An Inquiry into Environmental Perception and Aesthetics," in *Innovative Approaches to Researching Landscape and Health*, ed. Catharine Ward Thompson, Peter Aspinall, and Simon Bell (New York: Routledge, 2010), 18.
19. The numbers that appear on Google Scholar in these last three categories fluctuate slightly, but the same pattern overwhelmingly holds. My thanks to Katherine Ellis, who retrieved these particular numbers in August 2023.

20. I am grateful to my research assistant Katherine Ellis for this research.
21. Latour mentions affordances as he describes the theory as useful for helping to name the "many metaphysical shades between full causality and sheer nonexistence." Bruno Latour, *Reassembling the Social: An Introduction to Actor-Network-Theory* (Oxford: Oxford University Press, 2005), 72.
22. Eleanor Gibson, "Perceptual Learning and the Theory of Word Perception," in Eleanor Gibson, *An Odyssey in Learning and Perception* (Cambridge, MA: MIT Press, 1991), 457; quoted in Namwali Serpell, *Seven Modes of Uncertainty* (Cambridge, MA: Harvard University Press, 2014), 22.
23. Eleanor J. Gibson, "Reading in Retrospect: Perception, Cognition or Both?" in Eleanor J. Gibson, *An Odyssey in Learning and Perception* (Cambridge, MA: MIT Press, 1991), 494; quoted in Serpell, *Seven Modes of Uncertainty*, 88.
24. Douglas Knight, *The Eschatological Economy: Time and the Hospitality of God* (Grand Rapids, MI: Eerdmans, 2006).
25. Hanna Reichel, "Conceptual Design, Sin and the Affordances of Doctrine," *International Journal of Systematic Theology* 22, no. 4 (October 2020): 538–561.
26. Hanna Reichel, *After Method: Queer Grace, Conceptual Design, and the Possibility of Theology* (Louisville, KY: Westminster John Knox, 2023).
27. Andrew Davison, "Home Is Where the Eternal Is," *Church Times*, May 29, 2020, https://www.churchtimes.co.uk/articles/2020/29-may/features/features/home-is-where-the-eternal-is. It was, in fact, through Davison and his graduate student Matthew Fell that I first encountered the term "affordances."
28. David Brown and Gavin Hopps, *The Extravagance of Music* (New York: Palgrave MacMillan, 2018).
29. Victoria Lebzyak, "Perceiving the Divine: Alexander Schmemann and the Sacramental Affordances of the Liturgy," *Modern Theology* 34, no. 4 (October 2018): 519–543.
30. Ted A. Smith, *The End of Theological Education* (Grand Rapids, MI: Eerdmans, 2023).
31. ANT has been misinterpreted by some as rejecting attention to power and social forces. Reviewing Felski's *Hooked* for the *Los Angeles Review of Books*, Sheila Liming claims the book "asks scholars to return to a halcyon age that predates critique" and accuses Felski of drawing "uncomfortably close to Trumpian logic." Part of what I take to be Liming's misjudgment of Felski's project derives from a confusion about ANT's relationship to political and socioeconomic realities. Liming sees Felski as "building off of Latour's denunciation of social constructivism" in her movement away from a hermeneutics of suspicion, as if she is sidestepping the conditions under which art and literature are made and the ways they participate in systems of power. But Latour insists again and again that he is both constructivist and realist; he resists their opposition. He is not a "social constructivist" because social constructivism, as he explains, is not sufficiently constructionist; it takes "the social" to name discrete building blocks, the "stuff" out of which something is really built, rather than as itself comprising an assemblage, made up of entities and

modes and vulnerable to failure. Another way to put it: Latour did not renounce a Foucauldian project of interrogating what and how a concept is made natural to us but took a step further toward it, to interrogate power itself. Latour himself discusses the difference between construction and constructivism in *Reassembling the Social*, 89–93. Sheila Liming, "Fighting Words," *Los Angeles Review of Books*, December 4, 2020, https://www.lareviewofbooks.org/article/fighting-words/.

32. In fact, the websites for women's studies programs often feature community engagement sections, describe political activities, or express a commitment to social justice that goes beyond the classroom. They post solidarity statements with Black Lives Matter (San Diego State, for example), promote the Anti-Detention Alliance (Cornell), or list local organizations that promote community involvement (Indiana).

33. Ellen Messer-Davidow, *Disciplining Feminism: From Social Activism to Academic Discourse* (Durham, NC: Duke University Press, 2002), 127.

34. A different version of this critique of feminism's relationship to actual women's liberation is picked up in Mikki Kendall, *Hood Feminism: Notes from the Women That a Movement Forgot* (New York: Viking, 2020), when Kendall points out the myriad ways feminism's attentions have deflected from the conditions of poor women of color.

35. Schüssler Fiorenza claims, "Feminist theology presupposes as well as has for its goal an emancipatory and theological praxis." Elisabeth Schüssler Fiorenza, "Feminist Theology as a Critical Theology of Liberation," *Theological Studies* 36, no. 4 (December 1975): 612. This end, she insists, can be pursued through academic work. She opens her article, "Writing an article on feminist theology for an established theological journal is as dangerous as navigating between Scylla and Charybdis. Radical feminists might consider such an endeavor as co-operation with the 'enemy' or at best as 'tokenism.' Professional theologians might refuse to take the issue seriously or might emotionally react against it. . . . Yet, since I consider myself a feminist as well as a Christian theologian, I am vitally interested in mediation between feminism and theology. And good theology always was a risky enterprise" (605).

36. As Schüssler Fiorenza puts it, "in the tradition, androcentric theology functions to justify the discriminatory praxis of the Church toward women." Schüssler Fiorenza, "Feminist Theology," 605.

37. Caroline Levine, *Forms: Whole, Rhythm, Networks* (Princeton, NJ: Princeton University Press, 2015), xi.

38. "We have typically treated aesthetic and political arrangements as separate, and we have not generally used the language of form for both, but we have routinely drawn on social scientific accounts of 'structure'; we have certainly paid attention to national boundaries and hierarchies of race and gender. And it is a commonplace practice in literary studies to read literary forms in relation to socials structures. . . .

This book proposes to bring together the field's dispersed insights into social and aesthetic forms to produce a new formalist method." Levine, *Forms*, 3.
39. Levine, *Forms*, 3.
40. "The bread-and-butterfly has wings made of buttered bread, a body of crust, and a head of a sugar cube. To sustain itself, it feeds on weak tea, which also dissolves it. This dissolving and reconstituting speaks for Fleckenstein to a way of continually updating one's understanding of affirming and taking responsibility for one's character as dispersed across ever-changing biological and abstract relations. So, as in the bread-and-butterfly, one's boundaries dissolve just in the place where one goes to find the locations, sustenance, and entanglements of subjectivity." Peter Khost, *Rhetor Response: A Theory and Practice of Literary Affordance* (Logan: Utah State University Press, 2018), 42–44.
41. Varnam writes of Kempe, "Gender identity is a 'doing' rather than a 'being'; it is produced and constituted in the individual moment of performance. The same, I would argue, is true of religious identity, especially for a laywoman such as Margery Kempe, who, as a married mother of fourteen children, could not assert her piety and holiness in the traditional ways available to women in the period, that is, as a virgin, nun, or anchoress. Unlike men, who could fix a religious identity through the ritual of ordination, for laywomen with religious aspirations, as Mary Suydam argues, the only option was to stage 'continuous performances of extraordinary piety.' And these performances must be recognized as such—that is, they must be citational, to use Butler's term. They must be a 're-enactment and a re-experiencing of a set of meanings already socially established.' Margery Kempe performs a range of socially established practices that are indicative of piety and sanctity as part of her attempt to reinvent herself as a 'self-styled saint,' to quote Gail Gibson. She wears white clothing, goes on pilgrimage to the most sacred sites in medieval Christendom, talks publicly about God, and, with the help of her scribes, transforms her experiences into narrative form in her Book. But she also draws upon the 'set of meanings' established in devotional objects such as the pietà, and it is her performance of extraordinary piety modeled on religious imagery that will be my focus here." Laura Varnam, "The Crucifix, the Pietà, and the Female Mystic: Devotional Objects and Performative Identity in the Book of Margery Kempe," *Journal of Medieval Religious Cultures* 41, no. 2 (2015): 212–213. Through the pietà, she adds later, Kempe "stages a devotional performance" (222). Quoting Mary Suydam, "Beguine Textuality: Sacred Performances," in *Performance and Transformation: New Approaches to Late Medieval Spirituality*, ed. Mary A. Suydam and Joanna Ziegler (Basingstoke, UK: Macmillan, 1999), 179; Judith Butler, *Gender Trouble: Feminism and the Subversion of Identity* (London: Routledge, 1999 [1990]), 178; Gail McMurray Gibson, *The Theater of Devotion: East Anglian Drama and Society in the Late Middle Ages* (Chicago: University of Chicago Press, 1989), 64.

42. All of this is not to dispute, of course, the negative affordances of the cross as well, which are well testified in feminist literature. The cross has been used to keep women in abusive relationships, to justify their suffering for others, to afford a logic of racialized surrogacy, and to relegate them to lives of silent humiliation.
43. Yves Citton, "Fictional Attachments and Literary Weavings in the Age of the Anthropocene," *New Literary History* 47: 317.
44. Citton, "Fictional Attachments," 318; quoting Jacques Rancière, *Le spectateur émancipé* (Paris: La Fabrique, 2008), 19 (Citton's translation).
45. According to Citton, Rancière develops this metaphor in Jacques Rancière, *Le fil perdu* [*The Lost Thread*] (Paris: La Fabrique, 2014).
46. This idea is one I have explored in more depth with Matthew Whelan in our forthcoming book *Why This Waste? Poverty and Art in a World of Need*.
47. As with much else, I am indebted here to Felski, whose 2021 Clark Lectures introduced me to the work of Kompridis.
48. Nikolas Kompridis, *Critique and Disclosure: Critical Theory between Past and Future* (Cambridge, MA: MIT Press, 2011), 245–247.
49. Kompridis, *Critique and Disclosure*, 245–247.
50. Kompridis, *Critique and Disclosure*, 213.
51. Kompridis, *Critique and Disclosure*, 213. It should be no surprise that Kompridis is also interested in the relation of the aesthetic and political, about which he has edited a volume. Nikolas Kompridis, ed., *The Aesthetic Turn in Political Thought* (New York: Bloomsbury Academic, 2014).
52. Phone interview with Mary Hunt, January 25, 2021.
53. Messer-Davidow, *Disciplining Feminism*, 6.
54. When the local bishop initially refused to allow Hildegard to move her monastery, she became debilitatingly ill, which was taken as divine visitation, and she was miraculously healed upon his relenting. Barbara Newman describes another vision that Hildegard relates to a "negligent bishop" in which a feminized Pure Knowledge appears in a bishop pallium as a likely double for Hildegard. Barbara Newman, "Hildegard of Bingen: Visions and Validation," *Church History* 54, no. 2 (June 1985): 174.
55. Citton, "Fictional Attachments," 310.
56. Ivone Gebara, "Feminism and Religious Identity," Pat Reif Memorial Lecture, Claremont College, March 2009, https://www.womensordination.org/2008/08/feminism-and-religious-identity-by-ivone-gebara/.
57. Gebara, "Feminism and Religious Identity."
58. Gebara, "Feminism and Religious Identity."
59. Skype interview with Ivone Gebara, March 4, 2021.
60. Thuy Anh Tran and Chaya Halberstam, "'I Think God Is a Feminist': Art and Action by Orthodox Jewish Women," *Journal of Feminist Studies* 37, no. 2 (Fall 2021): 5–24.

61. For other examples of how art can be implicated in feminist, political work, see Natalie Carnes, "Feminism, Religion, and Art in the North Atlantic," in the *Oxford Research Encyclopedia of Religion*, forthcoming online. I trace examples that include Israeli women filmmakers, the French Muslim group NiqaBitch, and the graphic illustrations of suffragists.
62. Nichole Flores, *The Aesthetics of Solidarity: Our Lady of Guadalupe and American Democracy* (Washington, DC: Georgetown University Press, 2021), 3.
63. Flores, *Aesthetics of Solidarity*, 38.
64. Flores, *Aesthetics of Solidarity*, 7.
65. Flores, *Aesthetics of Solidarity*, 8.
66. Bruno Latour, "Why SPEAP?" http://blogs.sciences-po.fr/speap-eng/20-2/why-speap/.
67. Latour, "Why SPEAP?"
68. Photos of *On Space Time Foam* and an interview with the artist can be found at https://studiotomassaraceno.org/on-space-time-foam/.
69. Bruno Latour, quoted in Laura Collins-Hughes, "A Potential Disaster in Any Language," *New York Times*, September 25, 2014, https://www.nytimes.com/2014/09/26/theater/gaia-global-circus-at-the-kitchen.html.
70. Francis Halsall, "Actor-Network Aesthetics: The Conceptual Rhymes of Bruno Latour and Contemporary Art," *New Literary History* 47, nos. 2–3 (Spring and Summer 2016): 458.
71. Francis Halsall, "An Aesthetics of Proof: A Conversation between Bruno Latour and Francis Halsall on Art and Inquiry," *Environment and Planning D: Society and Space* 30, no. 6 (2012): 964.
72. Graham Harman, "De-Modernizing the Humanities," *New Literary History* 47, nos. 2–3 (Summer 2016): 272.
73. J. Gibson, "A Theory of Affordances," 138.
74. Claire Dederer, "What Do We Do with the Art of Monstrous Men?" *Paris Review*, November 20, 2017, https://www.theparisreview.org/blog/2017/11/20/art-monstrous-men/. Dederer's article was so popular it became the basis for her book *Monsters: A Fan's Dilemma* (New York: Knopf, 2023).
75. Sarah Stewart-Kroeker, "'What Do We Do with the Art of Monstrous Men?': Betrayal and the Feminist Ethics of Aesthetic Involvement," *De Ethica* 6, no. 1 (2020): 51–74.
76. Stewart-Kroeker, "'What Do We Do?,'" 65. Hilary Jerome Scarsella et al. use similar criteria in their document, "Show Strength: How to Respond When Worship Materials Are Implicated in Abuse," http://voicestogetherhymnal.org/wp-content/uploads/2021/01/Show-Strength.pdf.
77. A. O. Scott, "My Woody Allen Problem," *New York Times*, January 31, 2018, https://www.nytimes.com/2018/01/31/movies/woody-allen.html; quoted in Stewart-Kroeker, "What Do We Do?," 57.

78. Scott, "My Woody Allen Problem"; quoted in Stewart-Kroeker, "What Do We Do?," 58.
79. Or it might have been important until early in 2023, when Scott left film criticism to be a critic at large for the *New York Times Book Review*.
80. In a clear, six-page resource, some from Into Account and other organizations offer guidance to communities seeking to respond to revelations of Haas's abuse. They write, "We choose not to sing a composer's songs when doing so causes injury to survivors or enables abuse. A decision not to use worship material written by a perpetrator of sexual violence has less to do with that person or the specifics of that person's behavior and more to do with the well-being of survivors and potential victims. This general principle should guide decisions [when] immediate family or survivors are still alive." Scarsella et al., "Show Strength."
81. I am grateful to the Into Account team for sharing their work and expertise, particularly to Hilary Scarsella for speaking with me further about what the survivor-centered approach looks like on the ground. The group's website features some valuable resources: https://intoaccount.org.
82. For an important treatment of Yoder as well as the broader issues his case raises, see Hilary Jerome Scarsella and Stephanie Krehbiel, "Sexual Violence: Christian Theological Legacies and Responsibilities," *Religion Compass* 13, no. 9 (September 2019): 1–13.
83. Tracy Fessenden, "'Woman' and the 'Primitive' in Paul Tillich's Life and Thought: Some Implications for the Study of Religion." *Journal of Feminist Studies in Religion* 14, no. 2 (1998): 45–76.

4
Repair

THE WAY THOMAS of Celano tells the story, it happens as Francis kneels in the ruined chapel of San Damiano, where the Spirit has led him to pray. Before the crucifix, Francis discovers he has changed since entering the church, and in that moment of recognition, Christ speaks to him through the lips of the painting. The image says, "Francis, go rebuild my house. As you can see, it is being destroyed."[1]

Thomas describes this as the moment when Francis receives the stigmata on his soul, foreshadowing his later marked flesh. "Go rebuild my house." His heart wounded, Francis obeys the image and repairs the building at San Damiano. Later, he will attempt a more spiritual repair, offering his life as a witness to the poverty of Christ and founding the Order of the Friars Minor to renew the church's own witness to Christ. Did Francis first misinterpret these words of the image, taking literally what he should have taken metaphorically? Or did the literal open analogically to the spiritual?

In summer 2020, I was addressed by an image, and perhaps you were, too. The image spoke words that rounded the world. Even if you did not see it, even if you never clicked on that video, you remember the last moments of George Floyd's life. He is lying on the ground, an officer's knee on his neck. A small crowd has gathered around him to witness the horror, and some try, unsuccessfully, to arouse mercy in the officer. "Mama!" Floyd cries through the lips of his image. "I can't breathe."

He is dying as he calls for his mama, who is dead and cannot save him. In calling for his mother, is Floyd conjuring an image of safety amid the violence bearing down on him? Does he remember a time when this woman, his mama, encircled a space of care for him in the world, affirming his claim to live? Maybe he is preparing to greet her on the other side of life. Maybe he sees how his death would pain her—she who raised a Black boy to successful adulthood in a world stacked against them. "Mama!" he cries. "I can't breathe." And it is finished.

Are these words of Floyd exhausted by their literal meaning? Or do they, too, open to other, analogical and spiritual, senses? Some protesters for Black Lives Matter have found in his words one analogical meaning. You may have seen the posters that read, "All mothers were summoned when George Floyd called out for his mama." "Mama" here opens up, addressing not just Floyd's mother but mothers everywhere. Invoking the mercy of maternal care, Floyd's image entreats mothers for relief, for succor, for justice. Three years later, Tyre Nichols repeats his cry, his final words, "Mom! Mom! Mom!" as he is beaten during a traffic stop, running to the refuge of his mother's house. After three days, he dies of his injuries. "For a mother to know he was calling them in their need—" his mother, RowVaughn Wells, said, "do you know how I feel right now because I wasn't there for my son?"

Before Wells entered this terrible grief and before Floyd's five children began theirs, iconographer Mark Doox (formerly Mark Dukes) made an image that seems to answer Floyd's and Nichols's calls with the Mother of God. It presents Mary as *Our Lady, Mother of Ferguson*.[2] Though it was made with Michael Brown and his mother in mind, those of us who inherit a cultural memory forged and carried by the Black Lives Matter movement know the litany that connects Brown, Nichols, and Floyd. And that litany helps us to see in this image the resonances of Nichols's mom, Floyd's mama, and Mother Mary.[3]

At the cross, Mary keeps watch with her son until he cannot breathe. Does she remember the slaughter of the innocents and how, against all odds, she protected her Jewish boy from Herod's murderous politics, only to lose him as an adult? The Romans crucify him because that is how they keep an empire going.[4] Christ's death is the byproduct of their exploitation, his dead body the debris in their ongoing efforts to maintain power, wealth, and the status quo. To them, he is waste. "The condition of black life," Claudia Rankine writes, "is one of mourning."[5] Mary stood near her son on the cross, his breaths fewer and shallower, and then it is finished.

Affordance and Repair

In chapter 3, we traced the way the artifacts of Christianity exist in relationships from which affordances arise and new affordances more generative to the flourishing of women and others marginalized by gender can be created. To enter into a constructive feminist relationship with these artifacts is not just to look on their brighter side, reconciling oneself to them through assurances that they are perhaps not so bad after all. It is to participate in the dynamism of an artifact's meaning, to co-create the text or image and thereby alter the landscape of Christian theology, rendering it more hospitable to the flourishing of all. The mode of interpretation I am calling attunement, then, is not just a way of assessing, decoding, or unmasking what is *there*; it is a way of repairing a text or image by making it again and in that way repairing and remaking the larger theological landscape. In this chapter, I want to explore repair by exemplifying what attunement might look like in the field of Mariology. Here I want to consider how a particular image—*Our Lady, Mother of Ferguson*—can be brought into conversation with the texts of Mariology in a way that offers a repair of the image of Mary at the heart of the field. By doing so, I want to show how attunement can intervene in even theology's most troubled conversations. As I reflect on Christian theology's problematic relationship to this mother, I also sketch a theology of attunement as one of receiving, co-creating, and becoming a mother.

The Gordian Knot of Mariology

Our Lady, Mother of Ferguson is an affordance that helps us to receive Mary and so to offer a repair both to the field of Mariology and to the world in which we live. It does so because of who Our Lady of Ferguson is and what *Our Lady of Ferguson* is. I'll defer the *who* until I have begun treating the *what*. And the *what* is an image, a mode of theological expression that affords the aesthetic, affective transformations central to attunement. It is also a theological form that, in the particular case of Mary, addresses a dilemma. From a feminist perspective, Mariology is bound in a Gordian knot. Maximalist Mariologies reaffirm gender essentialism, and both maximalist and minimalist Mariologies risk reinscribing female subordination. The more ardently one pulls in one direction, the more tethered Mariology becomes to either or both problems.

A maximalist, or high, Mariology emphasizes Marian titles such as the Queen of Heaven to construe Mary as the eternal feminine principle or the divine feminine. This approach may sound promising. Shouldn't maximizing the importance of the most blessed among women also maximize the power and authority of the women among whom the blessed one is identified? That the opposite has, in fact, happened is so widely acknowledged among feminist theologians that Schüssler Fiorenza can open her analysis of Mariology by observing, without controversy or footnote, "Feminist theologians largely agree in their criticism of the malestream image of Mary and of patriarchal mariology."[6] In particular, many feminist theologians have detailed problems in maximalist Mariologies—their negative affordances—four of which I'll briefly outline.[7]

The first negative affordance that feminists identify with high Mariologies is their elevation of femininity within a hierarchy that still subordinates it to masculinity. Mary's representation of the eternal feminine contrasts with and complements the patriarchal imagery of God the High King.[8] The very role of Mary as divine mother, Johnson points out, presupposes a God who is properly conceptualized and imagined through male language and imagery. In this way, Mariology sanitizes God of femininity. Mary becomes the repository for all that is feminine so that God—who is always higher than Mary, however exalted she is—can stay safely masculine. The inescapable subordination of the eternal feminine to the eternal masculine in this schema translates into a political and ecclesial order in which temporal females are also subject to temporal males, instantiated for Catholics and Orthodox in an all-male priesthood. The critique here is biting: the elevated femininity of high Mariologies is not only held firmly in place by a more elevated masculinity, but it is the very means of creating a wholly masculinized imagination of God.

The vexed gender complementarity named by the first negative affordance suggests the second, which is that the eternal feminine trades on a feminine–masculine binary that entrenches gender essentialism. In this dualism, women are supposed to embody the femininity Mary is said to exemplify. Perhaps the most familiar version of this critique points to the way Mary holds up for women an impossible ideal of virginity and motherhood, subjecting women to the judgments of purity culture and the cult of motherhood as true womanhood. This gender dualism is deep and wide—deep enough to sustain an entire cosmic view of the masculine and feminine that goes all the way through political and economic orders and wide enough to reach women beyond their roles vis-à-vis sex and family to prescribe an entire posture, a manner of being in the world. This Marian essentialism reduces the plural possibilities for being a woman and circumscribes women's sphere of activity, binding women to humility, obedience, and forever saying yes.[9] The gender scripts for everyone are narrowed by such essentialism but particularly for women. The scripts for those who identify as nonbinary or trans are functionally eliminated. In the Latin American context, there is even a word for how Mary has been used to support patriarchal *machismo* ideals and circumscribe women's roles: *marianismo*.[10]

The understanding of femininity sustained by high Mariology, moreover, is often covertly racialized, romanticized by what Schüssler Fiorenza calls "the ideology of the (White) Lady."[11] This third problem with high Mariology, then, is that the version of femininity advanced under its banner is solidified by images and scripts that exclude or marginalize Black, Indigenous, and women of color, reproducing the problems that plagued the first feminist theological writings. "Ain't I a woman?" Sojourner Truth famously asked in the nineteenth century, as she pointed out that while White women were treated as objects of chivalric courtesy, her own Black womanhood was not included in the gender ideology of the day. That antebellum ideology was recapitulated in Victorian ideals of the White Lady, which continue to fund pictures of the ever-Virgin Mary today. The pure and virginal body that Mary typifies is imagined as White, and countless statues, prayer cards, and stained-glass windows featuring an alabaster Mary sustain that imagination and carry it forward into cultural norms and valuations.[12] Stripped of her concrete life and reality, she is made White to be made universal, "unmarked" (unstigmatized) by race. There are centuries of examples in which church officials literally whitened Black Madonna statuary to strip them of local associations and "catholicize" them.[13] Further, not only is Mary pictured or made pale, but she is also often pictured as royal, wreathed in gold and elegantly robed, further distancing her from the Gospel story of the Galilean peasant girl and aligning her with symbols of power.[14] The modern story of Mary's racialization reinforces a long trajectory in high Mariologies of interpreting her on the side of the powerful, conserving a political and social order.

The fourth problem with high Mariologies is that the Marian feminine does not include actual female bodies. Denying Mary's actual female body, like refusing racial marking, is a way of rendering her a universal and transparent signifier. The more Mary is lifted up as emblematic of the divine feminine, the more literal female bodies disappear from that status.[15] Often the exclusion of actual female bodies from the exalted status of Mary is explained in terms of the impossibility for women to emulate her virgin motherhood, but it also happens simply because of how Mary is abstracted from her body and history. She becomes an idea or a principle more than a person; her body disappears along with other women's. We can see such disappearing happen right before our eyes in the theology of Schmemann, who writes rhapsodically of Mary as "the climax, the personification, the affirmation of the ultimate destiny of all creation," conflating her with the feminine that transfigures and triumphs in the new creation.[16] In the midst of such lyricism about Mary, he turns to concrete women. "Unfortunately," he writes, "some women today think that they should also become priests and bishops. They are wrong.... It is symbolic indeed that on Mount Athos, the great monastic center of the Orthodox East, no woman is admitted. Yet, the whole mountain is considered to be the particular possession of the Mother of God."[17] That the mountain belonging to Mary, the Mother of God, admits no female bodies exemplifies a problem for Marian maximalism in a strikingly literal mode: the higher Mary is elevated, the more actual women are left in the valley of her shadow. The irony is doubled in its contrast with the maleness of Jesus, whose historical male body forms the basis for Catholic and Orthodox justifications of an all-male priesthood. Observing the "extreme dichotomy" of Mary's exaltation and ordinary women's degradation, Daly explains the contrast in terms of both a "compensation mechanism" and a means of attracting and harnessing feminine energy while maintaining the full patriarchal control of an all-male priesthood.[18] It is a way of elevating the feminine to do work for the church while peeling it apart from female bodies, who do not benefit from this elevation.

To summarize these four problems, then. High Mariologies reaffirm the male–female hierarchy and essentialize women, offering a romanticized view of femininity that obscures the identities of non-White and marginalized women and excludes actual female bodies. High Mariology universalizes Mary, rendering her transparent, which means stripping away her raced, sexed body. These are the well-documented cliffs of a high Mariology, the negative affordances that seem to keep offering support to gendered hierarchies and the oppression of women and the gender-marginalized. It has been a sad truth for feminist theologians that one of the few parts of the Christian story featuring a woman—and in such a role!—has been a source of so much disappointment. And worse than disappointment for many women. Observing Marian piety in Latin America, Althaus-Reid's assessment is harsh: "We must honestly face the fact that although in Latin America Mary is sometimes hailed as a powerful liberator of women and the poor, we have yet to see any evidence of it. The reality is that the Virgin Mary has become a white, rich God." The high Mariology in Latin America, she claims, is "at the root of 500 years of oppression of women."[19]

What is a feminist to do with Mary? For if high Mariology is not necessarily liberative for women, if it can even be a source of degradation, a low, or minimalist, one cannot provide an answer to this dilemma. In the wake of Vatican II and centuries of Protestant theology, a historicizing and demythologizing trend emerged in Mariology. In a spirit of ecumenism, the Council did not explicitly reaffirm her title as Mediatrix, for example.[20] But it turns out that extricating women from an essentializing and subordinating vision of the eternal feminine vis-à-vis Mary only confirms female subordination by another direction. Remembering the examples of the Protestant Reformation and Vatican II, Schüssler Fiorenza points out how diminishing the status of Mary leaves the church bereft of female symbols of the divine. Without her as a quasi-divinity, the church has a patriarchal God, his male Son, and a thoroughly masculinized imagination of the divine.[21] The more Mary's meaning is limited to her role as a historical figure, the less purchase she has on our current lives and imaginations. Less imaginative purchase, moreover, means less reflection on Mary. In the wake of Vatican II, it has become obvious that a lower Mariology also means less Mariology. The Mary of the minimalists is severed from who we are and what we hope, leaving us enthralled to what in fourth-century theologian Gregory of Nyssa's language constitutes "conceptual idolatry."[22] Our ways of imagining divine working in the world are even more bound to the masculine; our God and the world of our God are fully captured by maleness.

Perhaps there are ways for a minimalist Mariology to work around this problem of our enthrallment to maleness. An especially enticing minimalist Mariology comes from Johnson, who follows Schüssler Fiorenza in calling for Mary of Nazareth to be approached as her own historical person, while reintegrating the feminine symbols, claims, and images traditionally associated with Mary back into God. This has the felicitous goal of returning attention to Mary in her historical conditions and biblical narrative and at the same time de-patriarchalizing God. But the cost is Mariology. To preserve the feminist significance of Mary, she is placed amid the saints of the church, and the traditional symbols and theologies of Mariology are subsumed into the doctrine of God. The solution is elegant and demanding—and perhaps less than satisfying. I wonder in practice about dissolving the claims about Mary into claims about God, whom the church still imagines in such masculine terms. Deep in the Christian tradition, important patristic voices that we continue to value and repeat assimilate holiness, sanctity, and virtue to maleness and masculinity, as discussed in chapter 2. Without Mary concretely figuring a divine feminine, will her former symbols extricate our imaginations from their masculine idolatries of God? Or will they simply be submerged and reintegrated into the masculine imagery, the conceptual idolatry that holds us captive? Then there is the problem of Marian piety. How do we understand the high Marian devotion over the centuries and particularly today in Latin America? Is it simply misdirected devotion to God, piety that can be severed from Mary as its incidental object and reconstituted as devotion to

God? Is the sacrifice of Mariology—or the risk of subsuming Mary's titles and roles into a masculine God—a cost we are willing to gamble?

What other choice does a feminist have? Rereading and rescuing images of Mariology, Althaus-Reid writes, cannot answer for the centuries of women's oppression.[23] Does this mean Mariology as a field is doomed to conserve a patriarchal, exploitative status quo? Though the field often has done so and may continue to do so for centuries to come, I believe Mary can bear more hopeful possibility for us. Even Althaus-Reid suggests the possibility of another Mariology when she describes where Mariology must begin: "sitting in our imagination among the defeated, raped, rag-dressed women."[24] This, I take it, is more than a rereading; it is a reimagining. And what does reimagining mean but reimaging? Reflecting on Mary in their context in Latin America, Ivone Gebara and Maria Clara Bingemer write, "At each new historical moment for Christians, the mystery of Mary unveils a different face, one that can deeply touch the needs of the poor and believing people."[25] This is why I find *Our Lady of Ferguson* a fitting way into Mariology. Like Mary herself, it is an image that reveals her face, extending to us the possibility of reimaging Mary and repairing Mariology.

Mary the Image

As an image, Mary is not bound by the territory outlined by either maximalists or minimalists. Rather, she can traverse a multilayered universe, opening up more fecund possibilities for women. As an image, she mediates absent presences, facilitating encounters with what and whom she images. She is like and unlike other images in Christianity. Christ is the Image of the invisible God who shows his disciples the Father whom he is not. Icons traditionally mediate the person of Christ to the prayerful beholder while remaining wood and paint. In a similar but different way from either Christ or icons, Mary mediates the presence of God, God's grace to us, and the hope of redeemed humanity, while remaining distinct from all of these. She does not sacrifice her historical identity in her imaging, for her imaging expresses her personal identity and rhymes with her history. To approach Mary as an image, further, does not require us to subsume Mariology into the doctrine of God or to its more familiar doctrinal companions of Christology, ecclesiology, and anthropology; but, as I will unfold, it connects Mariology closely to them, particularly to the doctrine of God. In so doing, Mary the image offers a way to take seriously the pietistic "excesses" of Marian devotion as not ancillary to Mary, as if we can just carry them off back to God because they have nothing to do with her—even as Marian devotion brings God's character more clearly into view. As an image, Mary is both particular rather than stripped of her sexed, raced, classed life and also able to connect to the particularity of the faithful. To approach Mary as an image is, in addition, fitting to the history of Marian piety, where Mary is always coming as an apparition as the faithful venerate her in statues, images, and icons. Besides apparitions such as Lourdes and Fatima, there are any number of conversions associated with her image, including Mary of Egypt's.[26] Mary, after all, is the only image that has been elevated to a patron, Our Lady of Guadalupe, Patroness of the Americas.

To approach Mary as an image is also fitting for the project of attunement I have been outlining, for several reasons. First, to approach Mary as an image that comes to us in different times and places is to acknowledge multiple appearances, modes, and melodies proper to Mariology. It is for this reason to suggest a way of dealing with problematic images through a Wittgensteinian iconoclasm, in which images repair us from our captivity to other images—or, to put it in other language, to approach Mary as an image that through images offers a way of addressing negative affordances through augmenting positive ones. Second, to approach Mary as an image is to underscore the aesthetic investments of attunement by taking as substantively theological a form normally treated by theologians as "simply" aesthetic or ornamental. In so doing, this approach continues the work many feminist theologians have done over time. Third, these aesthetic investments afford the transformation that attunement offers. The image has an aesthetic immediacy that works on multiple levels—converting us, moving us, speaking to us in ways I will aspire to be faithful to in my writing. Fourth, and related, this aesthetically immediate, theologically laden encounter with an affordance-rich image that augments the positive affordances of the tradition while building new positive affordances is exemplary of the repair I see as attunement's gift and demand. I repair the text; the text repairs me. Here we extend "text" to include image, the image of Mary at the heart of Mariology. How can I repair the texts and artifacts of Mariology by staging an encounter with *Our Lady of Ferguson*? How can this encounter repair me?

My proposal is not unprecedented. To recognize Mary as an image is to touch on a Marian identity rooted deeply in the tradition, to rehabilitate the title of Mediatrix that Vatican II minimized. It has long been considered integral to Mary's role that she mediates; what I am suggesting is that her mediation correlates with forms of revelation—that Mary mediates as she images. And the way she reveals, her multidirectionality toward God and humans, yields her distinct form of mediation.

In elaborating Mary as Mediatrix, Karl Rahner first affirms that Christ is the sole mediator. Besides Christ, there is no other; only Jesus is the "God made [human]." Only Christ is the "efficient cause of our salvation," and in this "definite and unambiguous sense," no one else mediates God and humanity.[27] And yet, as Rahner goes on to remind us, all humans are called to be intermediaries, to mediate grace to one another.[28] We are all called to bear one another's burdens, pray for one another, administer the sacraments to one another, and bear the common weight of our guilt.[29] We do not produce grace. We can only access grace that God has already given. Yet God intends that the grace of Jesus Christ "reaches one member through another."[30] Mary's role as Mediatrix is an elevated form of that shared task of mediation, one that is dependent on Christ as the sole mediator and speaks to her similarity to us as intermediaries.[31]

Rahner's descriptions of Mary's role as Mediatrix imply a bidirectionality to Mary's imaging. Her mediation images the Christ who enables it while also imaging humans in their calling to mediate grace to one another.[32] It images Christ and also gives Christ, as Mary at the Annunciation began mediating Christ. As her body became our first image of Christ, she literally bore Christ to us.

The Annunciation suggests a more concrete picture of Mary's mediation, giving content to what and how Mary images, to who Mary the image is and why her identity as image rhymes with her history. To call Mary a Mediatrix who shows us our calling as mediators is perhaps simply a more abstract way of saying she is a mother who shows us that we are all called to be mothers, midwives, and grandmothers. Expressing how Mary pictures our redeemed humanity by the language and imagery of "mothering" has important advantages over the language of "mediating" alone.[33] First, "mother" names Christ's relationship to Mary differently from "mediator." Mary's mediation depends on Christ's sole mediation, but Christ's motherhood is in a human sense learned, supported, and first pictured for him through Mary. In a very ordinary and mundane sense, Jesus learned from Mary that "mother" names someone who nurtures you in your need, tends to your wounds, cares for your life, and supports your growth. Through Mary's example, Jesus grows in wisdom and stature toward his own motherhood. Her maternal love and support accompany him all the way to what some medieval theologians such as Julian called the labor pains of the cross and the gift of his nourishing body in the sacraments, which express the tender mercies of our maternal Christ.[34] On the cross, in other words, Christ becomes our mother, a role Jesus first learned from Mary, his mother, that we might all become mothers. And our motherhood, though funded by Christ's, is more akin to Mary's. We do not become like Christ in that we save the world by our sacrifices. We do not birth the new creation or feed the world with our saving bodies. We become like Christ by becoming mothers like Mary, giving birth to Christ in the world and nurturing Christ's presence however and wherever we can. To conceive of Mary as an image—the whatness of *Our Lady of Ferguson*—is fitting given who she is as a mother. As an image, in other words, Mary mediates to us a divine encounter, which is fitting for her role as a mother, by which she mediates to us Christ's life.

A second benefit of identifying mediation with Mary's motherhood is that it elevates a role women often occupy in the world without essentializing either that role or women as occupants of it. Motherhood is already an analogical term, which we apply to biological motherhood, adoptive motherhood, and fostering. We refer to academic advisers as *doktor-mütters*, and sometimes pet owners call themselves mothers, too. Mentors, teachers, grandmothers, and aunts can all also play the role of mothers for us in different ways. Evolutionary biologists even have a term for this feature of mammalian life: "allomothers," *other mothers* who help care for young.[35] Mothering is an activity of bearing, fortifying, and caring for life. Literal mothers among us are important, not because they have by their sex or biological motherhood an essential tie to Mary, God, or redemption. After all, non-procreating female, intersex, male, and nonbinary individuals, too, are called to become mothers who bear Christ into the world, as Christ became the mother of a new creation. And they can also be earthly analogical mothers, allomothers, even if their motherhood is not as obvious to us. Still, the bodies of visible mothers remain important to us as concrete images, sites, and reminders of the vocation to which we are all called and by which we imitate God. To say that motherhood pictures for us our human vocation is not to say that it is the only way of picturing that vocation. But in a world sick with patriarchy and misogyny, it is important that women's bodies can so powerfully signify for us our human calling; the pedagogy of women imaging God and redeemed humanity for us is like a medicine that can expunge our idolatrous views of men and maleness, working to heal us from our conceptual idolatry.[36] It is a reversal of that influential early Christian trope associating maleness and masculinity with virtue and holiness. As those early figures did not foreclose the possibility of sanctity for women, but made men figures of sanctity whose bodies visibly symbolized holiness, so the bodies of the pregnant and of those we see mothering visibly figure holiness and divinity to us, inviting us into liberation from our captivity to a masculinized picture of God.[37]

This manner of elevating motherhood will, I know, raise anxieties among some feminist theologians sensitive to the way motherhood has marked the limits of women's vocational horizons. As Schüssler Fiorenza puts it, "Malestream mariology and cult of Mary . . . devalue women . . . by unilaterally associating the ideal of 'true womanhood' with motherhood."[38] The cult of true womanhood would have all women be mothers. Doesn't exalting Mother Mary risk once again limiting women to valuation by their roles as mothers? And the answer is yes. Yes, it does—unless we emphasize the analogical character of motherhood, the way literal motherhood symbolizes and helps us to value the multiple modes of motherhood to which all people, all genders, are called, all the ways we are summoned to bear life into the world and care for it so that this life, too, can bear new life. And the way literal motherhood opens up to nonliteral motherhood means that the "we" who are called to motherhood also opens up to include those who have no vocation or desire for childbearing and childrearing as well as all those who, for any number of reasons, find themselves in a troubled or complex relationship with literal motherhood. It also includes men. By expanding women to include all humanity and drawing on the analogical meanings of motherhood to include the myriad nonbiological relationships that motherhood points to, the exaltation of Mary, the Mother of God, can move beyond our collective enthrallment to the cult of true womanhood.

Though it is uniquely pictured by the pregnant body, motherhood is not restricted by sex and gender, nor is it bound by biology—yet neither is it an abstraction that floats unmoored from concrete conditions. Its concreteness, in fact, is the third benefit of seeing redeemed humanity through Mary's motherhood. For Mary tells us what that motherhood looks like in the world. At the end of Gabriel's Annunciation to Mary, the angel points the way for her, informing her that her kinswoman Elizabeth has also conceived (Luke 1:36). Mary takes the hint, and in the verse after Gabriel departs, we find her "setting out with haste" to Elizabeth. The visitation of these mothers celebrates and multiplies their joy. Mary greets Elizabeth. Elizabeth's child leaps in her womb. Elizabeth is filled with the Holy Spirit and blesses her kinswoman. "Blessed are you among women, and blessed is the fruit of your womb." Through this visit, Mary enters more deeply into the joy of bearing Jesus and breaks forth in a song that echoes her foremother Miriam's celebration of God's deliverance of Israel from Pharaoh's army:

> *My soul magnifies the Lord,*
> *and my spirit rejoices in God my Savior . . .*

> *He has brought down the powerful from their thrones*
> *and lifted up the lowly;*
> *he has filled the hungry with good things*
> *and sent the rich away empty.*
> *He has come to the aid of his child Israel,*
> *in remembrance of his mercy.*[39]

The joy of Mary's motherhood is the mercy of God, who lifts up the lowly, fills the hungry, sends the rich away empty, and brings down the powerful. Standing faithfully by the cross, watching her son birth new creation, Mary also receives the expansion of her motherhood, which is realized at Pentecost when the Spirit arrives in wind and flame to give us Mother Church in whom we can be reborn into Christ-likeness and learn to bear Christ ourselves. Now we can become co-laborers with Mary in her work of birthing Christ into the world. We, too, have been invited to take up the Magnificat as the joy of our motherhood, the joy of entering and participating in the mercy of God.

The joy of this motherhood is costly. It will take us into and through forms of violence. Mary knew this from the slaughter of the innocents. As a picture of redeemed humanity, Mother Mary gives us not a Hallmark version of motherhood as our human vocation but a vision of motherhood as passage into the merciful life of God, with a community that can celebrate the joy of that mercy, through the violence and death-dealing regimes that would extinguish mercy and its joy. In this vein, Gebara and Bingemer quote Saint Oscar Romero, who wrote, "the true homage a Christian can pay the Virgin is, like her, to make the effort to incarnate the life of God in the trials of our transitory history."[40] I think it must have been partially in appreciation of this conviction that Romero's canonization ceremony ended with a call-and-response meditation on the angel coming to Mary and Mary's words of consent. The call-and-response resolved into a Hail Mary before the final words, given as both a remembrance and a charge, as if the congregated people had collectively given birth: "The Word became flesh. And lived among us."[41] Romero's life was one of Marian Christ-bearing, yet it warns us that Mary's motherhood is not to be sentimentalized. Romero's divine motherhood, alive with the joy of the Magnificat, aflame with the presence of Christ, took him to his own cross, and in his stand for truth and justice on behalf of the poor and exploited ones of El Salvador, he died a martyr. Now so many photographs and icons picture him with children, a hint of the mothering work he did throughout his life.

When the Theotokos pictures for us our redeemed humanity, what she shows is a human imitation of God, a picture of God at work in human life.[42] To put this point in other terms, in an earthly sense, Mary's motherhood preceded Christ's motherhood; but in a divine sense, her motherhood is preceded by God's own. God is our mother in whose womb we are reborn to new life, the one who has swallowed death that we may receive life abundant, the one who nurtures us in this new life. Our own motherhood follows this motherhood of God, pictured for us by Mary. Conceiving of Mary as an image means that Mary's importance is *not* that she offers a motherhood that balances out God's fatherhood but that in Mary's divine motherhood, we see how the motherhood that pictures the vocation to which all humanity is called imitates the motherhood of God. Mary in this way assists us in the project Johnson commends, that of reintegrating femininized imagery into the Godhead. We might put it this way: Mary's motherhood is a theophany of the Mother God. Mary here is not simply aligned with the church, a new humanity, or an eternal feminine principle. As an image, she connects the historic with the transcendent, offering glimpses into the God who is our mother and the motherhood that pictures our human vocation. As such, Mary is a central image in a chain of images that names a set of deeply dependent relationships rather than contrastive ones. We can bear Christ only because Mary did, and Mary could bear Christ only because God bears Mary, as God bears all created life. Mary is not the feminine human counterpart to a masculine God. No, our human motherhood images Mary's, which images God's. Mary as image speaks both of our humanity *and* of God's divinity.

Once Mary is understood as an image that pictures for us the creator God, Mariology as a doctrine becomes closely bound to the doctrine of God. This approach is both similar to and importantly different from the low Mariology of Johnson and Schüssler Fiorenza. After noting the way Mariology has over time displaced aspects of the doctrine of God, these feminist theologians responded by migrating the claims of Mariology back to the doctrine of God. They return Mary to her historical conditions of life in Nazareth, in a sense demoting her and dissolving Mariology into the doctrine of God, which could receive the feminine images as proper to God. In response to essays reviewing her book *Truly Our Sister*, Johnson writes of two distinct alternative spiritualities with respect to Mary, the patronage and companionship models, what she calls Mary the mother and Mary the sister. "In rough outline, mother, at least in traditional Mariology, coheres with the patronage model while sister fits with the companionship model. Thus, the answer to 'how is my mother my sister?' cannot be given in a logical line of reasoning within the framework of the question itself, for it requires a shift of paradigm, including one's understanding of God, Christ, human beings, and the church."[43] She goes on to affirm that the mothering imagery belongs more properly to God than to Mary, though both are options for spirituality. Having spent my childhood and adolescence in the evangelical church, I am convinced that we can relate to Mary as both sister and mother, as Mediatrix and companion. In those dual roles, Mary refracts the two roles by which evangelicals relate to Christ: as intimate friend and mighty king. Both patron and companion, evangelicals have proven, can be held together in a robust spirituality, and even though the roles of Mary are different, evangelical piety around Christ points to the way humans are capable of a complex and multifaceted spirituality that can accommodate this duality of intimacy and exaltation.[44]

The dichotomy of terms that apply either to Mary or to God is one I want to resist. Instead of the doctrine of God vying for territory with Mariology, these two doctrines can be understood to inhabit it differently. The symbols, claims, and pictures that accrue to Mary do so because Mary of Nazareth is an image God gives to us of who God is. When we look at Mary, we perceive God's relationship to us as creatures. It is because Mary has not been taken seriously as an image that her connection to the doctrine of God has been underappreciated. For Mariology opens onto the doctrine of God precisely in its aesthetics, in the way Mary images God for us. And once we see Mary's imaging of God, we can begin to order and make sense of her connections to other doctrines, including the doctrines traditionally associated with Mariology, ecclesiology, and Christology and the doctrine of theological anthropology, which Ruether turned to as she articulated Mary as the summation of redeemed humanity. This is, I want to affirm, the other side of Mary's imaging: she pictures for us God and she also pictures for us our humanity.

To speak to us of our humanity and our human redemption, Mary speaks to *us* and *our* redemption. The spiritual and the political, theological truth and cultural interpretation, are not two poles to be precariously balanced. Divine life is found in intimacy with those living under political conditions of oppression, need, and vulnerability. Christ tells us this in the Gospel of Matthew: "Truly I tell you, just as you did it to one of the least of these brothers and sisters of mine, you did it to me."[45] It is the hungry, the thirsty, the naked, the stranger, the sick, the imprisoned who bear Christ's face.[46] Christ is found not in the idea of Christ but in the concrete negotiations of living in this world. Where do we expect to find Christ's mother?

Black Maternity and Insurrectionary Potentials

Our Lady, Mother of Ferguson locates Christ's mother for us in the suffering of Black life in America.[47] Doox's icon presents Mary the image through and as Black maternity, in tensions of Black motherhood that reverberate in Mariology. Mary cannot be resolved into transcendental symbol or historical figure, nor can the tensions of Black motherhood be dispelled, and these irresolvable tensions that exist at multiple levels illustrate and help interpret one another. A conversational stream in Black studies illumines this complexity.

In 1987, literary critic and Black feminist scholar Hortense Spillers published her landmark essay "Mama's Baby, Papa's Maybe."[48] Rejecting the narrations of the 1976 government-sponsored Moynihan report—which establishes the trope of "the absent Black father" to describe the Black family's "social pathology" and underachievement, attributing these to the Black family's matriarchal structure—Spillers responds with a historically informed picture of Black life in America that is both much more pessimistic and, paradoxically, more attuned to the promise of such life.[49] The particular importance of the mother for Black families, Spillers maintains, dates back to slavery, when Black children were born outside the law of the father. Whereas White children gained their names and social status through fathers, enslaved children legally followed the condition of the mother, who also gave them their name. In this way, and in the way Black bodies were reduced to flesh, as sites that could be "invaded/raided" by White desire, Black women and men existed on the boundary of patriarchal gender norms, which were established and enforced in America together with capitalistic conceptions of property and race.[50] At these margins, this boundary condition, the possibility for life otherwise lingers. Drawing on psychoanalysis to describe the ongoing legacy of this *otherwise*, Spillers writes:

> The African-American male has been touched, therefore, by the *mother*, handled by her in ways that he cannot escape, and in ways that the white American male is allowed to temporize by a fatherly reprieve. This human and historical development . . . takes us to the center of an inexorable difference in the depths of American women's community: the African-American woman, the *mother*, the daughter, becomes historically the powerful and shadowy evocation of a cultural synthesis long evaporated—the law of the Mother—only and precisely because legal enslavement removed the African-American male not so

much from sight as from *mimetic* view as a partner in the prevailing social fiction of the Father's name, the Father's law.

Therefore, the female . . . breaks in upon the imagination with a forcefulness that marks both a denial and an "illegitimacy." Because of this peculiar American denial, the black American male embodies the *only* American community of males which has had the specific occasion to learn *who* the female is within itself, the infant child who bears the life against the could-be fateful gamble, against the odds of pulverization and murder, including her own. It is the heritage of the *mother* that the African-American male must regain as an aspect of his own personhood—the "power" of "yes" to the "female" within.[51]

As the male has the power to say yes to the female within, so the female has the power to "[claim] the monstrosity (of a female with the power to name)."[52] Amid the horror of slavery and its ongoing legacy, there is, in other words, "insurgent ground" to be gained in the boundary situation of these gender roles.[53]

Recent work by Black theorists and writers has returned to Spillers to explore the "insurrectionary potentials" of Black motherhood that live even amid deep pessimism born of these theorists' attention to the "fungible" structures of White supremacy.[54] Though she sees no recompense or final overcoming of the social death of slavery, Saidiya Hartman outlines transformative promise in the mother's labor of care and its political-social potential.[55] She writes: "Those of us who have been 'touched by the mother' need acknowledge that . . . [t]his brilliant and formidable labor of care, paradoxically, has been produced through violent structures of slavery, anti-black racism, virulent sexism, and disposability. The forms of care, intimacy, and sustenance exploited by racial capitalism, most importantly, are not reducible to or exhausted by it. . . . This care, which is coerced and freely given, is the black heart of our social poesis, of making and relation."[56] Hartman insists in this brilliant and beautiful passage that the care of Black motherhood is both coerced and nevertheless free, produced within a violent system that cannot fully determine it. Black maternity, Hartman and Spillers claim, funds an alternative way of inhabiting gender outside the patriarchal norms of our gender practices.[57] The Black mother holds insurrectionary potentials that our world, our performance of gender, might be otherwise. This potential exists within and cannot be prised apart from tragedy, from the horrific conditions of slavery and its afterlives. There is a terrible danger in passing over the tragedy in order to claim maternity's hope, to overlook the fungibility of White supremacy's structures and claim a victory that is too easy, too uncommitted. It is to refuse to see that the brilliant care, the potentially transformative maternal touch, was pressured by the conditions of slavery. Yet there is a temptation that twins this one, which is to reject the potential for tragedy's transformation promised by the Black mother's swelling womb, to refuse to appreciate her brilliant and formidable labor of care, to insist on ignoring how the Black mother jars the patriarchal-racial imagination of gender. Slavery produces the conditions of and yet cannot subsume the mother's labor of care or her touch. This is not a tension to solve but one to acknowledge. When we celebrate the promise at the expense of reckoning with the tragedy, or when tragedy swallows any glint of a promise, we deny the Black mother and her queer and costly labors of care.[58] For similarly to how Mariology of the image holds together historical figure and transcendent sign, death-dealing politics and liberative hope, so Black maternity holds together the realities of deep tragedy and transformative promise. In this way, the Black mother is an especially compelling Marian image of our time.

Our Lady, Mother of Ferguson *and the Virgin of the Sign*

Our Lady, Mother of Ferguson is crowned with a nimbus of victory. She is marked by the sight of a gun. This contemporary icon imagines the Virgin of the Sign or Oranta icon under the pressures of our present moment, as the iconographic traditions of Christian Byzantium and Black Lives Matter coalesce in complex ways. Mary raises her arms in the traditional *orans* position, as a prayer—or does she raise them to say "hands up, don't shoot"? The Christ child is a silhouetted figure, raising his arms to say "hands up, don't shoot"—or is he praying? A shooting, at any rate, is imminent; a gun is trained on the child in utero and, by extension, on the mother. Observing this, the viewer will recognize—I recognize—the impossibility of neutrality. My view of Our Lady comes through the scope of this gun.

Our Lady of Ferguson draws on the two traditions of iconography not to resolve the tension of tragedy and hope but to exemplify it. The image speaks of the mother of Michael Brown, the eighteen-year-old Black man shot by a police officer in 2014 in Ferguson, Missouri, even though his hands, Brown's companion affirmed, were in a "hands up, don't shoot" position. *Our Lady of Ferguson* speaks also to a history of oppression and violence, invoking a litany of victims that includes Trayvon Martin, Eric Garner, Philando Castile, Walter Scott, Tamir Rice, Alton Sterling, Breonna Taylor, Ahmaud Arbery, Atatiana Jefferson, Stephon Clark, Sandra Bland, Daunte Wright, Tyre Nichols, and George Floyd. Yet the image is not simply a spectacle of violence and death. As in most images of Mary, this mother has sorrowful eyes, communicated principally by the light semicircles below her bottom lid. And still vitality radiates from her—in the blue and red aureole behind her, in the slender fingers pointing deliberately upward, in the energetic lines of her garment, and in the golden nimbus surrounding her head.

Borrowed from a "pre-Christian Greek and Roman . . . way of representing preternatural light and glory," the golden nimbus communicates holiness and victory.[59] It signifies that this Black mother is not defeated. Even as her child is marked for death, she stands as a testament to life. And in this way, the halo underscores the promise in Black maternity, which functions symbolically or iconographically to signal and affirm the insurrectionary potentials of the Madonna of the image. As Byzantine iconography drew the golden nimbus from Greek and Roman imagery to communicate glory, so Doox draws insurrectionary Black maternity from contemporary imagery to communicate the death-defying motherhood of Mary. The images interact in complex ways. The Black maternity of *Our Lady of Ferguson* does not just confirm the nimbus but shifts the way we perceive it, the way we recognize how and where such haloed victory is claimed.[60]

Our Lady is almost engulfed by violence. With the gun trained on her child, her situation is desperate—and yet she creates a space of nurture and care, touching her child in a "brilliant and formidable labor of care."[61] In her life-bearing, which the death-dealing structures of the world cannot extinguish, *Our Lady* figures forth the possibility of another politics, another way of being together. But her way of being with her child will be destroyed any moment. There is death and violence in this image. There is life and the promise of transformation. The Black Lives Matter imagery inscribes the tragic conditions of social death for Black women, men, and children in America today into the Oranta icon, helping us more powerfully encounter the Gospel story of Mary, her sorrow and her strength. The Byzantine iconography connects the possibility for political transformation expressed in Black Lives Matter and in the Black maternity literature to the story of Christ, the sacred heart testifying to love's ongoing life and victory in the world but also to the way such hope is alloyed to the tragic confession that we crucified love.[62] The proclamation of resurrection cannot be wrested away from acknowledgment of death.

And the hope of resurrection, of the life-from-death that Christ extends, is imaged in the insurrectionary potentials of Black maternity amid social death. For Spillers and her interpreters, the possibility of life otherwise figured by the Black mother neither overcomes social death nor compensates for it. Yet such hope is expanded, emboldened, and realized in Mary's body, for the shadowy, lost Law of the Mother in Black maternity points to Mary's virgin motherhood of Christ, a child with no biological father and one who is thus uniquely "touched by the mother." Defying all social convention, the earliest Gospel refers to Jesus as the "Son of Mary" (Mark 6:3).

Too often, we pass over the violence to gaze at the nimbus as we gloss current tragedy to delineate hope. But *Our Lady of Ferguson* helps us interpret and locate Christian hope by the more difficult and tragic elements of the Gospel stories. As icons tend to do, the image plays with multiple temporalities, connecting several key scenes in Mary's life. As a Virgin of the Sign icon, it images the Annunciation not in the moment of Gabriel's invitation but in the moment of Mary's "yes" that fulfills the prophecy, "The Lord will give you a sign. Behold, a virgin shall conceive" (Isaiah 7:14). As an interpretation of the Virgin of the Sign, *Our Lady of Ferguson* presents Mary not as the one hailed by Gabriel but as the one whose "yes" inaugurates the rebirth of the world. This is not about Gabriel's message of invitation; it is about Mary's active embrace of her vocation, the moment she receives the person of Christ and accepts her role as the Mother of the Lord, thus becoming a sign of messianic hope. And she signs this hope as a Black Madonna, recovering a class of Marian figures that the church hierarchy tried to subdue, embodying the darker skin of the very first image of Mary.[63]

Like almost all images of Mary, this one also references the cross, where Mary stood as part of the faithful remnant. Images of Mary and the Christ babe usually allude to the cross in Mary's solemn sorrow, but *Our Lady of Ferguson* is much more explicit. The gunsights form a literal cross on the body of the Christ, who is still a child, still even in utero. This is a child marked for violence before he is born, as Herod marked young Jewish males in the vicinity of Bethlehem. The specter of violence against children thus adverts to the infancy narratives in Matthew, a much less common source of Mariology than the other Gospels—when Mary and Joseph flee through Egypt to escape Herod's murderous designs on Jewish children, repeating the flight of God's people from Pharaoh's hard-heartedness to the Hebrew babes in an earlier age. It reminds us that Jesus, too, was marked for death, that he lived in an empire that saw him as threatening and disposable. That is why Mary's motherhood, her formidable labor of care for his life, is celebrated by her Magnificat, a song of lifting up the lowly and bringing down the powerful from their thrones. Unlike the White Lady, whose body has become transparent, de-stigmatized, the Black Mary of Ferguson rhymes with the Mary of Nazareth and her historical, Jewish flesh.

Like many Sign icons, *Our Lady of Ferguson* also recalls our last glimpse of Mary in scripture: Pentecost. It is not just the prominence of the color red. It is also that in *Our Lady of Ferguson*, we see Mary depicted as the first dwelling place of Christ, in her role as the first church as well as a figure and type of the church, thus foreshadowing the birthday of the church on Pentecost. On that feast, Mary is spiritually filled with the Holy Spirit just as she is in the image physically filled with Christ. At Pentecost, when Mary is so alive that she is like a red flame of divine presence, we receive the Mater Ecclesiae that the Mater Dei figures. The literal and metaphorical are intertwined in ways that yield multiple forms of divine presence. Mary expresses and mediates the human vocation to bear Christ, which is enabled by the way her literal motherhood of physically bearing Christ opens to her spiritual motherhood as the first church, displayed in her faithfulness at the cross and her presence at Pentecost, where she celebrates the birth of the church that will outlive her earthly life. Bearing Christ literally and metaphorically, birthing Christ and Christ bearers, Mary exemplifies our human vocation to bear Christ and the way such bearing is related to the birthing of other Christ bearers.

In these ways, *Our Lady, Mother of Ferguson* references and associates several important Marian scenes—the Annunciation, the flight to Egypt, the cross, and Pentecost—which are then overlaid with the story of Black motherhood in a way that transforms the viewer's relationship to those stories. Traditional Byzantine icons present a window into eternity, into God's peaceable kingdom where injustice and violence have been overcome. Yet they are windows meant not for passive gazing but for passing through. As so many theologians of the icon have reminded us over the years, icons are thresholds, invitations to divine encounter. We met one such icon in the figure of Hagar, as Delores Williams presents her. *Our Lady of Ferguson* reminds us of the icon's divine encounter and its stakes by confronting us with the sights of a gun through which we gaze and connecting divine presence to politically urgent conditions. Here the living Mother of God shows us and calls us into our redeemed humanity in the concrete and tragic conditions of our time. Like the cry of Floyd, this image is a summons to all mothers. Also like that cry, the summons extends to all of us mother-born.

Neighbor Love as the Summons to Motherhood

What does it mean to answer the summons to motherhood? What does it mean even to hear it? According to *Our Lady, Mother of Ferguson*, the mother is one who shares the suffering and danger with the one she mothers. The gun trained on the child is also aimed at the mother, whose body embraces her child. The mother of Brown knows, viscerally, what it means to suffer the shot of a gun, as Nichols's mother is forever marked by her son's death, as Floyd's mother—he understood—would have shared his own suffering of racialized violence. This maternal co-suffering is inseparable from Mary's picturing of redeemed humanity. We are all summoned to the co-suffering Mary exemplifies.

Russian theologian Mother Maria Skobtsova describes maternal co-suffering as central to the Christian commandment to neighbor love.[64] Taking her cues from Simeon's warning to Mary that a sword would pierce her heart also, Skobtsova identifies the cross cleaving the earth of Golgotha as the sword through Mary's heart, which is to say, the sword that pierces Mary is none other than the cross bearing the pierced body of her son, as the bullet that tears the flesh of the son also wounds the Mother of Ferguson.[65] This is what it means to love your neighbor as yourself, Skobtsova affirms—not as a moralistic program to be taken up as fundamental to Christianity or as "an outward manifestation of an inner spiritual state."[66] The former puts an individual decision at the center, as if neighbor love is a triumph of the ego, and tempts us into heroic pictures of neighbor love that feed White savior complexes. The latter makes neighbor love accidental to Christianity rather than its very essence, representing piety as a set of spiritual practices primarily involving God and the soul, only secondarily touching the neighbor.[67] For Skobtsova, these will not do. We are for her implicated in the suffering of others by the given solidarity of humanity, and our vocations to Marian motherhood are recognitions and realizations of that givenness.

The givenness of human solidarity in Christ expresses for Skobtsova why maternity is such a crucial image. Maternal neighbor love means being involved in the pain of another as instinctively and unquestioningly as a mother is involved in the pain of her child. Rowan Williams describes her approach this way: "Our given entanglements in the mutuality of Christ's Body, the absence in the Body of any secure boundaries between one subject and another, is analogous to Mary's entanglement in the suffering of her son. . . . The 'adoption' of the whole Body, our mothering love towards each and every other, is not another version of the heroic venture out from the castle of the soul to embrace something alien, but the recognition of the full character of our prior relation with and 'investment' in the other."[68] To be in the body of Christ is to be exposed to the suffering of all humans, with whom we are already in a relation of given solidarity. Usually, such solidarity is identified with the church, which Mary traditionally figures; why, for her, does it identify all humanity?

Williams points to her undefended conception of universal human solidarity as a lacuna in Skobtsova's theology, and it is true that her theology offers only suggestions about how to theologize such solidarity. One explicit suggestion is her icon theology. Given the strong theology of the icon in the Russian Orthodox church, Skobtsova's repeated claim that all humans bear the image of God means that to see a human properly is to see her as a sacred icon of Christ to whom Christ is therefore present. She links this explicitly to maternal neighbor love when she writes that love of one's neighbor rightly flows from "a single law. . . . Our relation is determined only by seeing the image of God in [the neighbor], and, on the other hand, in adopting him as a son [or daughter]."[69] Everywhere, in every neighbor we encounter, is the child of Mary, awaiting a mothering relationship and inviting us to open ourselves to entanglement with these bodies as a mother mingles her flesh with a child's, as Mary shares hers with Christ.[70]

The theology of maternity, of entangled flesh, of interdependency, can help us understand the solidarity in any particular encounter with a neighbor, but Skobtsova also speaks of this solidarity as collectively given, not just the summation of individual relations of solidarity. Perhaps we can complete this vision of solidarity by coupling her emphasis on humans as icon bearers with a more implicit vision of Mary as an image, whose motherhood signifies God's own. For God is the mother who bears in the divine womb the human race, united as God's creation. God's maternal relation to creation is one that we are invited into through the commandment of neighbor love, and Mary embodies and points us toward that relation of Creator–creation. To claim solidarity with all humankind is to enter into a Marian imitation of God's own maternal relation to creation and in such solidarity to find our own Marian vocation to love the neighbor. We are invited to imitate and participate in both motherhoods through the commandment of neighbor love.[71] To love one's neighbor like Mary is to acknowledge the divine image in the other, to imitate divine motherhood, to share in another's Golgotha, and so "to give birth to Christ within [oneself]."[72]

As the repeated yoking of motherhood and Golgotha suggests, maternal love is dangerous. Like her namesake, Mother Maria Skobtsova lived under an empire exterminating Jewish children, all Jewish people, in fact. As a Russian exile in Paris during the 1940s, Skobtsova remained in the city when she could have escaped, to continue her ministries and to start others, living increasingly in solidarity with the Jews. When 6,900 of the city's 12,884 Jews were rounded up in a stadium to be sent to Auschwitz, Skobtsova used her monastic robes to smuggle in goods to them. She used trash cans to smuggle out children. She helped forge documents to set out routes of escape and secure food for them. For this work, she was arrested and sent to Ravensbrück, where she continued her life of neighbor love for another two years, sharing her food, organizing discussion groups, and offering encouragement as her health declined. On Good Friday, March 30, 1945, she was executed. Reports are conflicted about whether she was simply chosen for execution that day or if she gave her life in exchange for another scheduled for death.[73]

Skobtsova's life is an icon of Mary—of Mary's faithfulness to her son, of her love that, like Christ's own motherly love, goes all the way to the cross and through the cross. And given the iconic power of her life, it is fitting that one of the last acts before she died in the concentration camp was to make an icon of Mary holding Christ on the cross—an aesthetic mediation of her own life, which was itself an icon of Mary and therefore of God, and in these ways also a perceptible form of her Mariology. She embodied the Mary she theologized. The act of writing this icon in a concentration camp, like the icon itself, is a thing of gorgeous beauty and excess in a place of toil, starvation, and death. An icon of the Theotokos was Skobtsova's answer to Nazis about whether she knew any Jews, and so it seems especially fitting that she wrote an icon of Mary and the Christ child in that concentration camp, where their iconic flesh mingled with that of their fellow Jews, ultimately sharing their fate. For the icon she wrote was lost, and today we have a reproduction based on memory. The life and theology of Skobtsova, the co-suffering of Mary, Christ, and Skobtsova with the Jewish people, identifies the Marian demands and commitments of maternal neighbor love.

Gathering these icons of Mother Maria, Mother Mary, Mother God, and the *Mother of Ferguson*, we return to our neighbor Floyd and hear again his call for Mama, a cry that searches out the one whose flesh is entangled with his own.

The Affordances of Our Lady, Mother of Ferguson

As an image of Mary, *Our Lady of Ferguson* solicits our attention away from notions of motherhood that are romantic, idealized, or infected with White supremacy. She offers an important pedagogy about where and how to find Christ in the world and about what motherhood looks like in our concrete conditions now. This is not to claim that *Our Lady of Ferguson* is invulnerable to being co-opted by White supremacy or other forms of violence, any more than I would want to claim that approaching Mary as an image protects Mariology from masculinist or idolatrous interpretations. As Schüssler Fiorenza puts it, "feminist G*d-talk is always in danger of . . . re-inscribing the Western, androcentric gender binary of Mariology that either devalues women and femininity or idealizes femininity as representing superior transcendent and salvific qualities."[74] All symbols, she writes, must submit to ongoing feminist testing within a discipleship of equals attentive to the lives of actual women. Copeland writes in a similar key that true change requires a community that acts as a community, with "nurture and interdependency; the acceptance, understanding, and appreciation of difference; and friendship."[75] Within a community of discipleship and nurture, approaching Mary as an image, like the image *Our Lady of Ferguson* itself, bears liberative potential.[76] *Our Lady* pictures the God-imaging, liberating Mary in the world today. But what exactly is that picture? According to *Our Lady of Ferguson*, how do we enter Mary's magnifying song, the joy of motherhood, in twenty-first-century America?

Joy, I realize, may seem a strange word for *Our Lady of Ferguson*. How can this image of sorrow and lament—this picture of maternal co-suffering—convey joy? I am acutely aware of the danger here of valorizing the suffering of Black women, of falling into the trap so many womanist theologians have identified of articulating a theology of redemption that justifies the subjugation of Black women. I see how wildly awry this could go. And yet I also see *Our Lady of Ferguson* beckoning us toward this danger—and overcoming it. Submitting to her vision, I want to remind us of three ways she embodies a joy undefeated by death.

First, visually, the image conveys in various details the joyful overturning that *Our Lady* promises. She is sober, but her gaze meets the world openly, steadily, unflinchingly. She is surrounded with gold that communicates an eternal life in holiness and glory. Her face and hands reflect light, which in iconology symbolizes divine presence. The child she bears is marked for death, and yet his heart opens a mandorla that the sights of the gun cannot mark. This sacred heart, we know, cannot be contained by death. *Our Lady* communicates in these visual details a fearlessness and freedom that meet the world's violence. Her serenity and commitment to life cannot be defeated by guns and brutality. And there is joy in the energy of these affirmations of life and freedom. In her refusal to succumb to or authorize the world's power structures, *Our Lady* figures their overturning.

Second, at a *historical* level, *Our Lady*, as an image of Black maternity, hints at insurrectionary potentials and insurgent possibilities that lie in those we have consigned to margins of this world, as she mothers forth the possibility of new worlds and ways of being together. This level, too, echoes the life and freedom that cannot be extinguished by even humanity's most brutal efforts to do so. The possibility of life "otherwise" that she signifies as a Black Madonna is the joy that funds the ongoing creativity and caregiving in and of Black life.

Third, these visual and historical intimations of joy are *theologically* affirmed by the icon's reference to Pentecost, when Mary, the Mother of God and the first church, is enflamed by the Spirit who gives Mother Church to us. Since at least the fourth century, Mary has shared titles with the church with which she is identified, and at Pentecost, Mary bodies forth a new way of our being together, a new political and social order that is the church, which is called to live out the vision of mercy that Mary sings in the Magnificat. *Our Lady, Mother of Ferguson* reminds us of that vocation and images it for us. The joy of this image is a joy that passes through life's most deeply suffering and discovers that God is not absent to them. It holds the tension of tragedy and hope together, refusing to deny either, showing us the Mother who images for us the possibility of transformed humanity, who images the God transformatively present to the bleakest tragedies. *Our Lady of Ferguson* displays and affirms that as an image, Mary traverses territories divided by minimalists and maximalists, speaking as both historical figure and transcendent sign, holding together our tragic conditions with transformative promise. It is only by their connection that hope is possible. In the denial of the promise—the danger of minimalism—we are left with the despair of tragedy. In the denial of tragedy—the danger of maximalism—hope is falsified and alloyed to the power structures of the moment. In these ways, *Our Lady of Ferguson* and images like it are important ways of discovering the Mary who remains with us as a model, guide, and revelation of divine work.[77] How exquisitely fitting that Lee's womanist Mariology culminates in a series of new Marian images: Keeper of Our Vineyard, Perpetually Her Own, Maker of Something with Nothing, Keeper of Good Company, Mother of the Movement.[78]

There is more to say about what and how *Our Lady, Mother of Ferguson* communicates, for images do more than convey information. As some experienced before the video of Floyd's death, as Francis experienced in front of the San Damiano crucifix, images can move us, speak to us, stigmatize us. Attuning us to possibilities for a way of being otherwise, they can summon us to change our life. This is, we might say, an affordance of images: that they can bear to us a vitality, a presence, that is potentially transformative. Gaston Bachelard expresses the power of images, writing, "But the image has touched the depths before it stirs the surface.... It takes root in us. It has been given us by another, but we begin to have the impression that we could have created it, that we should have created it. It becomes a new being in our language, expressing us by making us what it expresses; in other words, it is at once a becoming of expression, and a becoming of our being. Here expression creates being."[79]

There is particular wisdom here, I think, for Mariology. Like pregnancy itself, Mary is the image that touches our depths before stirring our surface. When we feed from Mary, receiving nourishment by her mediation of Christ, Mary touches our deep hunger, nourishing us with new images by which she comes to us. Those new images, too, touch our depths; *Our Lady of Ferguson* touches our depths. In *Our Lady*, Mary expresses us by making us what she expresses. She expresses, that is, our motherhood, and with our depths and surfaces stirred, we become her motherhood. Those of us who have been touched by this mother "regain an aspect of our own personhood" (to paraphrase Spillers); we gain the power of "yes" to the Christ birthed within us and thus to the grace of the motherhood given to us. To put it differently, we attune to Mary, and she comes in the magnifying music of our age, drawing and expanding us into divine life. We attune; we are attuned. We repair; we are repaired. Expression creates being, like a rebirth.

So easily we lose sight of our vocation to bear Christ into the world. The demands of that vocation wither and wane as we become inured to violence. Images like *Our Lady of Ferguson* jolt us out of that spell. We see her, and we see anew the image of Floyd, a police officer kneeling on his neck. "Mama!" he says. And *Our Lady, Mother of Ferguson* helps us see that when Floyd called for his mama, he summoned all of us to become mothers.

Attunement, Motherhood, and Mariology

By centering *Our Lady, Mother of Ferguson* and constellating around her the image, story, and theology of Mother Maria Skobtsova; the story and image of George Floyd; the work of Hortense Spillers and her interpreters; and some important Marian moments in scripture, I offer a repair to the image of Mary funding much theology, augmenting a positive affordance in an effort to transform the environment of Mariology. Through Mary as an image and through the particular image of the *Mother of Ferguson*, I retune the core Marian image from the powerful, White Lady who conserves the status quo to the one who figures for us our vocation and God's life with us, the one who calls us into the joyful song of God's mercy by passing through the death-dealing regimes of our time. Attuning our image of Mary, tuning to her, entails reimagining and expanding the significance of her motherhood and the claims it makes on us, the way we are all called to become mothers in imitation of our Mother God.

This emphasis on motherhood returns us to where we started. Mariology as a summons to mother-becoming rhymes with the description in chapter 1 of attunement as a way of giving birth to one's own mother. It resonates with the conviction that the condition of theology is one of having a mother. Attunement, I said in that first chapter, is fitting for who we are as creatures (those who do not sustain themselves but are mothered into existence) and for who we are by the Spirit (those who sustain others and mother them and therefore our world into existence). In tuning (to) the image of Mary our mother in this last chapter, I return to these dual theological aspects of attunement, learning to receive the mother anew and giving her anew to others—and thereby becoming a mother.

In this way, this entire book is a study in pneumatology, a human picture of the work of the Holy Spirit, who is always coming to creation and making it new. The Holy Spirit is, after all, the one who inspires the attuned writings and readings that have become canonical to the church—the ark of Noah as a figure of baptism, the Akedah as the sacrifice of Christ, the beloved of the Song of Songs as Mary, as the church, as the soul. My descriptions of attunement as co-creating images and texts through their affordances in order to offer a repair is a literary description, a creaturely imprint of how the Spirit has so often moved in the history of Christian interpretation. My summons to a mode of interpreting accountable to the concrete conditions in which we live, answerable to and reparative of a world sick with racialized, patriarchal violence and greed, is also a translation of what I take the Spirit's work to be: befriending matter, resting on creation, making Christ present.[80] What is the work of the Spirit but constructing niches, transforming the environment, heralding the kingdom, converting earth to be as it is in heaven? And my turn to Mary as the one who images both God and our human vocation is likewise a turn to a picture of the Spirit's work in drawing human life into the divine. For Mary and the Spirit are intimate, so intimate that Protestants often speak of the Spirit where Catholics and Orthodox speak of Mary, as if the two roles are interchangeable. Such interchangeability is more than I want to claim for the Spirit's relation to Mary, though I think it is important to remember that Mary became pregnant with Christ when the Holy Spirit hovered over the waters of her womb, that Francis became stigmatized like Christ when the Holy Spirit animated an image to speak Christ's words, that we can become bearers of Christ, converted to Christ, only by the Holy Spirit who makes us like Mary. Another way to frame my exhortation to attunement, then, is a prayer to the Spirit to come and do a new thing among us, to inspire us to follow after God our Mother, to surface in our lives and interpretations the marks of the God of the living: stigmata pictured for us by Mary, like novelty, movement, recreation, creation, and birth.

A Summons

By the San Damiano crucifix, Francis was changed. He received the blessed wounds on his soul and embraced his vocation to repair the church that was weighed down with luxury and indifference to the poor. Accepting the literal sense, which opens to the metaphorical, Francis received the joy of mothering Christ's presence into the world.

Our Lady, Mother of Ferguson is summoning us, and by her summons, she blesses and wounds us. The image speaks. *May you all be pregnant with Christ, stigmatized with the hope that accompanies this world's deep sufferings. Yes, may you all be reborn as Christ bearers in the womb of the Mother God. May you carry in your person the life of the Crucified and, embracing your motherhood, sing the joy of God's mercy.*

Notes

1. Thomas of Celano, "The Remembrance of the Desire of a Soul by Thomas of Celano," in *Francis of Assisi, The Founder: Early Documents*, Vol. 2, ed. Regis J. Armstrong, J. A. Wayne Hellmann, and William J. Short (New York: New City Press, 2000), 249.
2. The full title is *Our Lady, Mother of Ferguson and All Those Killed by Gun Violence*, though it is often also called simply *Our Lady of Ferguson*.
3. Other images that use traditional forms to speak to present realities of racial violence have appeared in the last several years. One particularly well-known image is a pietà in an iconographic style, called *Mama*, made by Kelly Latimore in 2020 and said to depict Christ as Floyd. The painting was stolen from where it was hung at the Catholic University of America, as was a smaller replacement painting later, and Latimore received many death threats. Reports of the two thefts can be found

at Jack Jenkins, "Second 'George Floyd' Pietà Stolen from Catholic University," *National Catholic Reporter*, December 17, 2021, https://www.ncronline.org/news/people/second-george-floyd-piet-stolen-catholic-university. There is, in fact, a tradition of reinterpreting Mary through images, one strand of which is analyzed in an article by María del Mar Pérez-Gil, who highlights images of nude or semi-nude Mary as figuring Mary entering life with the marginalized. María del Mar Pérez-Gil, "Undressing the Virgin Mary: Nudity and Gendered Art," *Feminist Theology* 25, no. 2 (January 2017): 208–221. One other striking example of an image and attunement is Ewan King's essay on David Jones's painting, which draws together a number of sources for a Mariological reflection. He ends the piece, "Having found in Mary's 'luggage' interweavings of biblical narrative, Greek myth, Celtic legend, late-medieval prose, and twentieth-century military history, we can now see a figure whose identity is irrevocably bound up with other human identities, just as in Jones' practice visual art and poetry are inextricably intertwined." Ewan King, "The Virgin and the Visual Artist as Theologian: Examining Two Marian Images by David Jones," in *Transforming Christian Thought in the Visual Arts: Theology, Aesthetics, and Practice*, ed. Sheona Beaumont and Madeleine Emerald Thiele (New York: Routledge, 2021), 92.

4. Courtney Hall Lee notes the similarities between the experiences of Black mothers like Floyd's, who witness their children "killed by the powerful empire of whiteness," and Mary in her womanist Mariology. She writes, "Mary had to witness her son's slow and gruesome death. At the same time, she had to witness his derision by those who mocked him and put him to death. Women like Mamie Till and Samaria Rice share a common bond with Mary, bound together in a shared experience that no one should endure." Courtney Hall Lee, *Black Madonna: A Womanist Look at Mary of Nazareth* (Eugene, OR: Cascade, 2017), 88.

5. Claudia Rankine, "'The Condition of Black Life Is One of Mourning,'" *New York Times Magazine*, June 22, 2015, https://www.nytimes.com/2015/06/22/magazine/the-condition-of-black-life-is-one-of-mourning.html. Several womanist theologians have also critiqued an overvaluation of suffering for the way it binds Black women to the conditions of suffering, absolving the world that created those conditions from reflecting on or ameliorating them. There is a fine, important line between acknowledging this suffering as an echo of Christ's and Mary's and hearing in that echo an affirmation that such suffering is therefore good or redemptive.

6. Elisabeth Schüssler Fiorenza, *Jesus: Miriam's Child, Sophia's Prophet: Critical Issues in Feminist Christology* (New York: Continuum, 1994), 180.

7. Though I am gratefully indebted to Schüssler Fiorenza's work, my own analysis of Mariology's dilemma does not map neatly onto hers. Schüssler Fiorenza articulates the four problems she sees this way: "Feminist the*logians have pointed out that malestream Mariology and the cult of Mary devalue wo/men in four ways. They do so *firstly* by emphasizing virginity to the detriment of sexuality, *secondly* by unilaterally associating the ideal of 'true womanhood' with motherhood, *thirdly* by

religiously valorizing obedience, humility, passivity, and submission as the cardinal virtues of wo/men, and *fourthly* by constructing an essentialized gender complementarity that sustains the structural oppression of wo/men." Elisabeth Schüssler Fiorenza, "Mariology, Gender Ideology, and the Discipleship of Equals," in Elizabeth Schüssler Fiorenza, *Transforming Vision: Explorations in Feminist The*logy* (Minneapolis: Fortress, 2011), 198. The reader will notice that the most important way I diverge from Schüssler Fiorenza concerns the elevation of motherhood, which she sees as wrongly constraining women's vocations, while I understand "motherhood" as an analogous term that need not constrain women in the way Schüssler Fiorenza worries about—as I explain later in this chapter.

8. As Schüssler Fiorenza puts it, Mariology "constructs not only the dualism between wo/men and wo/men but also between wo/men and men. Mary, the Queen of Heaven, is not quite divine because divinity is male defined; she thereby inscribes the pattern of subordination as a feminine divine-human pattern." Schüssler Fiorenza, "Mariology," 202.

9. As Schüssler Fiorenza puts it, "In holding up to women the image of the perpetual virgin and sorrowful mother Mary, churchmen preach a model of femininity that ordinary women cannot imitate. Mary, as the completely desexualized 'plaster being from the grotto of Lourdes' and the symbol of humble obedience, serves to religiously inculcate normal women with dependency, subordination, and inferiority." Schüssler Fiorenza, *Jesus: Miriam's Child*, 180–181.

10. The classic article here is Evelyn P. Stevens, "Machismo and Marianismo," *Society* 10 (September 1973): 57–63. The term is not without controversy, and a trenchant criticism can be found in Marysa Navarro, "Against *Marianismo*," in *Gender's Place: Feminist Anthropologies of Latin America*, ed. Rosario Montoya R., Lessie Jo Frazier, and Janise Hurtig (New York: Palgrave Macmillan, 2002), 257–272. Nevertheless, the term continues to gain traction, particularly within the field of psychology, where some scholars have developed a Marianismo Beliefs Scale and given "Marianismo" its own entry in *The Wiley Encyclopedia of Personality and Individual Differences*. Alejandro Morales, Oscar Fernando Rojas Pérez, "Marianismo," in *The Wiley Encyclopedia of Personality and Individual Differences: Models and Theories*, Vol. 1, ed. Bernardo J. Carducci et al. (New York: Wiley Blackwell, 2020), 247–251.

11. Schüssler Fiorenza, "Mariology," 202.

12. That Mary's pure and virginal body is White and that purity and virginity are exemplified in U.S. purity culture through White bodies are mutually implicated realities. Lee testifies to this reality in her book *Black Madonna*, where she opens with a meditation on her experience of pregnancy as a Black woman and the judgment about her own sexuality she noted during it.

13. Lucia Chiavola Birnbaum, *Black Madonnas: Feminism, Religion, and Politics in Italy* (Boston: Northeastern University Press, 1993), 3.

14. Schüssler Fiorenza has pointed out the way Mary's alignment with power has often served the interests of the powerful. "It is no accident that the classic

mariological dogmas were articulated at a time when the Greco-Roman imperial form of Christianity became institutionalized and historically operative: The images of heavenly rulers developed parallel to secular imperial iconography. The imperial Christ, already the norm in the time of Constantine, was followed after the Council of Ephesus in 431 by the empress-like Mary.... Such politically conservative tendencies have also influenced the articulation of mariology in modern times. Barbara Corrado Pope, for instance, has documented that the 'century of Mary,' which opened in 1854 with the dogma of Mary's immaculate conception and climaxed in 1950 with Pius XII's dogmatic proclamation of Mary's assumption into heaven, propagated a defensive antimodernist attitude. Its conservative, backward-looking nostalgic politics yearned for the traditional order of monarchy and was afraid of social upheavals." Schüssler Fiorenza, *Jesus: Miriam's Child*, 180. The essay she references from Barbara Corrado Pope is "Immaculate and Powerful: The Marian Revival in the Nineteenth Century," in *Immaculate and Powerful: The Female in Sacred Image and Social Reality*, ed. Clarissa W. Atkinson, Constance H. Buchanan, and Margaret R. Miles (Boston: Beacon, 1985), 173–201.

15. Natalie K. Watson, among others, discusses this issue. Natalie K. Watson, "Feminist Ecclesiology," in *The Routledge Companion to the Christian Church*, ed. Gerard Mannion and Lewis S. Mudge (New York: Routledge, 2008), 461–475.

16. Alexander Schmemann, "On Mariology in Orthodoxy," *Marian Library Studies* 2, no. 4 (1970): 30–31. I discuss this in Natalie Carnes, "Gender and Ecclesiology," in *T&T Clark Handbook of Ecclesiology*, ed. Kimlyn J. Bender and D. Stephen Long (New York: Bloomsbury, 2020), 375–390.

17. Schmemann, "On Mariology," 30–31.

18. Daly, *Beyond God the Father*, 89–90.

19. Althaus-Reid, *From Feminist Theology to Indecent Theology*, 13. She also writes: "How can we explain Mariology in Latin America, with its emphasis on motherhood and a culture of 'purity,' having produced five centuries of disrespect for poor mothers and abuse of women?" (39).

20. The dogmatic constitution of Vatican II, *Lumen gentium*, mentions this title but with some care, reflecting the ambivalence of those attending the Council and crafting the document. It simply lists Mediatrix once as among Mary's recognized titles and then quickly qualifies that this detracts not at all from Christ as the sole mediator. Vatican II Council, *Lumen gentium: Dogmatic Constitution on the Church*, November 21, 1964, https://www.vatican.va/archive/hist_councils/ii_vatican_council/documents/vat-ii_const_19641121_lumen-gentium_en.html, §62.

21. Schüssler Fiorenza, "Mariology," 202, 203.

22. This is particularly a concern of Gregory's in *The Life of Moses*. See, for example, II, 165. It is taken up and developed by Pseudo-Dionysius in his apophatic theology.

23. Althaus-Reid, *From Feminist Theology to Indecent Theology*, 80.

24. Althaus-Reid, *From Feminist Theology to Indecent Theology*, 40.

25. Ivone Gebara and Maria Clara Lucchetti Bingemer, *Mary, Mother of God, Mother of the Poor* (Maryknoll, NY: Orbis, 1989), 25.
26. For more on Mary of Egypt and her relation to Mother Mary, see Sonia Velázquez's excellent book *Promiscuous Grace: Imagining Beauty and Holiness with Saint Mary of Egypt* (Chicago: University of Chicago Press, 2023).
27. Karl Rahner, *Mary, Mother of the Lord: Theological Meditations*, trans. W. J. O'Hara (New York: Herder and Herder, 1963), 94–95.
28. Rahner, *Mary, Mother of the Lord*, 97, 96.
29. Rahner, *Mary, Mother of the Lord*, 96.
30. Rahner, *Mary, Mother of the Lord*, 97.
31. Rahner, *Mary, Mother of the Lord*, 97.
32. Glossing Rahner's *Mariology*, Peter Joseph Fritz writes of Mary, "She shares in the same pilgrim journey as all human persons. Indeed, she is distinct from other pilgrims in that she has already arrived at a destination toward which others still travel. But the fact that 'the redemption of the world came through her redemption to its goal does not separate Mary from the rest of humanity; in fact, it is precisely why 'her redemption is not a merely "private matter" ["Privatangelegenheit"]... but something that belongs to the conditions of our own redemption.'" Peter Joseph Fritz, "Karl Rahner's Marian 'Minimalism,'" in *Mary on the Eve of the Second Vatican Council*, ed. John Cavadini and Danielle Peters (Notre Dame, IN: University of Notre Dame Press, 2017), 162; quoting and translating Karl Rahner, "Assumptio Beatae Maria Virginis," in *Sämtliche Werke*, Vol. 9, 308.
33. Both *Lumen gentium* and Pope John Paul II's 1987 encyclical *Redemptoris Mater* connect Mary's maternity and mediation; however, they do so in a way that continually exemplifies a problem with high Mariology. Mary's maternity is elevated but then firmly and continually subordinated to Christ and aligned instead with the church. Mary's maternal mediation, in other words, is linked to humanity, while Christ's mediation is founded on Christ's divinity.
34. For two treatments of some of these themes of Christ as mother, see, for example, Caroline Walker Bynum, *Jesus as Mother: Studies in the Spirituality of the High Middle Ages* (Berkeley: University of California Press, 1982); Barbara Newman, *Sister of Wisdom: St. Hildegard's Theology of the Feminine* (Berkeley: University of California Press, 1987).
35. Drawing on the work of Hrdy (*Mothers and Others*), I treat this theme in Carnes, *Motherhood*.
36. The fact that women are still targets of misogyny in the very traditional role of mother reveals the depth of misogyny and the work yet to be done, even in affirming motherhood. In an editorial piece following the revelation of some sexist remarks by then–U.S. presidential candidate Michael Bloomberg, Elizabeth Bruenig writes, "Misogyny reserved specifically for mothers is a curious thing. Discussions about sexism these days usually involve the consequences women face for being insufficiently feminine—for transgressing their prescribed roles by being too loud, too

angry, too big, too strong, too much. But the great paradox of misogyny is that its object is womanhood itself—not traditional womanhood or nontraditional womanhood, but the very fact of being a woman. One can't dodge it by hewing to her place. Even in the archetypally feminine role of mother, women can find themselves the subjects of that old and storied hatred." Elizabeth Bruenig, "Michael Bloomberg and the Long History of Misogyny toward Mothers," *New York Times*, February 28, 2020, https://www.nytimes.com/2020/02/28/opinion/mike-bloomberg-women-discrimination.html?smid=url-share

37. Virginia Burrus criticizes Gregory of Nyssa for invoking his sister Macrina as a literary figure "marked by both a sublimated and maternalized fecundity and a radical transcendentalization of erotic passion via its transformation into an agapic love"—a "reflection," then, "of masculine erotics . . . initially displaced or masked via its feminized representation" (120). According to this critique, femininity is for Gregory a mask, a trope, a tool for the true subject, the man. Virginia Burrus, *Begotten Not Made: Conceiving Manhood in Late Antiquity* (Stanford, CA: Stanford, 2000). I think this argument overlooks the way such maternity is grounded ultimately in God—which destabilizes patriarchy's gendered order, even if Gregory does not overcome it.

38. Schüssler Fiorenza, *Jesus: Miriam's Child*, 181.

39. Luke 1:52–54 (NRSV).

40. Bingemer and Gebara, *Mary, Mother of God*, 136. The passage is translated differently and included in Romero's *The Violence of Love*, where it is identified as a homily from December 24, 1978: "The true homage that a Christian can make to Mary is, like her, to make the effort to incarnate God's life in the fluctuations of our fleeting history." Oscar Romero, *The Violence of Love*, trans. James R. Brockman, S.J. (Maryknoll, NY: Orbis, 2004), 128. http://www.romerotrust.org.uk/sites/default/files/violenceoflove.pdf. The original is found in Oscar Romero, *Homilías* (San Salvador: UCA Editores), Vol. 3, 96.

41. The canonization ceremony for Romero, which included Pope Paul VI and five other saints, was in Latin with readings in various vernacular languages, and video is available at the Vatican website. http://w2.vatican.va/content/francesco/en/events/event.dir.html/content/vaticanevents/en/2018/10/14/messa-ritocanonizzazione.html.

42. It is not *the* picture of God. The image of the invisible God is not made with wood and paint, after all. It is Christ, the only begotten Son of God. But *Our Lady, Mother of Ferguson* is *a* picture of God. Mary offers *a* picture of God. She shows us who God is and how God loves.

43. Elizabeth Johnson, *Truly Our Sister: A Theology of Mary in the Communion of Saints* (New York: Continuum, 2003); Elizabeth Johnson, "Author's Response," *Horizons* 31, no. 1 (Spring 2004): 181.

44. Johnson in her response declines the temptation to veto certain titles, claims, or images of Mary, taking care to leave the Marian titles in places and insist that some

will fade in importance, while others will be taken up and reinterpreted in fresh ways. In this way, her approach to Marian titles accords very much with the larger project of attunement that I am elaborating. It is, to put it in other terms, a type of Wittgensteinian iconoclasm.
45. Matthew 25:40 (NRSVUE).
46. For example, Gregory of Nyssa claims in a sermon on Matthew 25:31–46 that the poor "bear the countenance [*prosopon*] of the Savior." Gregory of Nyssa "On the Love of the Poor, 1: On Good Works," in Susan R. Holman, *The Hungry Are Dying: Beggars and Bishops in Roman Cappadocia* (New York: Oxford University Press, 2001), 195. For a more extensive discussion of the Cappadocian use of this trope, see Carnes, *Image and Presence*, 125–129.
47. It is also a way of, in the words of Shawn Copeland, "subvert[ing] the aesthetic taxonomy of the West, in which blackness is constructed as a deficient and negative signifier." Copeland goes on to name contesting the Western canon as one way of reordering the aesthetic, and I suggest that *Our Lady of Ferguson* exemplifies another, of aesthetically reordering canonical sources such as the *Virgin of the Sign*. M. Shawn Copeland, "Thinking Margin: The Womanist Movement as Critical Cognitive Praxis," in *Deeper Shades of Purple: Womanism in Religion and Society*, ed. Stacey M. Floyd-Thomas (New York: New York University Press, 2006), 231.
48. Hortense Spillers, "Mama's Baby, Papa's Maybe: An American Grammar Book," *Diacritics* 17, no. 2 (1987): 64–81.
49. The government-sponsored Moynihan report of 1976 describes the Black family's "deterioration," attributable, according to the report, to its matriarchal structure. The Moynihan report established the trope of the "absent Black father" that named a supposed moral inferiority of Black families and has had a damaging legacy in the racial policies and imagination of the United States.
50. Spillers, "Mama's Baby," 77.
51. Spillers, "Mama's Baby," 80.
52. Spillers, "Mama's Baby," 80.
53. Spillers, "Mama's Baby," 80–81. Spillers writes of the problematizing of gender of the Black mother that "places her . . . out of the traditional symbolics of female gender, and it is our task to make a place for this different social subject. In doing so, we are less interested in joining the ranks of gendered femaleness than gaining the *insurgent* ground as female social subject."
54. The term "insurrectionary potentials" is from Annie Menzel, who contrasts Frank B. Wilderson III's reading of Spillers—one that "effaces her accompanying gesture towards its insurgent possibilities"—with that of Fred Moten, who, according to Menzel, "broadly amplifies Spillers's gesture toward Black maternity's insurrectionary potentials." Annie Menzel, "Maternal Generativity in the Afterlife of Slavery," *Contemporary Political Theology* 17, no. 1 (2017): 112–113. Saidiya Hartman uses "fungibility" to describe the afterlives of slavery, which remain foundational for modern liberal society in America. Saidiya Hartman, *Scenes of Subjection: Terror,*

Slavery, and Self-Making in Nineteenth Century America (New York: Oxford University Press, 1997).

55. Copeland describes the terrible conditions of maternity under slavery, which "devalued motherhood and mother-love" and left mothers to rage and despair—and yet still labor, even at great cost to themselves. Copeland, *Enfleshing Freedom*, 48–49.

56. Saidiya Hartman, "The Belly of the World: A Note on Black Women's Labors," *Souls: A Critical Journey of Black Politics, Culture, and Society* 18, no. 1 (January–March 2016): 171.

57. Others make similar points. Zakiyyah Iman Jackson writes similarly of a new mode of being: "the black mater(nal) holds the potential to transform the terms of reality and feeling," and "if an essential feature of your existence is that the norm is not able to take hold, what mode of being becomes available, and what mode might you invent?" Zakiyyah Iman Jackson, "Sense of Things," *Catalyst: Feminism, Theory, Technoscience* 2, no. 2 (2016): 11. Shulman affirms both that slavery is a kind of "social death," and also Spillers's discernment of "opportunity hidden" in those conditions, and that "children inherit the chance to do gender and kinship otherwise." Shulman, "Theorizing Life against Death," 127.

58. The mother's labors are queer because they are, as Spillers puts it, "outside the traditional symbolics of female gender" ("Mama's Baby," 81) but also because they are expressive of an ambivalence that Sedgwick saw as central to the vitality of queer theory, a holding together of the paranoid and the reparative positions. Writing on Afro-pessimism's description of social death and Spillers's discernment of opportunity yet hidden within it, Schulman claims, "Sedgwick is often read in a 'paranoid' way, as if she posed an either-or between the paranoid and reparative positions, partly because at moments she herself does this splitting. But a truly 'reparative' view of paranoid theory or radical politics would have to value and sustain ambivalence, a tension between the hermeneutic of suspicion and quest for deep truth that characterizes 'critique,' and a generosity that seeks and welcomes possibility, in the form of unexpected changes, actions, attunements." Shulman, "Theorizing Life against Death," 127.

59. Jaroslav Pelikan makes this point in *Imago Dei: The Byzantine Apologia for Icons* (Princeton, NJ: Princeton University Press, 1990), 100. He also observes that the nimbus is "akin to the Buddhist art of India." In these ways, it is exemplary of the way Byzantine iconography was forged from non-Christian sources reimagined for Christian purposes.

60. In the way *Our Lady, Mother of Ferguson* holds tragedy together with promise, the image answers to the icon anxieties of those such as Ian McFarland, who worries about the way icons "depict the glorified destiny of the material order under the triumphant lordship of Christ"—in other words, in the way he sees them offering an overrealized eschatology inappropriate for creatures who live within the travails of history. While I don't think his critique is right about the intention of icons, I do

believe a virtue of *Our Lady, Mother of Ferguson* is that it dramatizes unmistakably our creaturely location within history, connecting that history with the eschatological hope while clarifying that this hope is one for which we yet wait. Ian A. McFarland, *The Divine Image: Envisioning the Invisible God* (Minneapolis: Fortress, 2005), 31.

61. Hartman, "The Belly of the World," 171.
62. The Russian version of the Oranta icon, Znamenie, has a fascinating resonance with *Our Lady of Ferguson*. In the twelfth century, as the Russian city of Novgorod was under assault, the people brought the icon to the city walls, where it was pierced with an arrow. Mary turned her face to the city and shed tears, as the Oranta suffered with the suffering people. This sign of Mary's co-suffering was for the bishop of Novgorod cause for hope. The story continues in a manner unlike *Our Lady of Ferguson*: "The tears dropped on the phelonion of Bishop John of Novgorod, who exclaimed: 'O wonder of wonders! How can tears be streaming from dry wood! O Queen! You are giving us a sign that you are entreating your Son that the city be spared.' Inspired by the wonderful sign, the people of Novgorod repelled the attacks of the Suzdal forces." "The Theotokos 'of the Sign': The Meaning of the Image and Its Name," *The Catalogue of Good Deeds*, December 10, 2018, https://blog.obitel-minsk.com/2018/12/the-theotokos-of-sign-meaning-of-image.html.
63. Birnbaum suggests the subversive political implications of many Black Madonnas, which embodied an "implicit liberation theology" and were associated with "universal salvation," "distributive justice," and "a politics of resistance." She also points out that the earliest-known Madonna is brown, quoting Georges Gharib, that "hers is a rich cocoa color that has withstood the centuries. Her skin, deliberately painted so much darker than that of the other women painted on these walls, gives pause for thought. The first Virgin Mary is a brown Virgin Mary." Birnbaum, *Black Madonnas*, 58, 33; quoting Georges Gharib, *Le icone mariane: Storia e culto* (Rome: Città Editrice, 1987), 19.
64. I am indebted here, as the notes make clear, to Rowan Williams's book *Looking East in Winter* for drawing my attention to Mother Maria's Mariology. Rowan Williams, *Looking East in Winter: Contemporary Thought and the Eastern Christian Tradition* (New York: Bloomsbury Continuum, 2021).
65. Skobtsova's interpretation of the cross and the sword also connects the suffering of the earth into maternal co-suffering and the commandment of neighbor love. She writes, "The earth of Golgotha with the Cross set up on it, piercing it, the earth of the Golgotha red with blood—is it not a mother's heart pierced by a sword? The Cross of Golgotha, like a sword, pierces the soul of the Mother-earth." Maria Skobtsova, *Essential Writings*, translated by Richard Pevear and Larissa Volokhonsky (Maryknoll, NY: Orbis, 2003), 67.
66. R. Williams, *Looking East*, 233.
67. R. Williams, *Looking East*, 233.
68. R. Williams, *Looking East*, 234.

69. Skobtsova, *Essential Writings*, 71.
70. R. Williams, *Looking East*, 221.
71. The motherly relation is not one of pride or superiority, nor is it a pious exercise in virtue, but simply "a humble and obedient striving to participate in another's Golgotha." Skobtsova, *Essential Writings*, 71. Sin is the refusal of this exposure by closing oneself off from the pain of another and thereby denying Christ. R. Williams, *Looking East*, 221.
72. Skobtsova, *Essential Writings*, 71. Skobtsova writes, "But insofar as we must strive to follow her path, and as her image is the image of our human soul, so we must also perceive God and Son in every man. God, because he is the image and likeness of God; the Son, because as it gives birth to Christ within itself, the human soul thereby adopts the whole Body of Christ for itself, the whole of Godmanhood, and every man individually."
73. This story is told in Jim Forest, "Introduction: Mother Maria of Paris," in Mother Maria Skobtsova, *Essential Writings*, translated by Richard Pevear and Larissa Volokhonsky (Maryknoll, NY: Orbis, 2003), 13–43.
74. Schüssler Fiorenza, "Mariology," 212.
75. Copeland, "Thinking Margin," 230.
76. In making an argument for attunement, I do not argue that all images are equal or even helpful or that all the images produced by popular piety should be venerated and carried forward. Images of Mary have helped solidify projects of nationalism, imperialism, and racism, after all, and in these ways, they betray Mary's own song, the Magnificat. They are deployed to crush the ones who bear Christ's face. But Mary, we know, does not oppose Christ; she bears Christ's sufferings in the way she bore his fetal body. She remained with the pierced body of Christ on the cross, the sword piercing her own heart also.
77. In his book on the Spirit, Simeon Zahl argues that pneumatologies need to keep in view that sanctification is made visible in a life and that visibility is the work of the Spirit. I wonder if the waning of Mariology might have contributed to our difficulties in picturing sanctification and whether the recovery of Mariology might be important to the recovery of a robust pneumatology. Simeon Zahl, *The Holy Spirit and Christian Experience* (Oxford: Oxford University Press, 2020).
78. Lee, *Black Madonnas*, 121–125.
79. Gaston Bachelard, *The Poetics of Space: The Classic Look at How We Experience Intimate Places*, trans. Maria Jolas (Boston: Beacon, 1994), xxiii.
80. My pneumatological descriptions are indebted to Eugene Rogers, *After the Spirit: A Constructive Pneumatology from Resources outside the Modern West* (Grand Rapids, MI: Eerdmans, 2005).

Acknowledgments

PIECES AND PROTO-PIECES of this book have been presented at various venues, where I received feedback both helpful and encouraging. In fall 2019, I presented an early version of what would become chapter 1 at the University of Chicago Divinity School. I workshopped a more developed draft of that chapter the following spring at an online graduate colloquium at St Andrews hosted by T. J. Lang. At Marquette University in spring 2021, I delivered the Annual Theotokos Lecture, which became the basis for chapter 4. And in summer 2021, I gave a presentation at the European Academy of Religion drawing from several chapters.

As I developed this book, I had the good fortune to speak to pioneers and pivotal figures in the fields of feminist theology and gender studies in Christianity. I am so grateful for the interviews and conversations with Tina Beattie, Shawn Copeland, Ivone Gebara, Mary E. Hunt, Margaret Miles, and Janet Martin Soskice. Their wisdom and generosity have made this a better book and their examples have made me a better scholar.

Other conversations sparked, quickened, or nourished the argument of this book. A few among the many include an early exchange with Kristen Pond on literary theory and religion; a graduate colloquium convened by Jonathan Tran on Rita Felski's *The Limits of Critique*; and *Political Theology*'s conversation on Felski's *Hooked*. A particularly important turning point was Andrew Davison and Matthew Fell's invitation to join them in a reading group on affordances. Additionally, the many conversations, podcasts, and presentation I did in the wake of my book *Motherhood* clarified what I was doing in that project and helped to generate this one.

Some individuals read whole drafts of *Attunement* and gave feedback— an immense gift to me. Among them, I thank the students in my Future of

Feminist Theology graduate seminar, especially Daniel Crouch, Katherine Ellis, Zen Hess, and Wemimo Jaiyesemi, who workshopped a draft of this book after the semester ended. I'd also like to thank Matthew Whelan, Lauren Winner, Jonathan Tran, and Alda Bathrop-Lewis, who offered both discerning advice and friendly support. Particular thanks go to Thomas Breedlove, my research assistant at the beginning of the writing process; Katherine Ellis, my research assistant through revisions and edits on more mature drafts; and Andrew Whitworth, who assisted with the final stages of production.

I want to express gratitude as well to Mark Doox, whose luminous, dense, and provoking image *Our Lady, Mother of Ferguson and All Those Killed by Gun Violence* draws me to it again and again. I am so grateful that he created the image and so honored that he granted permission to use it as the cover.

Then there are my deepest debts—to my family, particularly and as always, Matthew. And also to my teachers and students, to whom this book is dedicated. I think especially of two of my earliest mentors, Kimerer Lamothe and Sarah Coakley. Kimerer guided me into new ways of reflecting on embodied life, modeled for me a scholarly life of joy and vitality, and advised me into a class on feminist theology at a key moment in my undergraduate life. The class she pointed me to was Professor Coakley's. Sarah Coakley's feminist theology course introduced me to academic theology and it marked me in ways I cannot fully identify, setting my initial intellectual grooves in theology and establishing my now-decades-long interests in aesthetics, feminist theory, and early Christianity. As for my students, who feature at various points in chapter 2, this volume emerged through years of conversations with them, particularly in my feminist theology class. The vulnerability, creativity, and conviction they have brought to theology over the years challenges me to do the same.

Works Cited

Althaus-Reid, Marcella. *From Feminist Theology to Indecent Theology: Readings on Poverty, Sexual Identity, and God*. London: SCM, 2004.

Anderson, Amanda, Rita Felski, and Toril Moi. *Character: Three Inquiries in Literary Studies*. Chicago: University of Chicago Press, 2019.

Angela of Foligno. *Complete Works*. Translated by Paul Lachance. New York: Paulist, 1993.

Augustine. *Confessions*. Translated by Henry Chadwick. New York: Oxford University Press, 1992.

Azzarello, Robert. *Queer Environmentality: Ecology, Evolution, and Sexuality in American Literature*. New York: Routledge, 2016.

Bachelard, Gaston. *The Poetics of Space: The Classic Look at How We Experience Intimate Places*. Translated by Maria Jolas. Boston: Beacon, 1994.

Bacon, Hannah. *Feminist Theology and Contemporary Dieting Culture: Sin, Salvation, and Women's Weight Loss Narratives*. London: T&T Clark, 2019.

Barnard, Mary. *Sappho: A New Translation*. Oakland: University of California Press, 2019.

Beattie, Tina. *The Good Priest*. Kibworth Beauchamp: Troubadour Publishing, 2019.

Beattie, Tina. *The Last Supper According to Martha and Mary*. New York: Crossroad, 2001.

Biale, David. "The God with Breasts: El Shaddai in the Bible." *History of Religions* 21, no. 3 (February 1982): 248.

Birgitta. *Revelaciones Lib. VI*. Edited by Birger Bergh. Stockhom: Almqvist & Wiksell, 1991.

Birnbaum, Lucia Chiavola. *Black Madonnas: Feminism, Religion, and Politics in Italy*. Boston: Northeastern University Press, 1993.

Bolz-Weber, Nadia. *Shameless: A Case for Not Feeling Bad about Feeling Good (about Sex)*. New York: Convergent Books, 2019.

Børresen, Kari Elisabeth. "Challenging Augustine in Feminist Theology and Gender Studies." In *The Oxford Guide to the Historical Reception of Augustine*, edited by Karla Pollman and Willemien Otten, Volume 1, 135–141. Oxford: Oxford University Press, 2013.

Børresen, Kari Elisabeth. *Subordination and Equivalence: The Nature and Role of Woman in Augustine and Thomas Aquinas*. Translated by Charles H. Talbot. Washington, DC: University Press of America, 1981.

Boyce Davies, Carol. *Black Women, Writing and Identity: Migrations of the Subject*. New York: Routledge, 1994.

Brekus, Catherine. *Strangers and Pilgrims: Female Preaching in America, 1740–1845*. Chapel Hill, NC: University of North Carolina Press, 1998.

Brown, David, and Gavin Hopps. *The Extravagance of Music*. New York: Palgrave MacMillan, 2018.

Brown, Peter. *The Body and Society: Men, Women, and Sexual Renunciation in Early Christianity*. New York: Columbia University Press, 1988.

Bruenig, Elizabeth. "Michael Bloomberg and the Long History of Misogyny toward Mothers." *New York Times*, February 28, 2020. https://www.nytimes.com/2020/02/28/opinion/mike-bloomberg-women-discrimination.html?smid=url-share.

Burrus, Virginia. *Begotten Not Made: Conceiving Manhood in Late Antiquity*. Stanford, CA: Stanford University Press, 2000.

Butler, Judith. *Gender Trouble: Feminism and the Subversion of Identity*. London: Routledge, 1999 [1990].

Bynum, Carolyn Walker. *Fragmentation and Redemption: Essays on Gender and the Human Body in Medieval Religion*. New York: Zone Books, 1992.

Bynum, Caroline Walker. *Jesus as Mother: Studies in the Spirituality of the High Middle Ages*. Berkeley: University of California Press, 1982.

Cannon, Katie G. *Katie's Canon: Womanism and the Soul of the Black Community, Revised and Expanded 25th Anniversary Edition*. Minneapolis: Fortress, 2021.

Cannon, Katie, and the Mud Flower Collective. *God's Fierce Whimsy*. New York: Pilgrim, 1985.

Carlson, Mary. "Making the Invisible Visible: Inviting Persons with Disability into Life with the Church." *Horizons* 45 (2018): 46–73.

Carnes, Natalie. *Beauty: A Theological Engagement with Gregory of Nyssa*. Eugene, OR: Cascade, 2014.

Carnes, Natalie. "Gender and Ecclesiology." In *T&T Clark Handbook of Ecclesiology*, edited by Kimlyn J. Bender and D. Stephen Long, 375–390. New York: Bloomsbury, 2020.

Carnes, Natalie. *Image and Presence: A Christological Reflection on Iconoclasm and Iconophilia*. Stanford, CA: Stanford University Press, 2017.

Carnes, Natalie. *Motherhood: A Confession*. Stanford, CA: Stanford University Press, 2020.

Cavell, Stanley. "Being Odd, Getting Even: Threats to Individuality." *Salmagundi* 67 (Summer 1985): 97–128.

Cavell, Stanley. "Excursus on Wittgenstein's Vision of Language." In Stanley Cavell, *Claim of Reason: Wittgenstein, Morality, Skepticism, and Tragedy*, 168–190. New York: Oxford University Press, 1979.

Cavell, Stanley. *Little Did I Know: Excerpts from Memory*. Stanford: Stanford University Press, 2010.

Cavell, Stanley. "Philosophy and the Arrogation of Philosophy." In Stanley Cavell, *A Pitch of Philosophy: Autobiographical Exercises*, 1–52. Cambridge, MA: Harvard University Press.

Chemero, Anthony. "An Outline of a Theory of Affordances." *Ecological Psychology* 15, no. 2 (2003): 181–195.

Chopp, Rebecca. "Poetics of Testimony." In *Converging on Culture: Theologians in Dialogue with Cultural Analysis and Criticism*, edited by Delwin Brown, Sheila Greeve Davaney, and Kathryn Tanner, 56–70. New York: Oxford University Press, 2001.

Citton, Yves. "Fictional Attachments and Literary Weavings in the Age of the Anthropocene." *New Literary History* 47 (2021): 309–329.

Clare, John. "The Yellowhammer's Nest." In *John Clare: Major Works*, edited by Eric Robinson and David Powell, 230. New York: Oxford University Press, 2004.

Clark, Elizabeth. "The Lady Vanishes: Dilemmas of a Feminist Historian after the 'Linguistic Turn.'" *Church History* 67, no. 1 (March 1998): 1–31.

Clark, Elizabeth. *The Origenist Controversy: The Cultural Construction of an Early Christian Debate*. Princeton, NJ: Princeton University Press, 1992.

Coakley, John. "A Shared Endeavor? Guibert of Gembloux on Hildegard of Bingen." In John Coakley, *Women, Men, and Spiritual Power: Female Saints and Their Male Collaborators*, 45–67. New York: Columbia University Press, 2012.

Coakley, Sarah. *God, Sexuality, and the Self: An Essay 'On the Trinity.'* Cambridge: Cambridge University Press, 2013.

Coleman, Monica. "Introduction." In *Ain't I a Womanist, Too? Third-Wave Womanist Religious Thought*, edited by Monica Coleman, 17–27. Minneapolis: Fortress, 2013.

Collins-Hughes, Laura. "A Potential Disaster in Any Language." *New York Times*, September 25, 2014. https://www.nytimes.com/2014/09/26/theater/gaia-global-circus-at-the-kitchen.html.

Congregation for the Doctrine of the Faith. *Inter Insigniores*, 1976, 5.12. https://www.vatican.va/roman_curia/congregations/cfaith/documents/rc_con_cfaith_doc_19761015_inter-insigniores_en.html.

Copeland, M. Shawn. *Enfleshing Freedom: Body, Race, and Being*. Minneapolis: Fortress, 2010.

Copeland, M. Shawn. *Knowing Christ Crucified: The Witness of African American Religious Experience*. Maryknoll, NY: Orbis, 2018.

Copeland, M. Shawn. "Thinking Margin: The Womanist Movement as Critical Cognitive Praxis." In *Deeper Shades of Purple: Womanism in Religion and Society*, edited by Stacey M. Floyd-Thomas, 226–235. New York: New York University Press, 2006.

Crary, Alice. "The Methodological Is Political." *Radical Philosophy* 202 (June 2018): 47–60.

Daly, Mary. *Beyond God the Father: Toward a Philosophy of Women's Liberation*. Boston: Beacon, 1973.

Daly, Mary. *The Church and the Second Sex*. Boston: Beacon Press, 1985.
Daly, Mary. *Gyn/Ecology: The Metaethics of Radical Feminism*. Boston: Beacon, 1978.
Daly, Mary. *Outercourse: The Be-Dazzling Voyage*. San Francisco: Harper Collins, 1992.
Daly, Mary and Jane Caputi. *Webster's First New Intergalactic Wickedary of the English Language: Conjured by Mary Daly in Cahoots with Jane Caputi*. Boston: Beacon Press, 1987.
Darwin, Charles. *The Formation of Vegetable Mould through the Action of Worms, with Observations on Their Habits*. London: John Murray, 1881.
Davison, Andrew. "Home Is Where the Eternal Is." *Church Times*, May 29, 2020. https://www.churchtimes.co.uk/articles/2020/29-may/features/features/home-is-where-the-eternal-is.
Dederer, Claire. *Monsters: A Fan's Dilemma*. New York: Knopf, 2023.
Dederer, Claire. "What Do We Do with the Art of Monstrous Men?" *Paris Review*, November 20, 2017. https://www.theparisreview.org/blog/2017/11/20/art-monstrous-men/.
DiMiele, Amanda. "Feminist Storytelling and the Problem of White Feminism." *Literature and Theology* 35, no. 2 (June 2021): 111–127.
Douglas, Kelly Brown. *Black Bodies and the Black Church: A Blues Slant*. New York: Palgrave Macmillan, 2012.
Douglas, Kelly Brown. *Stand Your Ground: Black Bodies and the Justice of God*. Maryknoll: Orbis Books, 2014.
Farley, Margaret A. "Sources for Inequality in the History of Christian Thought." *Journal of Religion* 56, no. 2 (April 1976): 162–176.
Felski, Rita. *Hooked: Art and Attachment*. Chicago: University of Chicago Press, 2021.
Fessenden, Tracy. "'Woman' and the 'Primitive' in Paul Tillich's Life and Thought: Some Implications for the Study of Religion." *Journal of Feminist Studies in Religion* 14, no. 2 (1998): 45–76.
Fleckenstein, Kirstie S. "Cybernetics, Ethos, and Ethics." *JAC* 25, no. 2 (2005): 323–346.
Fleissner, Jennifer. "Romancing the Real: Bruno Latour, Ian McEwan, and Postcritical Monism." In *Critique and Postcritique*, edited by Elizabeth S. Anker and Rita Felski, 99–126. Durham, NC: Duke University Press, 2017.
Flores, Nichole. *The Aesthetics of Solidarity: Our Lady of Guadalupe and American Democracy*. Washington, DC: Georgetown University Press, 2021.
Forest, Jim. "Introduction: Mother Maria of Paris." In Mother Maria Skobtsova, *Essential Writings*, translated by Richard Pevear and Larissa Volokhonsky, 13–43. Maryknoll, NY: Orbis, 2003.
Fritz, Peter Joseph. "Karl Rahner's Marian 'Minimalism.'" In *Mary on the Eve of the Second Vatican Council*, edited by John Cavadini and Danielle Peters, 156–178. Notre Dame, IN: University of Notre Dame Press, 2017.
Fulkerson, Mary McClintock. "The *Imago Dei* and a Reformed Logic for Feminist/Womanist Critique." In *Feminist and Womanist Essays in Reformed Dogmatics*, edited by Serene Jones and Amy Pauw, 95–106. Louisville, KY: Westminster John Knox, 2006.

Gafney, Wilda. *Womanist Midrash: A Reintroduction to the Woman of the Torah and the Throne*. Louisville, KY: Westminster John Knox, 2017.

Gebara, Ivone. "Feminism and Religious Identity." Pat Reif Memorial Lecture, Claremont College, March 2009. https://www.womensordination.org/2008/08/feminism-and-religious-identity-by-ivone-gebara/.

Gebara, Ivone, and Maria Clara Lucchetti Bingemer. *Mary, Mother of God, Mother of the Poor*. Maryknoll, NY: Orbis, 1989.

Gharib, Georges. *Le icone mariane: Storia e culto*. Rome: Città Editrice, 1987.

Ghodsee, Kristen R. *Everyday Utopia: What 2,000 Years of Wild Experiments Can Teach Us about the Good Life*. New York: Simon & Schuster, 2023.

Gibson, Eleanor J. "Perceptual Learning and the Theory of Word Perception." In Eleanor J. Gibson, *An Odyssey in Learning and Perception*, 453–470. Cambridge, MA: MIT Press, 1991.

Gibson, Eleanor J. "Reading in Retrospect: Perception, Cognition or Both?" In Eleanor J. Gibson, *An Odyssey in Learning and Perception*, 493–495. Cambridge, MA: MIT Press, 1991.

Gibson, Gail McMurray. *The Theater of Devotion: East Anglian Drama and Society in the Late Middle Ages*. Chicago: University of Chicago Press, 1989.

Gibson, James J. "A Theory of Affordances." In James J. Gibson, *An Ecological Approach to Visual Perception*, 127–143. Boston: Houghton Mifflin, 1979.

Gilbert, Olive. *Sojourner Truth: Narrative and Book of Life*. 1850 and 1875; reprint ed. Chicago: Johnson, 1970.

Grant, Jacquelyn. *White Women's Christ, Black Women's Jesus: Feminist Christology and Womanist Response*. Atlanta: Scholars, 1989.

Gregory of Nyssa. *Life of Macrina*. Translated by Kevin Corrigan. Toronto: Peregrina, 1998.

Gregory of Nyssa. *Life of Moses*. Translated by Abraham Malherbe and Everett Ferguson. New York: Paulist Press, 1978.

Gregory of Nyssa. "On the Love of the Poor, 1: On Good Works." In Susan R. Holman, *The Hungry Are Dying: Beggars and Bishops in Roman Cappadocia*, 195–199. New York: Oxford University Press, 2001.

Halperin, David. *One Hundred Years of Homosexuality and Other Essays on Greek Love*. New York: Routledge, 1990.

Halsall, Francis. "Actor-Network Aesthetics: The Conceptual Rhymes of Bruno Latour and Contemporary Art." *New Literary History* 47, nos. 2–3 (Spring and Summer 2016): 439–461.

Halsall, Francis. "An Aesthetics of Proof: A Conversation between Bruno Latour and Francis Halsall on Art and Inquiry." *Environment and Planning D: Society and Space* 30, no. 6 (2012): 963–970.

Hanson, Ellis. "The Languorous Critic." *New Literary History* 43, no. 3 (Summer 2012): 547–564.

Haraway, Donna J. *Modest_Witness@Second_Millennium. FemaleMan©_Meets_OncoMouse™: Feminism and Technoscience*. London: Routledge, 1997.

Haraway, Donna. "Situated Knowledges: The Science Question in Feminism and the Privilege of Partial Perspectives." *Feminist Studies* 14, no. 3 (Autumn 1988): 575–599. https://www.jstor.org/stable/3178066.

Harman, Graham. "De-Modernizing the Humanities." *New Literary History* 47, nos. 2–3 (Summer 2016): 249–274.

Hartman, Saidiya. "The Belly of the World: A Note on Black Women's Labors." *Souls: A Critical Journey of Black Politics, Culture, and Society* 18, no. 1 (January–March 2016): 166–173.

Hartman, Saidiya. *Scenes of Subjection: Terror, Slavery, and Self-Making in Nineteenth Century America*. New York: Oxford University Press, 1997.

Harvey, Susan Ashbrook. *Scenting Salvation: Ancient Christianity and the Olfactory Imagination*. Berkeley: University of California Press, 2006.

Harvey, Susan Ashbrook, and Margaret Mullett, eds. *Knowing Bodies, Passionate Souls: Sense Perceptions in Byzantium*. Washington, DC: Dumbarton Oaks, 2017.

Heft, Harry. "Affordances and the Perception of Landscape: An Inquiry into Environmental Perception and Aesthetics." In *Innovative Approaches to Researching Landscape and Health*, edited by Catharine Ward Thompson, Peter Aspinall, and Simon Bell, 9–32. New York: Routledge, 2010.

Heras-Escribano, Manuel. "The Evolutionary Role of Affordances: Ecological Psychology, Niche Construction, and Natural Selection." *Biology and Philosophy* 35, no. 2 (2020): 1–27.

Hildegard of Bingen, *Hildegard: Selected Writings*. Translated by Mark Atherton. New York: Penguin, 2001.

Hildegard of Bingen. *Scivias*. Translated by Columba Hart and Jane Bishop. New York: Paulist, 1990.

Hrdy, Sarah Blaffer. *Mothers and Others: The Evolutionary Origins of Mutual Understanding*. Cambridge, MA: Belknap, 2009.

Hunt, Mary E. "Feminist Theologians Bring Wisdom to Fiction." *National Catholic Reporter*, May 29, 2019. https://www.ncronline.org/news/opinion/feminist-theologians-bring-wisdom-fiction.

Jackson, Zakiyyah Iman. "Sense of Things." *Catalyst: Feminism, Theory, Technoscience* 2, no. 2 (2016): 1–48.

Jenkins, Jack. "Second 'George Floyd' Pietà Stolen from Catholic University." *National Catholic Reporter*, December 17, 2021. https://www.ncronline.org/news/people/second-george-floyd-piet-stolen-catholic-university.

John Paul II. *Redemptoris Mater: Encyclical on the Blessed Virgin Mary in the Life of the Pilgrim Church*. March 25, 1987. https://www.vatican.va/content/john-paul-ii/en/encyclicals/documents/hf_jp-ii_enc_25031987_redemptoris-mater.html.

Johnson, Elizabeth. *Creation and the Cross: The Mercy of God for a Planet in Peril*. Maryknoll: Orbis Books, 2018.

Johnson, Elizabeth. "Author's Response." *Horizons* 31, no. 1 (Spring 2004): 174–186.

Johnson, Elizabeth. *She Who Is: The Mystery of God in a Feminist Theological Discourse*. New York: Crossroad, 1992.

Johnson, Elizabeth. *Truly Our Sister: A Theology of Mary in the Communion of Saints.* New York: Continuum, 2003.

Jones, Clive G., and Moshe Shachak. "Fertilization of the Desert Soil by Rock-Eating Snails." *Nature* 346 (1990): 839–841.

Jones, Serene. "Glorious Creation, Beautiful Law." In *Feminist and Womanist Essays in Reformed Dogmatics*, edited by Serene Jones and Amy Pauw, 19–39. Louisville, KY: Westminster John Knox, 2006.

Jones, Serene. *Trauma and Grace: Theology in a Ruptured World.* Louisville: Westminster John Knox, 2009.

Juster, Susan. "'Neither Male nor Female': Jemima Wilkinson and the Politics of Gender in Post-Revolutionary America." In *Possible Pasts: Becoming Colonial in Early America*, edited by Robert Blair St. George, 357–379. Ithaca, NY: Cornell University Press, 2000.

Kang, Namsoon. *Diasporic Feminist Theology: Asia and Theopolitical Imagination.* Minneapolis: Fortress Press 2014.

Kendall, Mikki. *Hood Feminism: Notes from the Women That a Movement Forgot.* New York: Viking, 2020.

Khost, Peter. *Rhetor Response: A Theory and Practice of Literary Affordance.* Logan: Utah State University Press, 2018.

King, Ewan. "The Virgin and the Visual Artist as Theologian: Examining Two Marian Images by David Jones." In *Transforming Christian Thought in the Visual Arts: Theology, Aesthetics, and Practice*, edited by Sheona Beaumont and Madeleine Emerald Thiele, 80–96. New York: Routledge, 2021.

Kierkegaard, Søren. *Fear and Trembling: And Sickness Unto Death.* Translated by Walter Lowrie. Princeton, NJ: Princeton University Press, 1974.

Kitzinger, Sheila. "Commentary." In *Breastfeeding: Biocultural Perspectives*, edited by Patricia Stuart-Macadam and Katherine A. Dettwyler, 385–394. New York: De Gruyter, 1995.

Knight, Douglas. *The Eschatological Economy: Time and the Hospitality of God.* Grand Rapids, MI: Eerdmans, 2006.

Kompridis, Nikolas, ed. *The Aesthetic Turn in Political Thought.* New York: Bloomsbury Academic, 2014.

Kompridis, Nikolas. *Critique and Disclosure: Critical Theory between Past and Future.* Cambridge, MA: MIT Press, 2011.

Krause, Nicholas Norman. *Political Theology and the Conflicts of Democracy.* PhD diss., Baylor University, 2021.

Kwok, Pui-lan. *Postcolonial Imagination and Feminist Theory.* Louisville, KY: Westminster John Knox, 2005.

Larson, Scott. "'Indescribable Being': Theological Performances of Genderlessness in the Society of the Publick Universal Friend, 1776–1819." *Early American Studies* 12, no. 3 (2014): 576–600.

Latour, Bruno. *An Inquiry into Modes of Existence: An Anthropology of the Moderns.* Cambridge, MA: Harvard University Press, 2013.

Latour, Bruno. *Pandora's Hope: Essays on the Reality of Science Studies.* Cambridge, MA: Harvard University Press, 1999.

Latour, Bruno. *Reassembling the Social: An Introduction to Actor-Network-Theory.* Oxford: Oxford University Press, 2005.

Latour, Bruno. Keynote Lecture for "SEEING / SOUNDING / SENSING," a 2014 Symposium by the Center for Art, Science and Technology and MIT. September 26, 2014. https://arts.mit.edu/cast/symposia/seeing-sounding-sensing/participants/bruno-latour/

Latour, Bruno. *We Have Never Been Modern.* Cambridge, MA: Harvard University Press, 1993.

Latour, Bruno. "Why Has Critique Run Out of Steam? From Matters of Fact to Matters of Concern." *Critical Inquiry* 30, no. 2 (Winter 2004): 225–248.

Latour, Bruno. "Why SPEAP?" http://blogs.sciences-po.fr/speap-eng/20-2/why-speap/.

Lebzyak, Victoria. "Perceiving the Divine: Alexander Schmemann and the Sacramental Affordances of the Liturgy." *Modern Theology* 34, no. 4 (October 2018): 519–543.

Lee, Courtney Hall. *Black Madonna: A Womanist Look at Mary of Nazareth.* Eugene, OR: Cascade, 2017.

Lee, Jarena. *Religious Experience and Journal of Mrs. Jarena Lee, Giving an Account of Her Call to Preach the Gospel.* Philadelphia: Jarena Lee, 1849. http://www.umilta.net/jarena.html.

Levine, Caroline. *Forms: Whole, Rhythm, Networks.* Princeton, NJ: Princeton University Press, 2015.

Liming, Sheila. "Fighting Words." *Los Angeles Review of Books*, December 4, 2020. https://www.lareviewofbooks.org/article/fighting-words/.

Love, Heather. "The Temptations: Donna Haraway, Feminist Objectivity, and the Problem of Critique." In *Critique and Postcritique*, edited by Rita Felski and Elizabeth Anker, 50–72. Durham, NC: Duke University Press, 2017.

Lutz, Catherine. "The Gender of Theory." In *Women Writing Culture/Culture Writing Women*, edited by Ruth Behar and Deborah Gordon, 249–266. Berkeley: University of California Press, 1995.

Lyons, Martyn. "Celestial Letters: Morals and Magic in Nineteenth-Century France." *French History* 27, no. 4 (December 2013): 496–514. https://doi.org/10.1093/fh/crt047.

Marrati, Paola. "Childhood and Philosophy." *MLN* 126, no. 5 (December 2011): 954–961.

McDougall, Joy Ann. "Keeping Feminist Faith with Christian Traditions: A Look at Christian Feminist Theology Today." *Modern Theology* 24, no. 1 (January 2008): 103–124.

McDuffie, Felecia. "Augustine's Rhetoric of Femininity in the *Confessions*: Woman as Mother, Woman as Other." In *Feminist Interpretations of Augustine*, edited by Judith Chelius Stark, 97–118. University Park: Pennsylvania State University Press, 2007.

McFague, Sallie. *Metaphorical Theology: Models of God in Religious Language.* Philadelphia: Fortress Press, 1982.

McFarland, Ian A. *The Divine Image: Envisioning the Invisible God*. Minneapolis: Fortress, 2005.

Menzel, Annie. "Maternal Generativity in the Afterlife of Slavery." *Contemporary Political Theology* 17, no. 1 (2017): 112–118.

Messer-Davidow, Ellen. *Disciplining Feminism: From Social Activism to Academic Discourse*. Durham, NC: Duke University Press, 2002.

Miles, Margaret. *Augustine and the Fundamentalist's Daughter*. Eugene, OR: Cascade Books, 2011.

Miles, Margaret. *A Complex Delight: The Secularization of the Breast, 1350–1750*. Berkeley: University of California Press, 2008.

Miles, Margaret. *Image as Insight: Visual Understanding in Western Christianity and Secular Culture*. Boston: Beacon, 1985.

Miles, Margaret. *On Memory, Marriage, Tears, and Meditation*. New York: Bloomsbury Academic, 2021.

Miles, Margaret. *The Word Made Flesh: A History of Christian Thought*. Malden: Blackwell, 2005.

Miller, Patricia Cox. *The Corporeal Imagination: Signifying the Holy in Late Antiquity*. Philadelphia: University of Pennsylvania Press, 2009.

Mitchell, Juliet. "Introduction." In *The Selected Melanie Klein*, edited by Juliet Mitchell, 9–32. New York: Free Press, 1987.

Moerer, Emily Ann. "Catherine of Siena and the Use of Images in the Creation of a Saint, 1347–1461." PhD diss., University of Virginia, 2003. https://doi.org/10.18130/V36P83.

Moi, Toril. "'Nothing Is Hidden': From Confusion to Clarity: or, Wittgenstein on Critique." In *Critique and Postcritique*, edited by Elizabeth S. Anker and Rita Felski, 31–49. Durham, NC: Duke University Press, 2017.

Moi, Toril. "Philosophy and Autobiography: How Stanley Cavell Welcomed Me into Philosophy." *ABC Religion and Ethics*, January 7, 2019. https://www.abc.net.au/religion/stanley-cavell-philosophy-and-autobiography/10696038.

Moi, Toril. *Revolution of the Ordinary: Literary Studies after Wittgenstein, Austin, and Cavell*. Chicago: University of Chicago Press, 2017.

Morales, Alejandro, and Oscar Fernando Rojas Pérez, "Marianismo." In *The Wiley Encyclopedia of Personality and Individual Differences: Models and Theories*, Vol. 1, edited by Bernardo J. Carducci, Christopher S. Nave, Jeffrey S. Mio, and Ronald E. Riggio, 247–251. New York: Wiley Blackwell, 2020.

Moten, Fred. "Blackness and Nothingness (Mysticism in the Flesh)." *South Atlantic Quarterly* 112, no. 4 (2013): 737–780.

Moyer, Paul B. *The Public Universal Friend: Jemima Wilkinson and Religious Enthusiasm in Revolutionary America*. Ithaca, NY: Cornell University Press, 2015.

Muers, Rachel. "The Ethics of Breastfeeding: A Feminist Theological Exploration." *Journal of Feminist Studies* 26, no. 1 (2010): 7–24.

Muers, Rachel. "Feminist Theology as Practice of the Future." *Feminist Theology* 16, no. 1 (September 2007): 110–127.

Navarro, Marysa. "Against Marianismo." In *Gender's Place: Feminist Anthropologies of Latin America*, edited by Rosario Montoya, Lessie Jo Frazier, and Janise Hurtig, 257–272. New York: Palgrave Macmillan, 2002.

Nelson, Maggie. *On Freedom: Four Songs of Care and Constraint*. Minneapolis: Graywolf, 2021.

Newman, Barbara. *From Virile Woman to Woman Christ: Studies in Medieval Religion and Literature*. Philadelphia: University of Pennsylvania Press, 1995.

Newman, Barbara. "Hildegard of Bingen: Visions and Validation." *Church History* 54, no. 2 (June 1985): 164–175.

Newman, Barbara. *Sister of Wisdom: St. Hildegard's Theology of the Feminine*. Berkeley: University of California Press, 1987.

Norman, Donald A. *The Design of Everyday Things*. New York: Doubleday, 1988.

O'Brien, Mary. *The Politics of Reproduction*. New York: Routledge, 1981.

Odling-Smee, John F., Kevin N. Laland, and Marcus W. Feldman. *Niche Construction: The Neglected Process in Evolution*. Princeton, NJ: Princeton University Press, 2003.

O'Donnell, Karen. *The Dark Womb: Re-Conceiving Theology through Reproductive Loss*. London: SCM Press, 2022.

O'Donnell, Karen, and Katie Cross, eds. *Feminist Trauma Theologies: Body Scripture and Church in Critical Perspective*. London: SCM Press, 2020.

Pandey, Shubham and Priyanshi Nagarkoti. "An Anthropological Analysis of the Invisibility of Dalits of India in the Environmental Discourse: A Tale of Subjugation, Alienation and Resistance." *Contemporary Voice of Dalit* 13, no. 2 (2021): 165–176.

Pelikan, Jaroslav. *Imago Dei: The Byzantine Apologia for Icons*. Princeton, NJ: Princeton University Press, 1990.

Pérez-Gil, María del Mar. "Undressing the Virgin Mary: Nudity and Gendered Art." *Feminist Theology* 25, no. 2 (January 2017): 208–221.

Pope, Barbara Corrado. "Immaculate and Powerful: The Marian Revival in the Nineteenth Century." In *Immaculate and Powerful: The Female in Sacred Image and Social Reality*, edited by Clarissa W. Atkinson, Constance H. Buchanan, and Margaret R. Miles, 173–201. Boston: Beacon, 1985.

Rahner, Karl. *Mary, Mother of the Lord: Theological Meditations*. Translated by W. J. O'Hara. New York: Herder and Herder, 1963.

Rancière, Jacques. *Le fil perdu* [*The Lost Thread*]. Paris: La Fabrique, 2014.

Rancière, Jacques. *Le spectateur émancipé*. Paris: La Fabrique, 2008.

Rankine, Claudia. "'The Condition of Black Life Is One of Mourning.'" *New York Times Magazine*, June 22, 2015. https://www.nytimes.com/2015/06/22/magazine/the-condition-of-black-life-is-one-of- mourning.html.

Raymond of Capua. *The Life of Catherine of Siena*. Translated by Conleth Kearns. Wilmington, DE: Glazier, 1980.

Reichel, Hanna. *After Method: Queer Grace, Conceptual Design, and the Possibility of Theology*. Louisville, KY: Westminster John Knox, 2023.

Reichel, Hanna. "Conceptual Design, Sin and the Affordances of Doctrine." *International Journal of Systematic Theology* 22, no. 4 (October 2020): 538–561.

Ricoeur, Paul. *Freud and Philosophy: An Essay on Interpretation*. Translated by Denis Savage. New Haven, CT: Yale University Press, 1970.

Rivera, Mayra. *Poetics of the Flesh*. Durham: Duke University Press, 2015.

Rogers, Eugene. *After the Spirit: A Constructive Pneumatology from Resources outside the Modern West*. Grand Rapids, MI: Eerdmans, 2005.

Romero, Oscar. *Homilías*. San Salvador: UCA Editores. http://www.romerotrust.org.uk/sites/default/files/violenceoflove.pdf.

Romero, Oscar. *The Violence of Love*. Translated by James R. Brockman, S.J. Maryknoll, NY: Orbis, 2004. http://www.romerotrust.org.uk/sites/default/files/violenceoflove.pdf.

Ruether, Rosemary Radford. *Sexism and God-Talk*. London: SCM Press, 1983.

Ruether, Rosemary Radford. "Virginal Feminism in the Fathers of the Church." In *Religion and Sexism: Images of Woman in the Jewish and Christian Traditions*, edited by Rosemary Radford Ruether, 150–183. New York: Simon & Schuster, 1974.

Ruether, Rosemary Radford. *Women and Redemption: A Theological History*. Minneapolis: Fortress, 1998.

Sahlin, Claire. "A Marvelous and Great Exultation of the Heart: Mystical Pregnancy and Marian Devotion in Bridget of Sweden's *Revelations*." In *Studies in Saint Birgitta and the Brigittine Order*, edited by James Hogg, Vol. 1, 108–109. New York: Edwin Mellen, 1993.

Saiving, Valerie. "The Human Situation: A Feminine View." In *Womanspirit Rising: A Feminist Reader in Religion*, edited by Judith Plaskow and Carol P. Christ, 25–42. San Francisco: Harper & Row, 1979.

San Roman, Magdalena, and Andreas Wagner. "An Enormous Potential for Niche Construction through Bacterial Cross-Feeding in a Homogeneous Environment." *PLOS Computational Biology* 14, no. 7 (2018): e1006340.

Scarsella, Hilary Jerome, Carolyn Holderread Heggen, Katie Graber, Anneli Loepp Thiessen, Sarah Kathleen Johnson, and Bradley Kauffman. "Show Strength: How to Respond When Worship Materials Are Implicated in Abuse." http://voicestogetherhymnal.org/wp-content/uploads/2021/01/Show-Strength.pdf.

Scarsella, Hilary Jerome, and Stephanie Krehbiel. "Sexual Violence: Christian Theological Legacies and Responsibilities." *Religion Compass* 13, no. 9 (September 2019): 1–13.

Schmemann, Alexander. "On Mariology in Orthodoxy." *Marian Library Studies* 2, no. 4 (1970): 25–32.

Schüssler Fiorenza, Elisabeth. *Bread Not Stone*. Boston: Beacon, 1985.

Schüssler Fiorenza, Elisabeth. "Breaking the Silence: Becoming Visible." In *The Power of Naming: A Concilium Reader in Critical Feminist Theology*, edited by Elisabeth Schüssler Fiorenza, 161–184. Maryknoll, NY: Orbis, 1998.

Schüssler Fiorenza, Elisabeth. "Feminist Theology as a Critical Theology of Liberation." *Theological Studies* 36, no. 4 (December 1975): 605–626.

Schüssler Fiorenza, Elisabeth. *Jesus: Miriam's Child, Sophia's Prophet: Critical Issues in Feminist Christology*. New York: Continuum, 1994.

Schüssler Fiorenza, Elisabeth. "Mariology, Gender Ideology, and the Discipleship of Equals." In Elizabeth Schüssler Fiorenza, *Transforming Vision: Explorations in Feminist The*logy*, 197–213. Minneapolis: Fortress, 2011.

Scott, A. O. "My Woody Allen Problem." *New York Times*, January 31, 2018. https://www.nytimes.com/2018/01/31/movies/woody-allen.html.

Sedgwick, Eve Kosofsky. *Novel Gazing: Queer Readings in Fiction*. Durham, NC: Duke University Press, 1997.

Sedgwick, Eve Kosofsky. "Paranoid Reading and Reparative Reading, or, You're So Paranoid, You Probably Think This Essay Is about You." In *Touching Feeling: Affect, Pedagogy, Performativity*, edited by Eve Kosofsky Sedgwick, 123–151. Durham, NC: Duke University Press, 2003.

Sedgwick, Eve Kosofsky. *Tendencies*. Durham, NC: Duke University Press, 1993.

Serpell, Namwali. *Seven Modes of Uncertainty*. Cambridge, MA: Harvard University Press, 2014.

Shachak, Moshe, Clive G. Jones, and Yigal Granot. "Herbivory in Rocks and the Weathering of a Desert." *Science* 236 (1987): 1098–1099.

Shieh, Sanford. "The Truth of Skepticism." In *Reading Cavell*, edited by Alice Crary and Sanford Shieh, 131–165. New York: Routledge, 2006.

Shulman, George. "Theorizing Life against Death." *Contemporary Political Theory* 17, no. 1 (February 2018): 118–128.

Silvas, Anna. *Jutta and Hildegard: The Biographical Sources*. University Park: Pennsylvania State University Press, 1998.

Simpson, James. *Under the Hammer: Iconoclasm in the Anglo-American Tradition*. New York: Oxford University Press, 2010.

Skobtsova, Mother Maria. *Essential Writings*. Translated by Richard Pevear and Larissa Volokhonsky. Maryknoll, NY: Orbis, 2003.

Smith, Ted A. *The End of Theological Education*. Grand Rapids, MI: Eerdmans, 2023.

Smith, Zadie. *On Beauty*. New York: Penguin, 2005.

Smith, Zadie. "Some Notes on Attunement." *New Yorker*, December 9, 2012. https://www.newyorker.com/magazine/2012/12/17/some-notes-on-attunement.

Soskice, Janet Martin. *The Kindness of God: Metaphor Gender and Religious Language*. Oxford: Oxford University Press, 2007.

Soskice, Janet Martin. *Metaphor and Religious Language*. Oxford: Clarendon Press, 1985.

Soskice, Janet Martin. *The Sisters of Sinai: How Two Lady Adventurers Discovered the Hidden Gospels*. New York: Alfred A. Knopf, 2009.

Sotgiu, Elisa. "Have Italian Scholars Figured Out the Identity of Elena Ferrante?" *Literary Hub*, March 31, 2021. https://lithub.com/have-italian-scholars-figured-out-the-identity-of-elena- ferrante/.

Spillers, Hortense. "Mama's Baby, Papa's Maybe: An American Grammar Book." *Diacritics* 17, no. 2 (1987): 64–81.

Stacey, Jackie. "Wishing Away Ambivalence." *Feminist Theory* 15, no. 1 (2014): 39–49.

Stark, Judith Chelius. "Introduction." In *Feminist Interpretations of Augustine*, edited by Judith Chelius Stark, 21–45. University Park: Pennsylvania State University Press, 2007.

Stevens, Evelyn P. "Machismo and Marianismo." *Society* 10 (September 1973): 57–63.

Stewart-Kroeker, Sarah. "'What Do We Do with the Art of Monstrous Men?': Betrayal and the Feminist Ethics of Aesthetic Involvement." *De Ethica* 6, no. 1 (2020): 51–74.

Suydam, Mary. "Beguine Textuality: Sacred Performances." In *Performance and Transformation: New Approaches to Late Medieval Spirituality*, edited by Mary A. Suydam and Joanna Ziegler, 169–210. Basingstoke, UK: Macmillan, 1999.

Tagliafelli, Lisa. "Lyrical Mysticism: The Writing and Reception of Catherine of Siena." PhD diss., City University of New York, 2017.

Tanner, Kathryn. "Social Theory Concerning the New Social Movements and the Practice of Feminist Theology." In *Horizons in Feminist Theology*, edited by Rebecca S. Chopp and Sheila Greeve Davaney, 179–197. Minneapolis: Fortress, 1997.

Tanner, Kathryn. *Theories of Culture: A New Agenda for Theology*. Minneapolis: Fortress, 1997.

Teresa, and Brian Kolodiejchuk. *Come Be My Light: The Private Writings of the Saint of Calcutta*. New York: Doubleday, 2007.

"The Theotokos 'of the Sign': The Meaning of the Image and Its Name." *The Catalogue of Good Deeds*, December 10, 2018. https://blog.obitel-minsk.com/2018/12/the-theotokos-of-sign-meaning-of-image.html.

Thistlethwaite, Susan Brooks. *Women's Bodies As Battlefield*. New York: Palgrave Macmillan, 2015.

Thomas of Celano. "The Remembrance of the Desire of a Soul by Thomas of Celano." In *Francis of Assisi, The Founder: Early Documents*, Vol. 2, edited by Regis J. Armstrong, J. A. Wayne Hellmann, and William J. Short, 233–393. New York: New City Press, 2000.

Tonstad, Linn Marie. "The Place, and Problems, of Truth." *Literature and Theology* 35, no. 1 (March 2021): 4–21.

Tonstad, Linn Marie. "(Un)wise Theologians: Systematic Theology in the University." *International Journal of Systematic Theology* 22, no. 4 (October 2020): 494–511.

Tonstad, Linn Marie. "Writing Theology." Paper presented at Christian Theology Senior Seminar Programme, University of Cambridge, February 10, 2021. https://www.facebook.com/2215193512141417/videos/743542639919348.

Tran, Thuy Anh, and Chaya Halberstam. "'I Think God Is a Feminist': Art and Action by Orthodox Jewish Women." *Journal of Feminist Studies* 37, no. 2 (Fall 2021): 5–24.

Turner, Denys. "'Sin Is Behovely' in Julian of Norwich's Revelations of Divine Love." *Modern Theology* 20, no. 3 (2004): 407–422.

Turman, Eboni Marshall. *Toward a Womanist Ethic of Incarnation: Black Bodies the Black Church and the Council of Chalcedon*. New York: Palgrave Macmillan, 2013.

Ursic, Elizabeth. "Imagination, Art, and Feminist Theology." *Feminist Theology* 25, no. 3 (2017): 310–326.

Varnam, Laura. "The Crucifix, the Pietà, and the Female Mystic: Devotional Objects and Performative Identity in the Book of Margery Kempe." *Journal of Medieval Religious Cultures* 41, no. 2 (2015): 208–237.

Vatican II Council. *Lumen gentium: Dogmatic Constitution on the Church*, November 21, 1964. https://www.vatican.va/archive/hist_councils/ii_vatican_council/docume nts/vat- ii_const_19641121_lumen-gentium_en.html.

Velazquez, Sonia. *Promiscuous Grace: Imagining Beauty and Holiness with Saint Mary of Egypt*. Chicago: University of Chicago Press, 2023.

Voaden, Rosalynn. "Mysticism and the Body." In *Oxford Handbook of Medieval Christianity*, edited by John Arnold. Oxford: Oxford University Press, 2014. https://doi.org/10.1093/oxfordhb/9780199582136.013.024.

Vogt, Kari. "'Becoming Male': A Gnostic and Early Christian Metaphor." In *Image of God and Gender Models in Judaeo-Christian Tradition*, edited by Kari Elisabeth Børresen, 170–186. Minneapolis: Fortress, 1995. (First edition Oslo: Solum Forlag, 1991.)

Walton, Heather. *Imagining Theology: Women, Writing, and God*. New York: T&T Clark, 2007.

Walton, Heather. "What Is Autoethnography and Why Does It Matter for Theological Reflection?" *Anvil: Journal of Theology and Mission* 36, no. 1 (n.d.: 6–10. https:// churchmissionsociety.org/resources/what-is-autoethnography-theological-reflect ion- heather-walton-anvil-vol-36-issue-1/.

Walton, Heather. *Writing Methods in Theological Reflection*. London: SCM, 2014.

Watson, Natalie, K. "Feminist Ecclesiology." In *The Routledge Companion to the Christian Church*, edited by Gerard Mannion and Lewis S. Mudge, 461–475. New York: Routledge, 2008.

Weil, Simone. "Reflections on the Right Use of School Studies with a View to the Love of God." In *Waiting for God*, trans. Emma Craufurd, 57–65. New York, NY: Perennial Classics, 2001.

Weisenfeld, Judith. "Invisible Women: On Women and Gender in the Study of African American Religious History." *Journal of Africana Religions* 1, no. 1 (2013): 133–149.

Wiegman, Robyn. "The Times We're In: Queer Feminist Criticism and the Reparative 'Turn.'" *Feminist Theory* 15, no. 1 (April 2014): 4–25.

Wilderson III, Frank. *Red, White, and Black: Cinema and the Structure of U.S. Antagonisms*. Durham: Duke University Press, 2010.

Williams, Delores S. *Sisters in the Wilderness: The Challenge of Womanist God-Talk*. Maryknoll, NY: Orbis, 1993.

Williams, Rowan. *Looking East in Winter: Contemporary Thought and the Easter Christian Tradition*. New York: Bloomsbury Continuum, 2021.

Withagen, Rob, and Margot van Wermeskerken. "The Role of Affordances in the Evolutionary Process Reconsidered: A Niche Construction Perspective." *Theory and Psychology* 20, no. 4 (August 2010): 489–510.

Wittgenstein, Ludwig. *Philosophical Investigations*, 4th ed. rev. German text with English translation by G. E. M. Anscombe, P. M. S. Hacker, and Joachim Schulte. Malden, MA: Wiley-Blackwell, 2009.

Wolfskeel, Cornelia D. "Some Remarks with Regard to Augustine's Conception of Man as the Image of God." *Vigilae Christianae* 30 (1976): 63–71.

Wright, James. "Sappho." In James Wright, *Above the River: The Complete Poems*, 33. New York: Farrar, Straus, and Giroux, 1990.

Yunporta, Tyson. *Sand Talk: How Indigenous Thinking Can Save the World*. New York: HarperOne, 2020.

Zahl, Simeon. *The Holy Spirit and Christian Experience*. Oxford: Oxford University Press, 2020.

Index

For the benefit of digital users, indexed terms that span two pages (e.g., 52–53) may, on occasion, appear on only one of those pages.

actor-network theory (ANT), 35–36, 69–70, 74–75, 93–94, 101–102n.31
aesthetics, xv, 2, 31–33, 37–38, 41–42, 44–45, 46–57
affect, 7–8, 9–10
affective, 10, 47, 50, 53, 109
affordance, xiv–xv, xvi–xviii, 70–74, 75–77, 79–98, 108–9, 115, 130–35
    negative affordance, 10–11, 82–83, 95–98, 109–12, 115
Althaus-Reid, Marcella, 2, 55–56, 112–14
ambivalence, xii–xiii, 8, 9–12, 15–16
Annunciation, 116–17, 118, 126
art, 31, 33, 48–49, 51, 54–56, 61n.45, 67–70, 76, 77, 83–84, 86–95, 143n.61
    art of monstrous men, 95–98
attention, 46–47, 71–72, 75–76, 79–81, 93
attunement, xv–xix, 2–3, 12–18, 19–24, 31–32, 69–70, 85–86, 108–9, 115, 134–35
    limits of attunement, 95–98
Augustine, 1–6, 16–23, 77
avoidance, 2–3, 6–8, 11, 31–32, 98

Beattie, Tina, 49–50
Bingemer, Maria, 114, 119
Black Lives Matter, 108, 124–25
Black Madonna, 111, 126, 132
body, 5, 21–22, 33, 44–45, 51–56, 78–79, 86–87
    body of Christ, 44, 48–49, 55, 126–27, 128–29
    body of Mary, 111–13, 116, 126–27, 128
breast, 19, 20, 23–24, 28n.48, 31, 37
breastfeeding, 3–5, 15, 18–19, 20, 21–22, 45
Brown, David, 73
Brown, Michael, 108, 124–25
Bynum, Carolyn Walker, 45

Catherine of Siena, 44–45, 77–78, 81–82
Cavell, Stanley, xvii–xviii, 14–15, 47, 56–57
Christ, 16, 40, 51–52, 53, 54–55, 82, 116–17, 119–21, 128–30
    Christ as image, 114–15
    Christ as a legitimizing form, 77–78
    Christ and race, 54–55
    giving birth to Christ, 23, 133, 134–35
    image(s) of Christ 44–45, 80–81, 107–8, 124, 126–27
    imagining Christ, 41, 44

Christology, 41, 82, 114–15, 121
Citton, Yves, 79–80, 85
Clark, Elizabeth, 34–36
Clement of Alexandria, 36–37
Coakley, Sarah, 48–49
Copeland, Shawn, 55, 130–31
creation, 2, 16, 17–19, 21, 22–23, 49–50, 80, 81–82, 111–12, 129, 134–35
    new creation, 23, 111–12, 116–17, 119
critique, xi–xii, xvii–xviii, 2–12, 31–32, 41–42, 83, 85–86, 93–94, 98
    critique of Mariology, 110–13

Daly, Mary, 47–48, 111–12
Darwin, Charles, xiv–xv
Davison, Andrew, 73
Doox, Mark, 108, 125

Ebner, Margaret, 45, 77–78
emotion, 5, 47, 52–53, 89–90

Felski, Rita, 10, 12–14, 35–36
feminism, 4, 6, 8, 22–23, 74, 75, 84, 86
feminist theology, xi–xix, 74–75, 81–89, 94–95, 115, 120–21
    aesthetics and the imagination, 31–34, 47–51, 54–57, 69–70, 71–72, 118
    feminist theology and attunement, 14–15, 18, 22–23
    feminist theology and repair, 21, 22–23
    feminist theology and Augustine, 1–8
    Mariology and feminist theology, 109–14, 120–21
    problem of the perceptibility of women, 37–41
Fiorenza, Elisabeth Schüssler, 40–41, 75, 109–10, 111, 112–14, 118, 120–21, 130–31
flesh, 4–5, 6, 52–53, 55, 81–83, 91–92, 107, 122, 129–30
    female flesh, 5, 18, 20–21, 22, 82
    fleshly longings, 36–37

lust of the flesh, 17
Flores, Nichole, 89–91
Floyd, George, 107–8, 124–25, 133
form, 42–51, 54, 69–70, 75–79, 80–81, 90–91, 93–95, 109, 115, 130
Francis of Assisi, 44–45, 55, 77, 80, 107, 134–35

Gebara, Ivone, 49–50, 86–89, 114, 119
genre, 33, 42, 46–51, 73, 94–95
Gibson, James G. 70–72, 95
Grailville, 84
Grant, Jacquelyn, 40, 54–56
Gregory of Nyssa, 35–37, 94–95, 112–13
Guadalupe, Virgin of, 31, 89–94

Haraway, Donna, xi–xiii, xviii–xix, 9
Hartman, Saidiya, 123–24
Hildegard of Bingen, 43–44, 45, 46, 78, 80–81, 84
Hopps, Gavin, 73
Hrdy, Sarah Blaffer, 15

iconoclasm, 4, 6–7, 10–12, 85–86, 96–97, 115
idol, 3, 4, 6–7, 19–20, 21, 85–86
idolatry, xiii–xiv, xviii–xix, 4, 10–11, 19, 20–21, 22, 112–14, 117, 130–31
image(s), 22, 61–62n.50, 107–8, 130–33
    aesthetic looking and images, 77, 80–81
    affordance theory and, 72
    images in feminist theology, 31–32, 41–47, 49–50, 51, 55, 58n.6, 63n.68
    image of God, 59–60n.24
    Mary as image, 114–21
    Mother Maria Skobtsova's icon theology, 129
    Our Lady, Mother of Ferguson as image, 109, 124–27
    Virgin of Guadalupe as image, 89–91
imagination, xvi, 6, 12, 32–33, 41, 47–48, 50, 55, 112–14, 123–24

infant, 3–4, 6, 9–10, 13–14, 15–16, 18–19, 123
Into Account, 97–98
invisibility, 34–42, 55–56, 58n.8, 92, 114–15

Johnson, Elizabeth, xvi–xvii, 48–50, 78, 82, 94–95, 110, 113–14, 120–21
joy, 53, 55, 118–19, 130–32, 133–35
Juana Inés de la Cruz, Sor, 46
Julian of Norwich, 42, 44, 77–78, 80–81, 116–17

Kempe, Margery, 45, 77–78
Kierkegaard, Søren, 13–14
Klein, Melanie, 9–10, 11
Knight, Douglas, 73
Kompridis, Nikolas, 83

Latimore, Kelly, 135–36n.3
Latour, Bruno, 8–9, 91–94
Lebzyak, Victoria, 73
Lee, Jarena, 52–53, 81–82
Levine, Caroline, 73, 76–77
Love, Heather, 10, 28n.39

Macrina, 23–24, 35–37, 94–95
Magnificat, 119, 132
Mama, 135–136n.3
Mariology, 109–15, 120–21, 130–35
Mary, 23, 59–60n.24, 89–92, 108, 109–21, 125–35
McFague, Sallie, 48–49
Messer-Davidow, Ellen, 75, 84
Miles, Margaret, 48–50, 74
monstrous men, 95–98
mother(s) xvii–xviii, 15–16, 19, 20–22, 23–24, 107–9, 124–30
  Black maternity, 122–24
  Christ as mother in Julian of Norwich, 44
  Macrina and Emmelia, 23–24, 37
  Mary as mother, 110, 116–21

mothers in Augustine, 3–5, 18–20
mothers in evolutionary biology, 15–16
mother in Kierkegaard, 13–14
mothers and Melanie Klein, 9–10
motherhood, 128–31, 133–35
Muers, Rachel, 4, 6, 11, 40–41
music, 12–13, 16–17, 46–47, 48–49, 73, 88, 97–98, 133

narrative, 46–47, 50, 54, 76–77
  declension narratives, 10–11, 82–83
niche construction, xv–xvi, 71, 74
niche construction theory, xiv–xv

Oranta icon, 124, 125
Origen of Alexandria, 1–2, 36–37
Our Lady, Mother of Ferguson and All Those Killed by Gun Violence, 108–9, 114, 124–27, 128, 130–34, 135

perceptibility, 32–42, 55–56, 71–72, 73
play(s), 31, 86–91, 93
pneumatology, 22–23, 134–35, 144n.77, 144n.80
politics, 33, 56–57, 85–86, 89–94, 99, 110–12, 121, 123–24, 125, 132
  attention and politics, 80–81
  disclosure and politics, 84–85
  Experimental Program in Political Arts, 91–94
  form and politics, 75–79
  politics and actor-network theory, 69–70, 74–75
  politics and critique, 8–10
  reparative politics, 12
pregnancy, 15–16, 19–20, 117–18, 133, 134–35
Public Universal Friend, 51–52
Pui-Lan, Kwok, 41, 48–49

Rahner, Karl, 116
Rancière, Jacques, 79–80

Reichel, Hanna, 73
repair, xiii, 16–18, 20, 21–24, 77, 107–9, 115, 133–35
representation, xvi, 45, 59–60n.24, 110
　crisis in representation, 91–94
　representational diversity, 50–51
Ricoeur, Paul, 11
Romero, Oscar, 119
Ruether, Rosemary Radford, 48–49, 59–60n.24, 82–83, 121

Saiving, Valerie, 7, 38
San Damiano crucifix, 77, 107, 132–33, 135
Sappho, 67–68, 79–80
Scarsella, Hilary Jerome, 105n.76, 106n.80
Sedgwick, Eve Kosofsky, 9–10, 11, 12, 16–17, 42
sin, 3–7, 19, 41–42, 53, 55, 73
sing, 53, 55, 68, 97–98, 99, 135
Skobtsova, Mother Maria, 128–30
Smith, Ted, 73
Smith, Zadie, 12–15, 67–69
song, 24, 31–32, 33, 51, 53, 55, 56, 80, 97–98, 118, 126–27, 130–31, 133–35
Soskice, Janet Marten, 48–50
Spillers, Hortense, 122–24, 126
Spirit, xvii–xviii, 52–53, 81–83, 107, 118, 127, 132, 134–35

Stewart-Kroeker, Sarah, 95–98
stigmata, 24, 44–45, 61–62n.50, 107, 134–35
　de-stigmatized, 126–27
　stigmatize(d), 132–33, 134–35
　unstigmatized, 111

Teresa of Avila, 44
Thistlethwaite, Susan Brooke, 49–50, 55–56, 94–95
Thomas of Celano, 107
Tonstad, Linn, 50–51

Ursic, Elizabeth, 32–33

Virgin of the Sign, 124–27
visibility, 6, 34–42, 50–51, 56, 60n.26, 65n.79, 77–78, 88–89, 94–95, 117
visitation, 118–19
　divine visitation, 84

Walton, Heather, 8, 49–50
Weil, Simone, 79
Williams, Delores, xvi–xvii, 38–40, 48–49, 55, 56
Williams, Rowan, 128–29
Wittgenstein, Ludwig, 11–12, 14–15, 85–86

The manufacturer's authorised representative in the EU for product safety is Oxford
University Press España S.A. of El Parque Empresarial San Fernando de Henares,
Avenida de Castilla, 2 – 28830 Madrid (www.oup.es/en or product.safety@oup.com).
OUP España S.A. also acts as importer into Spain of products made by the manufacturer.

Printed in the USA/Agawam, MA
January 17, 2025

881168.010